SOONER NATION

OKLAHOMA'S GREATEST PLAYERS TALK ABOUT SOONERS FOOTBALL

JEFF SNOOK

TRIUMPH
BOOKS

Material previously published in the book *What It Means to Be a Sooner* © 2005 by Jeff Snook (Chicago: Triumph Books)

This book is available in quantity at special discounts for your group or organization. For further information, contact:

Triumph Books LLC
814 North Franklin Street
Chicago, Illinois 60610
(312) 337-0747
www.triumphbooks.com

Printed in U.S.A.
ISBN: 978-1-62937-127-6
Design by Patricia Frey
Photos courtesy of the author unless otherwise indicated

Contents

Foreword *by Barry Switzer* v

Foreword *by Bob Stoops* xiii

Introduction xvii

Chapter 1: The Forties 1
Paul "Buddy" Burris • Jack Mitchell • Darrell Royal • Wade Walker

Chapter 2: The Fifties 27
Eddie Crowder • J. D. Roberts • Prentice Gautt • Jerry Thompson

Chapter 3: The Sixties 51
Wayne Lee • Jim Grisham • Carl McAdams • Granville Liggins • Steve Zabel • Steve Owens

Chapter 4: The Seventies 99
Jack Mildren • Tom Brahaney • Joe Washington • Tinker Owens • Lee Roy Selmon • Jimbo Elrod • Thomas Lott • Uwe von Schamann • Billy Sims

Chapter 5: The Eighties 177
J. C. Watts • Terry Crouch • Jackie Shipp • Rick Bryan • Spencer Tillman • Brian Bosworth • Mark Hutson • Anthony Phillips

Chapter 6: The Nineties and the New Millennium 243
Rocky Calmus • Josh Heupel • Roy Williams • Jason White

Foreword

My story begins in South Arkansas, in a little town of about 3,000 people called Crossett.

I was interested in athletics at a very young age, and it was in the late forties when I began my football career in junior high school. I loved the game from the beginning. On Saturdays, I would go outside to sit in Daddy's car, roll down the windows and open the doors because it was so hot, and just sit there and listen to college football games.

I became an Oklahoma football fan for one reason—the Sooners always played afternoon ballgames, and I could listen to them. At night, I could get the Razorback Network and listen to Arkansas.

And sometimes, we listened to the Grand Ole Opry.

What some people don't know is that Oklahoma played afternoon games only because there were no lights at Owen Field, and Bud Wilkinson wanted their games to make all the newspapers' deadlines on the East Coast. That was a tremendous advantage in those days, and I thought it was a pretty good strategy to gain exposure.

When I was a kid, I had this map of the USA pinned to my bedroom wall, but this was a college football map, including all of the major football schools and featuring their mascots. For example, there was a Trojan out in L.A., a big Leprechaun in the northern part of Indiana, and an Indian logo right over Norman, Oklahoma. That was long before political correctness forced Oklahoma to abandon the Indian mascot.

So while I was growing up, the Oklahoma Sooners were on my mind at that time, through listening to their games on the radio and staring at that map.

My last season of high school football was 1954, and I was considering attending either LSU or Arkansas. Crossett was closer to Baton Rouge than it was to Fayetteville, but I had a really tough decision. Charlie McClendon, the head coach at LSU, was a great coach and he later became a very good friend of mine. If I had gone there, I would have played on the 1958 national title team with Billy Cannon, but I decided to go to Arkansas with my high school buddies.

As I played at Arkansas, that Oklahoma influence still followed me.

Being in Fayetteville, we were somewhat isolated from the world. TV was in its infancy, but we did get the Tulsa network that carried the Oklahoma games on replay and *The Bud Wilkinson Show*. The only newspaper I read was the *Tulsa World*. So I was immersed in Oklahoma politics and Oklahoma football tradition because of all of those things.

OU was in the middle of that 47-game winning streak during my freshman, sophomore, and junior years.

This is one thing I will never forget: we had played SMU and Don Meredith in the Cotton Bowl one Saturday and as we flew home to Arkansas, I was reading *Sports Illustrated*. I remember the exact date: November 16, 1957. I was sitting there in that DC-3, twin-engine plane [it took two of them to fly the football teams around then], reading a story titled, "Why Oklahoma Is Invincible."

As I was in the middle of that article, the pilot came over the audio system and said, "I have a college football score that may interest you: Notre Dame 7, Oklahoma 0."

And that started the *Sports Illustrated* jinx.

It was the end of the greatest streak in college football history.

* * *

Bud Wilkinson never remembered this story of meeting him, but I do vividly.

Six years later, in 1963, Bud resigned to run for the U.S. Senate. In January 1965, I was at the national coaches convention at the Hilton Hotel in Chicago. I was in my late twenties and was the assistant offensive line coach at Arkansas, and Merv Johnson was the offensive line coach at the time. Jim MacKenzie was our defensive coordinator. We had just beaten Nebraska in the Cotton Bowl to win the national championship.

I had grown up with Larry Lacewell, and his mommy had dated coach Bear Bryant years earlier. In fact, I used to kid him that his profile looked just like the Bear! Anyway, I called Larry, who had just won the junior-college national championship at Kilgore Junior College, and asked, "Are you coming to the coaching clinic in Chicago?"

He said, "No, our budget doesn't allow that."

"You hop your butt on a bus and come up here," I told him. "I will pay for your meals and we can put you on a roll-away in my room."

So he did. At night, Larry and I would sit at the hotel bar and point to all the coaching legends who walked by. After a while, we had a few drinks and he said, "Let's go see coach Bryant."

We went to the front desk, and they told us he was in suite so-and-so. We got on the elevator, got up to his floor, and started that long walk down the hall to his suite. There were big double doors at the entrance, but we could still hear all of this laughter behind those doors.

As we were about to knock on the door, Larry froze.

Just as I said, "Larry, if you don't knock on that door—" Duffy Daugherty came through the door with two ice buckets under his arm.

Duffy looked at us and said, "Hey guys, come on in! But go fill up these ice buckets first."

After Larry and I filled up the ice buckets, we walked back into the suite and set them up on the bar. Duffy then walked up said, "Hey, why don't you mix a drink for Coach over there."

Over there with the Bear were Woody Hayes, Ara Parseghian, Bob Devaney, and Bud. So Larry and I started mixing drinks for those guys, the greatest coaches in the history of college football.

Coach Bryant noticed Larry, but he didn't know who the hell I was. I figured they must have thought the hotel had sent us up to mix drinks for them. As it ended up, we spent the entire evening with them, listening to their stories and mixing their drinks. It was one of the greatest evenings of my life—and it was the first time I met Bud Wilkinson.

I never told Bud that story when I got to know him later, but I wish I had.

After Bud had retired from coaching, he was only 47. I was shocked when he lost the Senate race because he was so popular, but I think he would have won had he changed political parties and been a Democrat. I think if he had done that, he could have become president of the United States. And I really believe that is what his aspiration was.

As soon as he was gone, Oklahoma fell on hard times. Gomer Jones got fired after only two years, and Jim MacKenzie, who not only was a colleague on Frank Broyles' staff with me but a great, great friend, applied for the job. I remember that they also interviewed Doug Dickey and Vince Dooley.

That season, 1965, Arkansas had gone undefeated again, and we were in San Antonio preparing for the Cotton Bowl. We were sitting in Frank's suite between our two-a-day practices one day and the phone rang.

Frank picked it up and said, "Jim, it's Oklahoma."

Jim took the call and then told me, "They want me to come interview for the job."

So Jim flew up there, but he made the mistake of falling asleep on the DC-3 before it landed in Oklahoma City. The stewardess didn't wake him up, and the airplane went on to Dallas. He had to get off that plane in Dallas and call Oklahoma to tell them what happened. Anyway, he went back up to Oklahoma and had a great interview.

Once Jim came back to San Antonio, we were sitting in Frank Broyles' suite when the phone rang again. Jim went into the bedroom to take the call and I could tell by his face that the news was positive. He hung up the phone and we all congratulated him.

It was a forgone conclusion that I would head to Oklahoma with him because Jim and I were very close.

We lost to LSU in the Cotton Bowl and I told Frank I would be leaving with Jim.

It was January 3, 1966, the day I landed in Oklahoma City for the first time. And I've been a Sooner almost every day since.

I think I may have driven through Norman once before, on a recruiting trip, but I never stopped. I never saw the campus. When I arrived once Jim hired me, I was shocked and dismayed a bit. Here Oklahoma had all this great tradition, but the facilities they had were at the bottom of the barrel.

Head coach Barry Switzer ponders his next move during Oklahoma's game against Texas in Dallas on October 12, 1985. *Photo courtesy of AP/Wide World Photos.*

Jim had told me, "Be prepared, because the facilities . . . "

He didn't need to finish the sentence. Everything we had at Arkansas was much, much better at the time. Oklahoma had no weight room and antiquated dressing rooms. Jones Dormitory at the time wasn't even air-conditioned.

Still, I knew we were going to win at Oklahoma, so I threw myself into the job because I was an unbridled young assistant coach full of enthusiasm.

The first thing we did was make those players physically and mentally tougher. We ran a hell of a lot of good athletes off that first year because we were trying to find out who was the toughest, who wanted it the most. We went at it hard for three and a half months, with only Fridays off. The culture of the kid was much different then. The demographics were different. We had only three or four black players on the team, and at Arkansas, we still didn't have any.

I had told Jim I really wanted to coach on the defensive side of the ball because I wanted to be a head coach some day. During that time, offensive line coaches rarely got the opportunity to become head coaches. Jim promised me if I stayed on offense for that first year, he would move me the following year.

I was the only one on the new staff who knew the offense he wanted to run. He hired Homer Rice out of Kentucky and Galen Hall, who had no college coaching experience, so I had to coach Homer and Galen on our offensive playbook when we got started.

That next spring, on April 26, 1967, following a 6–4 season in which three of our losses were by a total of seven points, Jim died of a heart attack.

Chuck Fairbanks was named head coach right away and he named me the offensive coordinator.

We had started to launch an all-out recruiting war in Texas, aggressively recruiting black players at every position. After a 10–1 season, we had two straight four-loss seasons and started to feel some heat. Then we lost to Oregon State early in the 1970 season and we made another major decision: we switched to the wishbone three games into the season.

In 1971, we had what was, statistically at least, one of the best offenses in the history of college football. We finished 11–1 that season and 11–1 again in 1972.

Then, on January 20, 1973, Chuck called me into his office.

"Barry," he said. "I am going to take a pro job."

I was stunned.

Then he said, "And I am going to support you for the head-coaching job here."

Six days later, Chuck announced he was leaving to become head coach of the New England Patriots.

On January 29, they named me the head coach at the University of Oklahoma. I was 35 years old. Over the next 16 years, I had a fun ride as the Oklahoma Sooners won a lot of games, three national championships, and 12 Big Eight championships.

I won't get into details of my resignation here because this is not the place for it, but it is true there was a time when not a lot of us wanted to be around the Oklahoma program after that, but Bob Stoops helped change that. Bob embraced our history and he realized nobody was a threat to him.

I like to tell people that Bob made us feel comfortable in our own home.

* * *

What does it mean to be a Sooner?

When I look at that Switzer Center on OU's campus, I realize it represents thousands of other people. We all did it here in Norman. We all accomplished the success that we all enjoyed. It wasn't just me. They put my name up there on that building because somebody's name had to be on it, but it represents everybody.

I think we have some of the greatest fans in the world. Now I sit up there and watch the games and I am one of them. They support Oklahoma, win, lose, or draw.

Sooners are proud people.

Like the song says, "I am Sooner born and Sooner bred, and when I die, I am Sooner dead."

I may not have been Sooner born, but I have spent most of my life here. I spend most of my time now being around my grandchildren and enjoying watching them grow here.

When I look back at my career and at my life here in Oklahoma, it wasn't all the games we won and all the championships we captured that matter now, it was the great relationships we built over time that mattered the most.

College coaches have a different mission in life. It is a mission of developing a young man for living his life. It is not just to win football games on a Saturday afternoon at Owen Field. It is a 365-day, 24-hour, 7-days-a-week job.

I was entrusted with the most precious gift a family can have: their child.

To most of them, I was a father, a friend, and everything else I could be. The coach-player relationship is a friendship that lasts a lifetime. It is a special bond, and only those who have been a part of it will understand it.

Billy Sims knows what it means. Joe Washington knows what it means. So does Steve Owens, Brian Bosworth, and Spencer Tillman. The list is so numerous that I can't mention them all.

Every player who played for me means so much to me. The fans know the names of the stars, but I also like to think that I took care of the second-team right guard and the third-team left tackle and made them feel just as good about themselves, as well.

For me, it is the substance of all of those relationships developed over time that defines being a Sooner.

—Barry Switzer

Barry Switzer is one of the winningest coaches in college football history, with a record of 157–29–4 (.837) at the University of Oklahoma from 1973 to 1988. His teams won three national championships (1974, 1975, and 1985) and 12 Big Eight championships. His teams also played in 13 bowl games, winning eight, including a 6–3 record in the Orange Bowl. A University of Arkansas graduate, Switzer served as an Oklahoma assistant coach from 1966 to 1972. Once named head coach, his teams started with a 29–0–1 record until a loss to Kansas late in the 1975 season. The Sooners produced 32 All-Americans during Switzer's head coaching tenure. From 1994 to 1997, he was head coach of the NFL's Dallas Cowboys, going 45–26. The Cowboys won Super Bowl XXX, defeating the Pittsburgh Steelers 27–17, making Switzer only the second coach in football history to have coached an NCAA national champion and a Super Bowl champion. Switzer was inducted into the College Football Hall of Fame in 2002. He currently resides in Norman, Oklahoma.

Foreword

I have admired Oklahoma Sooners football since my grade-school days in Youngstown, Ohio.

I first remember watching the OU-Nebraska games and seeing players such as Steve Owens, Tinker Owens, Greg Pruitt, Joe Washington, and the Selmon brothers. I was completely amazed that a guy as big as Steve Owens could be a running back and be as fast as he was.

Of course, I am too young to remember Bud Wilkinson's great teams, but as a coach, having a 47-game winning streak is really difficult to imagine. It is an incredible feat that probably will never be surpassed in today's game of college football. I can think back to when we won 20 in a row and we weren't even halfway there, so that might be a record that stands forever.

As a redshirt freshman at the University of Iowa, our second game of the 1979 season was against Oklahoma at Memorial Stadium. I had heard so much about Norman and what it was like on game days, and I can remember pulling into town and thinking what a neat place this was.

Twenty years later, when I was hired as the head coach at the University of Oklahoma, I believed I had a great, great job and I also believed history has a way of repeating itself. The positives that were here in the Wilkinson and Switzer eras were still here. I felt that way coming in and I feel that way now and, fortunately, we have been able to do something about it.

Sometimes, people mention how I welcomed coach Switzer when I got here, but that was never meant to be a political move on my part. I believe in what is right, and that was right. I believe in his legacy and all that he accomplished here, and it was the decent thing to do. This was his place as much as anybody else's. He deserves to be around here and greeted with open arms by everybody.

And this is still his place, along with his assistant coaches and all of his players.

I believe that what you earn, you keep. Coach Switzer certainly earned quite a bit while he was head football coach here. We have a great relationship and he knows my feelings toward him are genuine.

At the same time, we won't shy away from all the expectations because of what he and his teams accomplished. They did great things and we want to do great things at the University of Oklahoma.

The relationships between our coaches and our players have been a big factor in what we have been able to accomplish. Our coaches and players know how to have a lot of fun while getting the job done. We're all coaching in a positive, confident manner, which all the players enjoy, and we don't beat ourselves up. We get our work done and work hard while we are here.

I want our coaches to be excited, fresh, and happy to go to practice because I think the players pick up on that. They see their coaches are excited to be at practice and not dragging.

After we won the national championship [in 2000], it is true that coach Switzer once told me not to expect to win a national championship every year. I wished he wouldn't have told me that! But he is right. You cannot win one every season, but you can shoot for it.

And we will continue to shoot for it.

I never want our players assuming an underdog role while they are at the University of Oklahoma. I don't believe in it. I want our coaching staff to be confident and positive heading into each game. I want them focusing on reasons why we should win instead of any reasons why we shouldn't.

That underdog stuff is for the media. It is for other people to talk about, and it's not for us to listen to. The same goes for being favored. That's not an issue for us, either. That's why you play the games. The game of football comes down to who is prepared, who is ready to play, and I want our players to understand that if they just prepare and play to their potential, the way they're capable of, then we should be fine.

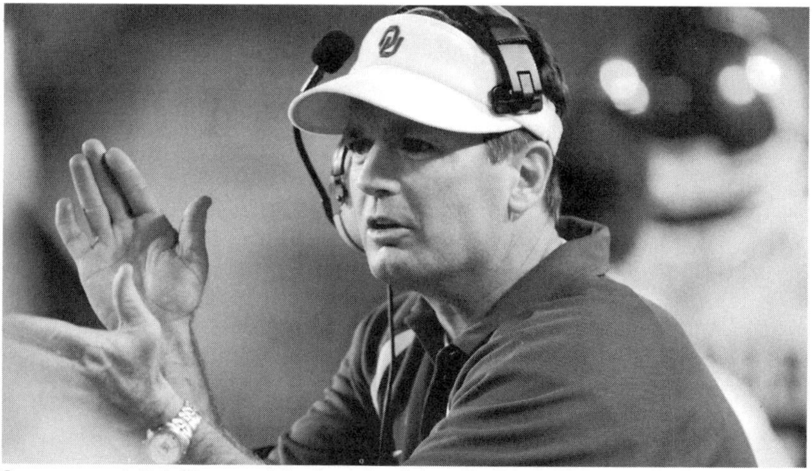

Sooners coach Bob Stoops celebrates a touchdown by Travis Wilson in the 2005 Orange Bowl. *Photo courtesy of AP/Wide World Photos.*

There should be great expectations here. This is a program with championships that should expect championships. I know we'll operate with no excuses. There are no excuses. You either succeed or you don't.

Most important of all, I want our teams to be full of strong character and unselfish players. I do believe in the integrity of the game. You play fast, physical, and with great effort. You play the game the right way, with a degree of sportsmanship, and with respect for whom you are playing.

We want our players to play unselfishly. Those antics on the field, such as showboating, are terribly selfish. We want our players to do their best to win and then to celebrate the right way.

It is true that people have approached me with other opportunities, but I have checked what path I want to be on in my career. That especially includes my family life. In any career, you have to address what is best for you and your family and that is no different in coaching. I feel fortunate to coach here at the University of Oklahoma. It is a great place to be.

I love it when spring rolls around and we have those lettermen functions. It seems that Oklahoma players mesh together like one big class reunion when they all come back to campus. I also love it when our younger players get to know some of these older guys and realize that Oklahoma football is one big family or fraternity.

Tradition like we have at Oklahoma is something that is built over decades, not measured by individual seasons. The story of the Oklahoma Sooners includes seven national championships and 44 conference championships dating back to 1915.

We have produced winners for every major individual college football award, including five Heisman Trophy winners, as well as more than 100 All-Americans. Our tradition has been built through the efforts of players named Burris, Vessels, Owens, Sims, Pruitt, Selmon, Davis, Bryan, and Cumby, to name a few. It has been built with great leadership of coaches named Owen, Luster, Stidham, Wilkinson, and Switzer, among others.

The tradition of Oklahoma football is something that drew me to Norman. We will continue to work together to add something to the rich legacy of excellence that we inherited and have been entrusted to carry on. As Sooners, we all know we have something special.

There are few feelings in the world comparable to the pride and excitement of gameday at Memorial Stadium. You have to love to coach at a place where there is great pressure and great expectations. Our fans have such passion for Oklahoma football. That is why there are more than 83,000 of them in the stands every week.

The University of Oklahoma is a magical place, a place where hard work and persistence make dreams come true any time a Sooner steps onto the football field.

—Bob Stoops

Bob Stoops is the winningest coach in Oklahoma Sooners football history. During his first 16 seasons in Norman, the Sooners have won one national championship, eight Big 12 championships, and eight bowl games, with a combined record of 168–44. Born September 9, 1960, in Youngstown, Ohio, Stoops was a defensive back at the University of Iowa, where he graduated with a bachelor's degree in marketing in 1983. He was an assistant coach at Iowa (1983–1987), Kent State (1988), Kansas State (1989–1995), and Florida (1996–1998) before becoming Oklahoma's 22nd head coach.

Introduction

It was September 24, 1977. As I sat on the 40-yard line in Ohio Stadium that afternoon, I was stunned by what was happening in front of me, as were 88,118 other fans on that gray, gloomy day in Columbus, Ohio.

Ohio State and Oklahoma, two college football powerhouses who had combined to produce 11 national championships, almost 200 All-Americans, and seven Heisman Trophies with more of each in their futures, had clashed for the first time in their respective and storied histories.

Along the far sideline, a young, brash head coach named Barry Switzer was on his knees, waiting for his place-kicker to either make his season or break his heart.

Along the near sideline, an aging legend named Woody Hayes paced back and forth, gathering a few defensive linemen around him, pleading to his players to make the last heroic play in a day full of heroic plays.

Between the two coaches stood a generation gap, figuratively, a contrast of styles, realistically, and a young German emigrant, literally.

Switzer's Sooners and Hayes' Buckeyes had smacked each other around for 59 minutes and 54 seconds in what would surely go down as one of the most exciting, intersectional games in college football history.

Oklahoma had busted out to a 20–0 lead barely into the second quarter. Ohio State then scored four straight touchdowns to take a 28–20 advantage. After the Sooners scored a touchdown, but failed to convert a two-point conversion to tie the game with only 1:25 remaining, it appeared the Buckeyes would win this epic battle.

That was until the Sooners, trailing by two points, recovered an onside kick and quickly moved to Ohio State's 24-yard line with only six seconds remaining. At that moment, a relatively unknown player named Uwe von Schamann trotted onto the field.

The scene was electrifying as Ohio State fans chanted, "Block that kick! Block that kick!" and von Schamann shocked everyone, including his teammates, by waving his arms to encourage the chant to grow even louder.

"I really don't know what made me do that," he said. "I guess I just got caught up in the moment."

Shakespeare couldn't have conceived more interesting characters for this dramatic moment.

There was Switzer, who grew up in a shack just outside of Crossett, Arkansas, having lived through his mother's suicide and his father's tragic death just a few years later, all by the time he became a collegiate head coach. As he kneeled on the Astroturf this day, he had already captured two national championships in his first four years at the Sooners' head coach and he surely was on a career path to become one of the game's central figures in years to come.

There was Hayes, a firm disciplinarian and beloved legend who had built his program into a perennial contender with a résumé that included five national championships and a slew of All-Americans. In another year and four months, he would be forced to resign after losing his senses momentarily and throwing a right hook at an opposing player during a bowl game.

There were Thomas Lott and Billy Sims, two Texas-grown kids who grew up poor but were on the brink of superstardom. Banged up and injured earlier in the game, they were forced to watch the drama unfold from the sideline, now unable to affect its outcome.

And there was von Schamann, raised in Germany by a young, single mother. Having emigrated to America only six years earlier, he never envisioned being the central figure of such a setting.

"When I first saw football, I thought it was a silly, stupid game," he said. "It looked like a bunch of guys with crash helmets on. And the ball was oblong, not round like a soccer ball. I just didn't see the attraction to it, didn't see the point."

At this moment in the Midwest of a country he had only dreamed of seeing as a kid, in front of the largest crowd in Oklahoma football history as well as millions more watching on national television, he saw the point. His life was about to change, one way or the other, whether he realized it or not.

At this moment, all of these lives intersected.

As the football was placed down, von Schamann approached and swung his right leg, and it was as if time stood still. The once-deafening noise of the crowd had eased into a shocking silence, resembling that inside a city library. As the oblong brown thing traveled end over end, heading directly between the two giant white posts, exactly where von Schamann had envisioned, every set of eyes followed it.

It was a simple field goal, one that traveled 41 yards to clinch a 29–28 victory for the visiting Sooners, but its effect would be remembered and talked about for decades to come.

"That kick changed my life," von Schamann said. "Here we are talking about it almost three decades later. I can't imagine what would have happened to me if I had missed that kick."

For me, a soon-to-be Ohio State student and future alumnus, von Schamann's kick would have hurt less if he had swung his powerful right foot into my stomach.

The pain has subsided somewhat over the years, as history has enshrined the game as one of the most memorable in the game of college football. And history cannot be changed, we learn quickly. Just as Nebraska's win over Oklahoma in the Game of the Century in 1971 can never be altered. As the decades pass, it's almost as if these storied games were meant to be forever remembered as they were, not as they could have been.

Therefore, I can now appreciate history's outcome. I can appreciate that I witnessed one of the greatest games in the sport I always loved. And I can appreciate how that day turned a young man into a hero for a lifetime—especially now that I have spoken with Uwe von Schamann and learned of his childhood, his single mother's struggle to raise him, their adventurous journey to America with little money and no food, but an abundance of hopes and dreams.

"The United States is a great country," von Schamann said. "My mother and I realized that in the first few days we were here through the kindness of strangers.

"And I was wrong—football is a great game."

That it is, Uwe.

As you read these chapters from the University of Oklahoma's greatest players, you will see that many have a common theme.

They were young men who arrived in Norman, Oklahoma, full of self-doubt, unsure of themselves, and apprehensive about their futures. Most wondered if they would ever succeed as Sooners. They figured they were either too slow, too small, or too timid to ever make a mark on Oklahoma's tradition-rich program.

Many, even future Heisman Trophy winners such as Steve Owens and Billy Sims, wanted to quit football and return to the comfort of their parents' homes, whether they were in Ada, Enid, Midwest City, Muskogee, or Miami, Oklahoma.

Most failed at first, but refused to quit and ultimately reached the absolute individual success: being named All-Americans.

I hope you find their stories entertaining, but most of all, I hope you realize they are human analogies for the most important lessons in life.

"Because you lose at times, doesn't make you a loser," J. C. Watts said. "And because you fail doesn't make you a failure."

Watts should know. He quit the OU football team not once but twice. He threw interceptions and fumbled, failed miserably twice in the annual showdown against Texas, and was booed on his home field.

But he overcame it all, picked himself up off the proverbial floor, and led the Sooners to eight consecutive victories, driving them the length of the field in the final minutes of the 1981 Orange Bowl to defeat Florida State 18–17. To say he ended his OU career in style would be an understatement. He then succeeded in the Canadian Football League and excelled in public office, serving Oklahoma for four terms in the House of Representatives of the U.S. Congress.

The Oklahoma Sooners football tradition was created by the men in this book, as well as countless others, including some who have reached

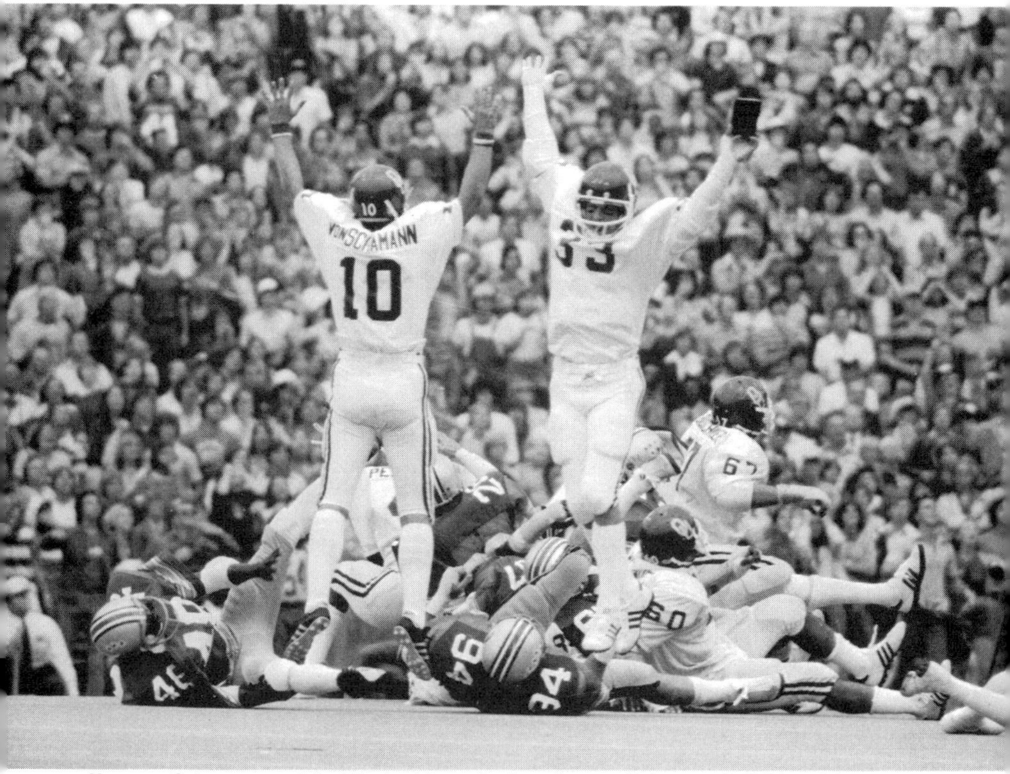

Uwe von Schamann and Bud Herbert jump for joy after von Schamann's field goal beats Ohio State 29–28 in the final seconds of the now legendary game played in 1977. *Photo courtesy of AP/Wide World Photos.*

the big end zone in the sky, such as Buck McPhail, Stan West, and Prentice Gautt.

I only regret never getting the chance to meet Bud Wilkinson and to experience all the qualities that made him so beloved to all of his players, such as Darrell Royal and Eddie Crowder.

I believe their stories, as well as those from nine other Sooners who played for coach Wilkinson, will provide an accurate picture of what a great coach, and perfect gentleman, he was while serving Oklahoma as assistant coach in 1946 and head coach from 1947 to 1963.

In reading these pages, I hope you can picture the ingenuity of Jack Mitchell and the burly toughness of Buddy Burris in the forties. I hope you understand the sweat and sacrifice from the men behind the NCAA's longest winning streak, such as Jerry Thompson. I hope you can realize the unwavering drive through adversity of Prentice Gautt, called by many OU's own Jackie Robinson. I hope you can feel the intensity of Steve Zabel or appreciate the endurance of Steve Owens in the sixties, the grittiness of Jack Mildren and the elusiveness of Joe Washington in the seventies, the creativity of Brian Bosworth in the eighties, and the intelligence of Josh Heupel in 2000.

* * *

I want to thank Barry Switzer for his contributions to this book.

He had the foresight to install the wishbone as an assistant under Chuck Fairbanks, and he had the courage to do it during the 1970 season. If there was a better recruiter of good football players during the seventies and eighties, I don't know whom it would have been. And what some people forget: Barry could coach a little, too.

His never-wavering encouragement and lifelong loyalty to his players is a constant theme in this book. To the Sooners who played for him, he is a beloved figure and rightfully so.

I also want to thank Bob Stoops.

I remember the day in 1996 when Steve Spurrier told me he was "bringing a real defensive ballcoach to town" as his defensive coordinator at the University of Florida. That season, the Gators won their first national championship, resulting directly from Spurrier's decision to hire Stoops.

Before the next season began, an interesting scenario unfolded one day inside the Gators locker room. It was August 23, 1997. Florida had just finished a scrimmage, and Spurrier and his staff relaxed in the locker room as Oklahoma played Northwestern on television in the Pigskin Classic at Soldier Field. The Sooners lost 24–0 that day, beginning what would become a 4–8 season under John Blake.

"As I watched a few plays from that game," Stoops remembered, "I had mentioned to some of our other coaches that it was a shame that the Oklahoma program was not living up to its potential. But most of Florida's other assistants were from the SEC and ACC and they didn't really understand. At the time, I called Oklahoma 'a sleeping giant.'"

A year and some five months later, ironically, Stoops would be hired to replace Blake and he promptly awakened that sleeping giant by guiding his 2000 team to OU's seventh national championship.

Just as Barry Switzer had admired Bud Wilkinson from afar, as you will read in his Foreword, Stoops had done the same of Switzer.

"Barry Switzer is one coach I always followed closely because I loved his style of football," he said. "I remember driving all night to meet my parents for a vacation at Lake Erie one time and I listened to an audiotape of his book, Bootlegger's Boy, to keep me awake. It was a fantastic story."

Wilkinson, Switzer, and Stoops are separated by the generations, but there is no generation gap in what was the objective of Wilkinson and Switzer and what is Stoops' ultimate goal: to win championships at the University of Oklahoma.

In other words, men named Bud, Barry, and Bob are connected in history by their mission and by their career paths. A Minnesota graduate, an Arkansas grad, and an Iowa grad, they made Norman their home to accomplish great things in life.

After all, what's more important than teaching young people to succeed?

"Nothing, in my opinion," Switzer said. "On, and especially off, the field."

As for that success that can be measured by statistics and numbers, it is truly only a part of the story of Oklahoma's football history:

- 47, as in the NCAA's longest winning streak
- seven, as in national championship teams
- five, as in Heisman Trophy winners
- more than 150, and counting, as in All-Americans

But the names tell the rest of the story. The Sooners themselves tell it best.

I want to thank them for spending the time, for sharing their splendid stories, and for making this book possible.

They were great players, but they are great and successful people. They were bonded by the work ethic it required to reach the top and forever linked by a love for their university—and for each other.

Their memories are worthwhile. Their stories are entertaining and priceless. And their experiences and contributions are invaluable. They are couriers of Oklahoma's history.

Here it is. Enjoy . . .

—Jeff Snook

| chapter one |

The Forties

Paul "Buddy" Burris | Guard | 1946–1948

I always knew from an early age that of all the sports, I was born to play football. In the third grade, I could do some things on the field that none of my friends could do. I know that several mommies around my area thought I played illegally or too roughly because I was hitting and tackling their boys. I guess I was knocking the wind out of them when I tackled them—there's nothing illegal about that.

I was raised on a farm—an Okie from Muskogee, Oklahoma. It was a town of about 50 people. There were six of us boys and we all were raised in a one-bedroom house. We had a water well, an outside john, and we slept on pallets. In the summer, we would take those pallets outside because it was too hot to sleep inside. There was no air-conditioning in those days. You could see the sunshine through the cracks in our walls. And in the winter, you could see the snow through the walls.

But we were happy.

By the time I got to high school, we had some pretty good football teams and won the state championship.

I had always wanted to go to OU, but after graduating high school in 1941, I went to Tulsa and we went undefeated that season—we actually beat OU 23–0. The thing I remember is that I got called for a 15-yard penalty in that game for holding Homer Simmons. Homer weighed about 370 pounds, so I *had* to hold him.

But then World War II was on and I had to leave Tulsa. I was attached to the Third Infantry, fighting in France, Germany, and Belgium. I always said that I had it better in the war, sleeping on the ground, than I had it at home. Sleeping on the ground was duck soup to me. After Europe, we went by ship through the Panama Canal to the Philippines to help out in the Pacific. That's a long trip—about three-quarters of the way around the world. It took us about 30 days.

One of the things I'll never forget is while I was stationed at Clark Field in Manila I noticed those B-29s. You didn't see them too often. While they were sitting out there, there were guards around them night and day, and I started to wonder about it. Then they used those planes to drop the big bombs that ended the war. It all made sense then.

When I got back home in February 1946, I looked forward to going back to school, but I wasn't going back to Tulsa. There was a new regime at Oklahoma: Jim Tatum had come in that year as head coach and he had been a Navy guy. So he brought a lot of those players with him from Jacksonville.

Jim recruited me hard. One day I was on a tractor in the field when a big, old car pulled up at the other end of the field. Jim took me off that plow and let me in that car and that was the end of it. I was going to Oklahoma.

That first year, the team was full of discharged veterans like me. I think we had 175 uniforms checked out at one time. It was simply a case of survival. They would line you up and run you as long as you could make it. Then we had jumping drills and more running drills. They wanted to make sure we had some athletes. At that time, I was 23 and I could run as fast and jump as high as any of them, and I could kick the football, too. In those one-on-one drills, I was pretty good. Plus, I had that year of experience while playing at Tulsa.

In the first game that season, we went to New York to play a big game against Army. President Truman was there at the time and we had a really big crowd for the game.

I remember we were all getting taped before the game. I was in the locker room, and Darrell Royal was complaining about not being able to sleep the night before. He said his roommate was scratching all night long

Buddy Burris, beloved by his teammates for his toughness, was Oklahoma's first three-time All-American. *Photo courtesy of OU Athletics Media Relations.*

and it had kept him up. I guess his roommate said he had a case of something that makes you scratch in a delicate spot. Anyway, Darrell didn't get much sleep that night.

We just screwed up every time we turned around that day. We could make three to five yards on every running play, but we couldn't pass. Darrell threw a couple of bad passes that day, and they took one of his fumbles back for a touchdown. Darrell later told me it wasn't his fault, but I always thought it was.

We outgained Army that day, but their two ends beat us. Doc Blanchard suited up that day, but didn't play [due to a knee injury]. And Glenn Davis didn't hurt us—I think he caught a pass or two.

That was Jim Tatum's first game, and he got all excited on the sidelines. He was complaining about some illegal plays and screaming at the officials. At one point, he wanted some water to drink, but they didn't have any nearby. So one of the guys was over there soaking his feet in water. Jim went over and picked that bucket up and drank it. I thought he had just about lost his marbles.

Anyway, we lost to Army 21–7.

We beat Texas A&M in the next game, but then lost to Texas. What I remember from that season was that game at Stillwater when they had sent me into the locker room after I got hurt. I thought I was walking into the locker room and I walked into the girls' restroom. A few girls were in there watching the game through a window and didn't notice me for a while. Once they did, one of them squealed and they all ran out. So did I.

We won eight games and lost three that season. Homer Paine and I were very good friends on that team and we agreed after that season that if Tatum stayed for another season, we would leave and sign pro contracts.

Tatum was a real charmer who was a very good coach, but he played favorites. He played all of those Navy guys over other players who should have been playing. He had been a commander in the Navy and he was very tough to play for.

At one point, Homer and I actually decided to leave, but Tatum had gotten into trouble by overspending his budget. He had given all the players some coupons for clothes and some money when we were down in Jacksonville to play North Carolina State in the Gator Bowl. They made a big stink about that.

At that time, all of the players loved Bud Wilkinson, and he was a very good assistant coach. We all wanted him to be the head coach, too. I don't know of a player on that team who didn't like Bud. So once Tatum left [for Maryland], it was natural that they would name Bud Wilkinson head coach.

And boy were we happy about it.

I was real tickled at the start of the 1947 season when we won the first two games. But against Texas just before halftime—I was playing nose guard at the time—Bobby Layne fumbled and picked up the ball and lateralled to another player who scored a touchdown. The thing was, Layne had his knee down when he picked up the ball, so he should have been ruled down. But they gave them a touchdown and the referees had to stop the game to clear the field of all the bottles the fans had thrown. That blew open a close game, and we lost 34–14.

I know one thing: Bobby Layne had ice in his veins. One time, I hit him so square on his chest and he threw the pass as he was going down. Then I rammed my elbow into his neck as we hit the ground. I really knocked the hell out of his face. After he went off the field, he was back in two plays. To get Bobby Layne off the field, you just about had to kill him.

At Nebraska that year I kicked off once, and the ball went straight up into the air against a strong wind and came straight down. We recovered it. It was just like an onside kick that they do these days, but it was by accident. After the game, Nebraska's coach came running up to Bud and asked how long we had been working on that play.

Bud just said, "Oh, we didn't work on it that long."

I had to laugh.

To start that 1948 season, we lost to Santa Clara 20–17, and Darrell made another bad play. On one screen pass we had called, he didn't throw it—he just put the ball in his belly and fell down. He lost 20 yards. He just froze up. We didn't get along too well after that. When the newspapers came out, someone had bad-mouthed him about it. Well, my locker was right next to his and I heard him say that he didn't play that badly.

I said something like, "Hell, Darrell, you've played a lot worse . . ."

He didn't like that too much.

A few years later, we had a reunion party and I guess I was drunk. Once the party was over, I was leaving and said something to Darrell, and he gave it to me—knocked me out with a punch. I was mad over it for a long time, but I finally got over it. I guess I had been telling him that night about all the things he had done wrong.

Even at that time, Darrell was working hard to become a head coach. He was up in Wilkinson's office 24 hours a day. He studied the game. He was a damn good defensive halfback—just not that good of a quarterback, in my opinion.

Heck, I sold Darrell the first car he ever owned. It belonged to a school teacher and I paid $2,000 for it, I think. I sold it to him for $1,000, but he wrecked it some place and it was beyond repair. I think he ran it off into a creek bed.

That 1948 team was a damn good team. We were better organized and that was the best Oklahoma team ever until the 1949 team won them all. Boy, I wish I had one more year to play on that team.

Before that first Sugar Bowl, when we beat North Carolina 14–6, they wanted to get a picture of me and Choo Choo Justice—North Carolina's great player. But Choo Choo didn't want to pose for a picture with the enemy. It really pissed me off. It made me play a better ballgame. I got in a couple of good licks on Choo Choo that day, too.

All my brothers went to OU, and four of us played football. Kurt [1951–1954] became an All-American, and Bobby [1953–1955] was pretty good. Bud thought Lynn [1956] was too small, but it was great to get to see them all play for OU. Everybody knows the Selmons had three bothers play for the Sooners in the seventies, but the Burris family had four long before that. Not bad for four guys who grew up on a river, just east of Muskogee and lived in a one-bedroom house with an outside john.

I think Oklahoma football means more to me now than it did when I played. It became very important over the years, and my memories of it remain very special to me.

Paul "Buddy" Burris was Oklahoma's first three-time All-American. He later played three seasons with the Green Bay Packers. Burris was the first OU player inducted into the Helms Athletic Foundation Football Hall of Fame.

Jack Mitchell | Quarterback/Halfback | 1946–1948

I was born and raised in Arkansas City, Kansas—about four miles from the Oklahoma border. My mom and dad went to Arkansas City High, and that is where they met. Dad played football at Washburn College in Topeka, and when the Depression came he got into the real estate business. Dad was a hell of an athlete, a really good track star. His name was Claude but everybody called him either "C.A." or "Mitch."

After my parents divorced, Mom moved to Norman for a few years to get her master's degree when I was young. I lived with her on campus—I was the only boy living in a girls' dormitory.

I had found this perfect spot where you could crawl under the fence at the football stadium, so on Saturdays I headed to the stadium to see all the Oklahoma football games—for free. All the kids would say, "Go see Mitch, he can get you into the game for free."

After my mother got her master's degree, we moved back to Arkansas City and she became the city's main librarian.

Every Saturday night in Arkansas City, the farmers would come to town and the stores would stay open until 9:00 p.m. That was a big deal in a place like Arkansas City back then. I was in the fifth or sixth grade, and my friends and I would race down the street from one block to the next to see who was the fastest. We were dodging people, sometimes knocking them down, to see who could get to the end of the block the fastest. I absolutely loved it because I beat them every time. I knew then that the Lord blessed me with a little bit of athletic ability.

One of my thrills as a kid would be to take a nickel and buy a big red apple each Saturday and turn on the radio and listen to college football games.

By the time I got to be a sophomore, our high school was running the old singe-wing and we had an A team for varsity and a B team for the sophomores. I started out on the B team that season, but the running back got hurt and they promoted me. I was the first sophomore ever to make varsity.

After football, I even made the varsity basketball team as a sophomore, and that really thrilled me. I couldn't wait to get to basketball practice. And then one morning I woke up and my ankle was killing me. It was as if someone had stuck it with a needle. On the way to school, I stopped at this store in town where my aunt worked and told her about it. By this time, I couldn't walk any further.

She felt my forehead and said, "You are hotter than a firecracker."

I had a 105-degree temperature, and they gave me a drug to get my temperature down and then put me to bed. It turned out that I had rheumatic fever. They took me to a specialist who told Mom, "This boy has a valve problem with his heart caused by that high temperature. You have to be very careful with this—he can never be very active again."

I remember my mother said, "What can I do? This boy is so active—I can't keep him in bed."

I had been one of those kids always running, always playing whatever sport was in season. I never stood still for a minute. All of a sudden they were telling me I had to be inactive for the rest of my life! You can imagine the thoughts that passed through my head.

My grandfather was a fairly wealthy man—he owned about half of the town—so we had found another doctor who was right out of medical school. This young doctor, Dr. Ward—I'll never forget that name—had followed athletics and he knew of me.

He said, "Look, I know he'll be a miserable kid if we don't do something."

My mother said, "Whatever it costs, we can afford it."

Dr. Ward explained that one of my heart's valves needed to completely close for me to be normal again and only one thing would do that: complete rest for about six weeks. I had to go home, crawl into bed, and stay there for six weeks! I couldn't even get up to go to the bathroom or to eat. I used a bedpan and was served all my meals in bed. I guess if you tie a horse up to a post long enough, the horse gets used to it. So I got used to it. I listened to the radio a lot, and my friends brought me my books to study. Mom had a teacher come in every once in a while so I didn't fall behind in school.

It kind of got to be a thing for the local kids to come by and see me in bed, like I was a circus act or something. But the neat thing was that when the girls would leave, they would give me a kiss—and on the lips, too, not one of those cheek kisses. That's how I met my high school sweetheart. She came by with some other girls one day and when I got out of that bed, she was the first one I asked for a date.

About six weeks later, that doctor came to examine me and said, "It's closing! It's closing!"

They could tell by its sound that my heart valve had returned to normal. When I first got up, my legs gave out. I could hardly walk. They had told me I couldn't be in athletics anymore, but I should start walking. So I started to walk. Then I would walk a little and jog a little. Then I started to run.

One day the doctor said, "You can run a little bit if you want, but don't overdo it."

Hell, I had been running already for weeks, but I didn't tell him that.

A little later, he said, "I believe this kid can go out for football again."

That was music to my ears, so I came back and had a good junior year. I had put on weight in bed because all I did was eat, so I was bigger. Then when I was a senior, I made all-state in basketball and football.

Life magazine had published one issue with the entire Texas starting team on the cover—all 11 of them. I remember thinking to myself, "Oh

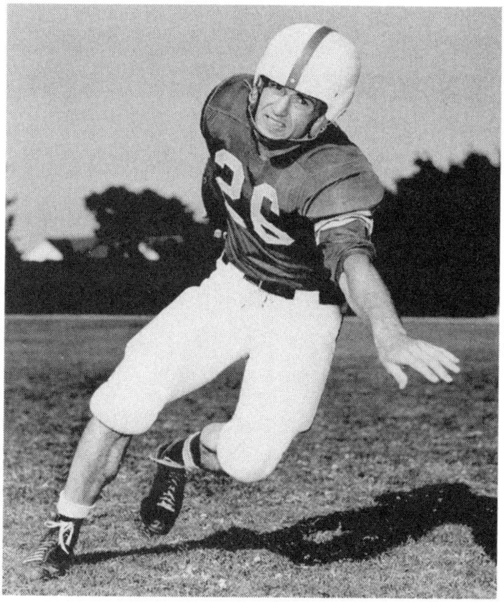

Jack Mitchell moved from halfback to quarterback shortly after he came to OU, where he played a role in the development of the option. *Photo courtesy of OU Athletics Media Relations.*

boy, wouldn't that be wonderful to be on the cover of *Life* magazine in my football uniform?"

One of the store owners in town had graduated from Texas and had gotten wind that I had really liked that *Life* magazine cover, so he sent a letter along with some of my press clippings to [Texas coach] D. X. Bible. Coach Bible offered me a trip to Austin on the train, and when I got down there I went to this dinner at one of the halls on campus. They served me like I was a king. It wasn't any buffet—they actually *waited* on me. That was enough for me: I decided to go to Texas.

The next year, I went to Texas and averaged a couple of touchdowns per game on the freshman team. Everybody there called me "Kansas."

My grandpa was a great guy, but he didn't always get his words right. He had told me, "Now Jackie boy, you're going to college and World War II is starting up, so when you get down there in college, get into that 'ABC' and join the 'battery.'"

What he meant to say was the "ROTC" and the "artillery." He knew that if you were in the artillery, you were not on the front lines, but I knew what he meant. I still laugh about what he told me when I think about it.

I really wanted to fly, but I was color-blind. I had joined the Air Force after that first year at Texas and had played some basketball right away. They came and asked for volunteers for the infantry. I figured they needed more front-line soldiers to get killed. I wanted to be commissioned, but one of the captains, Captain Reid, who coached and played on the basketball team, said to me, "Listen, Jack, you have a lot of potential in college athletics and you are a smart guy . . . you have a real future. I am not going to sign off on this and send you to the infantry to get your ass shot off."

Finally, I convinced Captain Reid that's what I wanted, so he signed my papers to release me from the Air Force. Well, fortunately, I didn't get my ass shot off and I came back home from the war in March 1946. Like a lot of boys returning home, I wanted to go back to school.

My idea was to go to Oklahoma that spring and practice for a week, then go back to Texas and do the same thing, and then make my choice of where I wanted to go to school.

It seemed that [Oklahoma coach] Jim Tatum, who was a hell of a recruiter, had about five classes of seniors out there. Three were hundreds of players for what was a tryout. South of the stadium was our practice field, and we made this circle of players. Why, the circle was so damn big, you could hardly see the other side of it. Pretty soon, they weeded many of them out.

Anyway, I was a halfback, and after a week of practice, Bud Wilkinson, then Tatum's top assistant, came to me and said, "Jack, I'd like to move you to quarterback."

Bud would never do anything unless the player wanted it, too. He knew if a guy was unhappy in a certain position, he wouldn't perform as well.

I said, "I don't think I want to do that. I am a runner—not a passer."

"I know that, Jack," Bud told me. "I know that. But the quarterback is the main runner in this offense. This is the 'Split-T.'"

"I don't care what kind of 'T' it is," I told him. "I don't want to be a quarterback."

Finally, I gave in. I said, "Ah, put me anywhere you want."

And I never made it back to Texas.

Heading into that fall, it was Tatum's first season as head coach. There was so much publicity and attention paid to that first game, at Army. All the fans and big-money alumni people wondered why Tatum had scheduled it and they were really on him about it. They figured Army would kill us.

We had practiced in these old leather helmets, and everyone knew that Army wore those modern Riddell helmets. Well, Tatum had made up his mind that he would order the Riddell helmets for the entire team. He told us that we would have helmets just like the Army team. They were much better helmets that offered you more protection, and once word got out on those helmets, that's all anyone talked about. We kept after our equipment man, Sarge Dempsey, always asking, "Sarge, when are those helmets coming in? When are those helmets coming in?"

That went on for a while and then one day Tatum was missing from practice. We looked over and saw this big truck coming down by the tennis courts, and it was full of helmets. Guess who was sitting on top of the truck? That's right, Tatum. He was sitting up there going through those helmets as the truck came down the road.

He then tossed all of those helmets out for us, and all the big ol' linemen got up there first and got theirs. Finally, I got mine and it was so big. By the end of practice, it had pivoted around and slid down and cut my nose. I still have a scar there.

I walked up to Sarge and said, "My helmet is too big for my head."

Tatum was standing there at the time, and he said, "No, Jack. Hell, there's nothing wrong with that helmet—that's just like the helmet Davis and Blanchard wear." I guess he didn't care about the size of it, but I'll bet Davis' and Blanchard's fit their heads.

Dave Wallace and I were to play equal time at quarterback. He was on one team and I was on another, and the two teams were even. We knew they were going to play one team two quarters and the other team two quarters. I wanted to start that game so badly. Stanley West, who was just out of high school, was on my team.

We were out practicing one day and Stanley was messing around and finally I said, "Damn it, Stanley, get serious with it, will you? Don't you want to start against Army? If you do, then straighten up and get with it."

And he did.

Tatum was so worried about our substitutions that we practiced coming on and off the field for a long time. He took Dave Wallace and Norman McNabb, a guard, and me over to the stadium one day. We went through it over and over.

It went something like this: Tatum would say, "McNabb, put your helmet on and go out to the hash mark. OK, now, Jack, I want you to go in for McNabb. Put your helmet on. McNabb come over here on the sideline and put your helmet between your legs. Now, Wallace, go in for Jack. Put your helmet on. Jack, over here and put your helmet between your legs."

This went on for some time with all three of us running back and forth, putting our helmets on and then putting them between our legs. He was scared to death of getting that 5-yard substitution penalty.

Come game time, Tatum was so nervous. He was taping ankles just to keep focused. Bud was up in the press box, and Dave Wallace's team started the game. So we were sitting on the sidelines and I heard Tatum talking to Bud upstairs.

Tatum would say, "Bud, how about this?" or "Bud, is it time to put McNabb in?"

Finally, it came time to kick the ball, and we kicked it, and then Bud must have told Tatum it was time for McNabb to go in. Tatum turned and handed the phone to McNabb, who was sitting there next to him with his helmet between his legs. Tatum then headed down to the end of the bench looking for McNabb. He was screaming, "McNabb! McNabb!" I was watching this whole thing and poor McNabb, who stuttered a little bit, was trying to get Tatum's attention. He was saying, "Co . . . Co . . . Coach . . . "

Tatum came running back and screamed, "McNabb, what are you doing with that phone in your hands? Get in there!"

And we got a 5-yard penalty!

We lost that big game to Army 21–7. We weren't laughing about it then, but as I have told that story over the years, we get a bigger kick out of it.

There's been much discussion over the years of how the option all started. Don Faurot, the head coach at Missouri, has always claimed he invented the option play. But this is my opinion of how it began. We had this little drill in practice where I would go down the line with the football, and if the play was called "28," I would pitch it, and if it was "26," I would keep it. If the defense played a 6–2 and the ends boxed out, I would keep it. If they played a 5–3 and stayed, I would pitch it. We had dummies set up for the linemen, and then there was a scout-team player on the end on defense. One day I was heading down the line and this scout-team player—he was either tired or didn't care—kept backing off and backing off. I followed him out and finally kept the ball and ran with it.

Bud asked me, "Jack, you had called the pitch play. Why'd you keep the ball?"

I told him, "There's no use following that guy all the way to the sidelines—he would just make the tackle after I pitched it."

He said, "You mean, you could tell what he was going to do?"

"It's just like basketball, coach," I said. "If you have a two-on-one and the defender comes to you, you pass it. If he doesn't, you keep it."

And we started running it that way. That's how I believe the option started, but Don Faurot thinks he invented it, so I won't argue with him. [Historians have credited Faurot with inventing the option in 1941]. But I never saw Missouri run the option the whole time I was at Oklahoma.

After Bud became head coach, he moved me back to halfback, but I still played both from time to time.

There was no question even then that Bud would become a great head coach. He wasn't like Tatum, who was a wild man. Bud was just a real nice guy. He kept his cool and treated you well. He really was ahead of his time. Bud was a great recruiter and he didn't cheat any more than any other coach at the time. He had things so organized. He had a practice schedule that was down to the minute. We didn't waste one minute of practice time.

After we got beat by Santa Clara [in the 1948 season-opener], Bud moved me back to quarterback after the first quarter of the Texas A&M game. We fell behind, and when I got to the line of scrimmage, I started changing plays. Our holes were 22, 24, 26, and 28 to the right, and 21, 23, 25, and 27 to the left. If I saw that the defense had a certain hole covered where we had called the play, I would just say "Add two" or "Drop two" to change the hole where the play was.

We picked up eight yards right away after that. Then boom, boom, boom, and we were in the end zone. That's how that nickname "General Jack" started, because I had changed some plays in that game.

In my final game, the Sugar Bowl after the 1948 season, we couldn't move the ball at all against North Carolina. We came to the bench one time after the first quarter, and I heard this drunk guy behind the bench yelling something like, "Jumper . . . toe ball on 'er line."

I couldn't make out what the heck he was saying because he was slurring his speech. He kept yelling that at us. Nobody else knew what he was talking about, but I finally made it out. It was, "Jump into the air and throw the ball over the line."

I thought, "Shit, we got that play in the playbook but we never use it."

The next time I was in there, I faked the handoff and jumped up and threw it to Jimmy Owens, and we did that two or three times to set up one touchdown.

Merle Greathouse intercepted a pass for us and ran it down inside the 5-yard line. I got in there and looked over the defense and just patted [center] Pete Tillman on the butt and he knew it would be a quarterback sneak. I did that a few times in a row and then, when they moved the guards in, I kept it wide, and it was wide open for a touchdown. We won that game 14–6, and they named me MVP of the game, but Merle Greathouse should have gotten it. He had a great game; I didn't even have a good game.

I want to talk a little about some of my teammates because I loved those guys.

Leon Heath ran up on his heels and he had so much power. He was a great runner. Buddy Burris was such a character. He was a tough guy who could whip anybody's ass. Man, he was good. Wade Walker was a hell of a player. Wade was so strong . . . he had the strongest hands I have ever seen. He could run, too. He was the finest tackle I ever saw.

When I think back on it now, I was very fortunate to end up at Oklahoma after the war ended. To come back and play under a coach like Bud Wilkinson, who taught me so much, remains a great thrill in my life. If it weren't for Bud, I don't know what I would have been in life, I really don't. I went into coaching because of what he taught me and what I learned while at Oklahoma.

I will end this by saying I was very proud to be an Oklahoma Sooner.

Jack Mitchell was named an All-American in 1948. He finished his career with 310 yards passing and he rushed for 1,520 yards and 16 touchdowns. He also was the nation's best kick returner of his era, totaling 927 yards and scoring seven touchdowns on 39 career punt returns and 665 yards on 29 career kick returns. His 23.8-yard punt return average on 22 returns in 1948 remains an NCAA record. He was named All–Big Six in 1947 and All–Big Seven in 1948. Mitchell was head coach of Arkansas 1955–1957 and Kansas 1958–1966.

Darrell Royal | Quarterback/ Defensive Back | 1946–1949

I was born July 6, 1924, and grew up in Hollis, Oklahoma. I never knew my mother, Katy, because she died when I was only four months old. My proper name is Darrell K. Royal—the K is an initial only—in memory of her. My father drove a fuel truck and then was a night watchman for a while. He worked at a lot of jobs just to put food on the table for us. I had three older brothers and two sisters, both of whom I also lost when I was fairly young.

By the time I was six, the land was parched during the Dust Bowl, farms were lost, and my father worked at whatever he could find. Roosevelt had started the WPA, which stood for Work Projects Administration. They built public buildings with local stone. Everyday, Dad would leave after breakfast and see if he could get WPA work that day. It paid 10 cents an hour. Some days he worked; some days he didn't.

You also could get canned food from the government, called "commodities." The cans had no labels on them, so it was obvious where they came from. I don't know how my father kept from accepting those commodities.

When it came to sports, I'll never forget this: there were four guys from Hollis who were quite a bit older than me and they all lettered in football at Oklahoma. Their names were Olin Keith, J. R. Manly, Alton Coppage, and Marvin Whited. They would come back home with those big lettermen jackets with the big white "O" on them. From that point on, after seeing them, that was my ambition.

I wanted to play football at Oklahoma and earn one of those letterman's jackets. I was always playing pickup games in the street—we didn't have organized football until high school.

When I was about 15 years old, my father moved us to California like a lot of other Okies. Our car was a Whippet that he bought before the bust.

He built a trailer and loaded it with our furniture. We were just Okies making the trek west. Times were hard and jobs were hard to come by.

Once we got out to California, I discovered they had a rule that you had to weigh "x" number of pounds to play varsity. If you didn't weigh that amount, and I didn't, you played on junior varsity. I went up to the coach and asked him if I could try out for the varsity no matter what I weighed. He said it didn't matter, that was the rule.

Because of that, I wanted to get back to Oklahoma. My high school coach from Hollis had written me a letter telling me he got me a job and wanted me to come back.

So Dad stayed in California and I started hitching for a ride down to Bakersfield. There, I found that I could get a ride to Texas, but the guy bounced me out in Abilene. It was night-time and I was carrying a little old Victrola box with all of my clothes in it. I found the courthouse in town, put my belt loop through that Victrola box, and crawled up behind some bushes to go to sleep for the night. I woke up with a bright light in my face. A policeman had found me. Right away, he thought I was a runaway.

Darrell Royal demonstrates a pitch during his All-American season of 1949, when the Sooners became the first undefeated team. *Photo courtesy of OU Athletics Media Relations.*

I told him, "I am headed back to Hollis, Oklahoma, to go to school and get a job my football coach promised me."

I had a letter from my high school coach in that Victrola box that proved I was telling the truth, so I showed it to him and he took me upstairs and put me in one of those cells so I could sleep on a cot that night. They didn't lock it. They woke me up the next morning and served me some breakfast while they were feeding the prisoners. Then that policeman drove me back to the highway so I could hitch a ride back to Hollis. All these years, I wished I would have gotten his name so I could have written him to thank him for his kindness.

When I got home to Hollis, I worked in the Ford Motor Company's plant, cleaning the grease wrack, mopping up the show floor, and washing cars. It paid $5 per week, and I was glad to get it. I learned how to shine shoes, and I found I could make more money on Saturdays and Sundays by shining shoes at Cecil Sumpter's Barbershop. I made a dime on a pair of shoes and if I got two or three shines, that was enough to buy lunch. Even on Sundays, guys in town knew I would be working and they would come down there to get their shoes shined before church.

In high school I was a quarterback who called all the plays and all that. We ran a running double-wing, and my position actually was that of a tailback. We had a good season during my senior year, finishing undefeated. My high school coach had taken me to see Oklahoma play, and I remember I was glued in to watching "Indian" Jack Jacobs punt. Boy, he was a great punter.

I graduated in 1943 and volunteered for the service right out of high school. I went into the Air Force and trained as a tail-gunner on B-24s. You had to know how to work the two 50-calibers back there and how to use oxygen and all that. I had an emergency appendectomy before we were to go overseas and I didn't go, but my crew did. And fortunately, they all came back in good shape.

I had played football on the Third Air Force team and that got me several college offers once the war ended. Once I was discharged, my wrist was still healing from a fracture while playing football for the Third Air Force, but I had my mind made up to go to Oklahoma as I had planned.

When I got to Norman, Jim Tatum was in his first year as head coach and he had an assistant named Bud Wilkinson. I had heard that when the school interviewed Tatum, they were more impressed with coach Wilkinson than they were with Tatum.

We had a whole bunch of guys out for football that year, too many to count.

Of course, the numbers were pared down quite a bit by the [1946] opening game at Army. It was a game we should have won, probably, but Arnold Tucker returned one fumble 85 yards for a touchdown after we had driven to the 15-yard line. It was a lateral play and somehow the ball got knocked up into the air and he picked it off and ran the entire way. I would like to see that play on film today just to see exactly what did happen on that play. They also blocked a punt [to set up another Army] touchdown. We lost 21–7, but I think our right halfback, Joe Golding, gained more yards in the game than their entire team.

I do remember that President Truman attended the game and delayed it some because he was late getting there.

I had been in a car wreck that December before we were to play in the Gator Bowl and had my chest all bruised up. I had bought that car from Buddy Burris. I made the trip to Jacksonville, but I didn't think I was going to play. I dressed out and Tatum told me, "Go down and be on the bench." Then he announced I was the starting defensive halfback. I played the game and it didn't hurt much.

Once Tatum left for Maryland after that season, we all thought naming Bud Wilkinson as the new head coach was the right thing to do. He was an excellent quarterback coach and situation coach. He was very, very organized and a very impressive man. I knew from the time I was in high school that I wanted to be a coach someday, so I listened to everything he said. And I spent a lot of time with [assistant] Gomer Jones, too. I wanted to know pretty much all aspects of the game.

Every off-season, I went to summer school—as a result I graduated in three and a half years in business management—so I would go over there to the coaches' office and look at film with them when they were around. You may not have heard much about Gomer receiving any credit, but he got a lot of credit from his players. He was a great coach.

We didn't start too well for coach Wilkinson's first season [in 1947], losing a few [to Texas and TCU, and tying Kansas] so when we got to that Missouri game, we knew we had to win. We were big underdogs that day, as I recall. When we got down to the 36- or 37-yard line a few times, coach Wilkinson decided to punt instead of going for it, and I knocked three of them out of bounds inside the 5-yard line. After that last one, they fumbled, Frankie Anderson recovered it, and we scored the winning touchdown soon after that. That 21–12 win was a big win for coach Wilkinson—and for Oklahoma. That got it all started for him.

We just had an off day, a real bad day to begin the 1948 season. Plus, Santa Clara had a good football team [OU lost 20–17]. But I never dreamed that we would never lose another football game in my career.

You want to win every game you suit up for, but you really don't expect to have a run like we did. [Oklahoma won their final 10 games of 1948 and all 11 in 1949 in Royal's senior season].

Over the years people have asked me about my 96-yard punt return [against Kansas State in 1948], and all I can say is that I never should have fielded it. You never field punts inside your 10-yard line, let alone inside your own five. When I got into coaching, we would put our punt returners on the 10 and tell them, "Now if it's a high kick, fair-catch it. If it's over your head, let it go."

But for some reason, I did field it that day and I got behind the wall. It wasn't clear sailing but it was pretty close to it.

I played defensive back and quarterback in 1948 and then spent the entire 1949 season at quarterback. It was a special season and we had a really good football team. Most of us had been there for four years.

What do you want me to say about the Texas games? It was sold out in 1946 when I played in it as a freshman, and it's been sold out every year since. What more can you say about a rivalry? There was an extreme amount of hard-hitting, and I always knew that both teams would be sore on the following Monday. That senior year, they put an offset guy on our center's nose, and I was having to check off quite a bit that day. We won [20–14], so I finished 2–2 against Texas as a player, which made it pretty easy to come here later on.

I was really close with some of my teammates. In fact, we were a very close team, but I suppose when you win them all it's easier to be close. Most winning teams are that way, I have discovered over the years.

Wade Walker and I always have been really close. As a matter of fact, I named my son David Wade Royal after him. When I got my first head coaching job at Mississippi State, Wade came to work for me there. We had an agreement: whoever became head coach first would bring along the other one. And I can say that he was a great tackle at Oklahoma.

Stan West was a close friend and an outstanding player, too. Boy, he was hard to block. George Thomas was a good friend and a great halfback. He had excellent balance. Jack Mitchell was an outstanding leader. He took control as well as anybody I had ever seen. Buddy Burris was a great football player. He had good speed. We had a little run-in once a long time ago, but when I saw him recently, I stuck my hand out to shake his hand. Buddy said, "The heck with that—give me a hug!"

You forget those old grievances as time passes on.

The sessions I had with coach Wilkinson . . . I copied the mold when I became a head coach. He was a great mentor, and I tried to use everything he taught me, but I couldn't copy his personality. I knew that would be a mistake. Nobody could copy that. I have seen several of coach "Bear" Bryant's assistants try to act like him over the years, and they couldn't do it effectively.

The things I learned from coach Wilkinson—like trying to make first downs, then make another first down instead of trying to break one for a touchdown on every play—stuck with me. He wanted to break the game down into a series of downs and it worked well for him.

He helped me get my first coaching job at North Carolina State. When I graduated, North Carolina State wanted somebody to coach who had a background in the Split-T. I always thought I would be a high school coach, but it came about all because of coach Wilkinson.

I went from North Carolina State to Tulsa, to a head coach at Mississippi State, to Washington, and then I got here to Texas in 1956.

When I came to Texas and we played against Oklahoma, I swear that I was so focused during the game, making the decisions I had to make, that I was never aware coach Wilkinson was on the other sideline. And I am sure he wasn't aware it was me on the other sideline. I had a team to run, an organization to run, and I competed the same way that I did as a player—to win. I competed all-out. [Royal had a 12–7–1 record coaching against OU, including a 6–1 record against Bud Wilkinson.]

I don't want to be cold about it, but when you are coaching, you are coaching. You are totally immersed in it. We were still close during those years, just as close as we were before. I gave his eulogy when he died in 1994. Texas-Oklahoma is a game that is special. I walked out of that tunnel of the Cotton Bowl four times as a player for Oklahoma and 20 times as a coach for Texas.

It really is amazing to think that we have been here in Texas for 48 years as of 2005.

I was contacted a couple of times about coming back [to become head coach at Oklahoma], but I felt I should stay here. It felt like I would be switching universities, and I had a good program going here. I had acceptance here. To tell you the truth, it wouldn't have been an easy chore to follow coach Wilkinson and I didn't want to do that. Later on, I still didn't want to do it.

It's really hard for some people to understand that you *can* have feelings for both Texas and Oklahoma. My alma mater is where I got my formal education, where I played, and where I knew all of my teammates. Some people can't understand my feelings for both, but it's not a complicated matter for me. It never has been.

Darrell Royal was an All-America quarterback in 1949 in leading Oklahoma to its first national championship. Considered one of the greatest all-around players in Sooners history, he passed for 1,268 yards and 13 touchdowns in his career and rushed for 641 yards and seven touchdowns. Oklahoma won 15 of Royal's 16 career starts at quarterback. He is OU's career interception leader with 17. His 96-yard punt return in 1948 against Kansas State remains a school record. He also punted 1946–1948 and had an 81-yard punt in 1948 against Oklahoma State. He went on to become head coach at the University of Texas 1956–1976, winning 11 Southwest Conference championships and three national championships.

Wade Walker | Tackle | 1946–1949

Growing up during the Depression, we lived through tough times. People who did not experience it have no idea how tough it was. My father was a used car dealer and my mom had five dollars to pay for groceries for a week. I was the youngest of six children. Our oldest brother went into the Navy just to send money home for us. But all these years later, I can honestly say that I have had a great life—because I played football for the University of Oklahoma.

Gastonia, North Carolina, was a great place to grow up. I hear all of these people on the national airwaves butcher the English language and I instantly think of Sarah McCurter. She taught ninth-grade grammar at Gastonia, and I promise you I still think of what she taught me. When one of our kids would say, "Where's it at?" I would answer "between the 'A' and the 'T'" because that was what Sarah would say.

I went to the University of North Carolina for three quarters before I went into the service. Even then, I always made the highest grade on grammar because Sarah taught us well. When the TV announcers use the wrong tense when I am watching a football game, I think of her. She must be rolling over in her grave at those TV guys.

I knew back then what I wanted to be. When I was playing high school football in Gastonia, I knew I wanted to become an All-American football player—and I wanted to be a head football coach someday.

When you reach those type of dreams, how lucky can you be?

But we all went into the service out of high school because we were in the middle of the war. I played three years of football in the service, two at the Jacksonville Naval Station. Don Faurot was the head coach and Jim Tatum was his assistant when I first got there in 1944. The next year, Tatum became the head coach. When Tatum took the job at the University of Oklahoma, he recruited me to come there.

I had no idea where Oklahoma was, I promise you. I was mustered out in Dallas, so I came to Norman for the weekend. Coach Tatum was staying in OU athletic director Jap Haskell's basement. When I walked in there to see him, a tall, younger-looking man was with them.

I asked him, "What position do you play?"

He looked at me and said, "Why, I am one of the coaches. My name is Bud Wilkinson."

Tatum said that if I came to OU, when I graduated he would get me a job with him. I had become very close to him at Jacksonville and I knew he was a good man.

I was so glad to get out of the Navy when I arrived at Oklahoma. I remember seeing the stadium for the first time. It was the biggest stadium I had seen. We had played in the Gator Bowl in the Navy, but it wasn't as big then as the stadium at the University of Oklahoma. When you first come into campus and you see that oval for the first time and then the loop to the law building, that's got to be impressive to anyone. It sure was to me.

The thing was, I was a 21-year-old freshman, like a lot of other guys right out of the service. Yep, we were all mature, 21- or 22-year-old freshmen.

I met Jean Herman in 1947 when Marshal Armstrong, one of my high school teammates, was a lifeguard at one of the resorts in Myrtle Beach, South Carolina. We met on the beach and I like to say the good Lord directed us together. We were married in 1949 and had five children. The ironic thing was that at Oklahoma at one time, 22 of us were married.

That's when coach Tatum started taking us over to Oklahoma City to stay in the hotel on the night before games. He wanted us rested and focused on the game, but that's the reason it all started, and Oklahoma has been doing it ever since.

Tatum was the funniest man . . . he used to tell us, "Now we are going to give you an aw-pul." That's an "apple" to you and me. He had that big Southern accent. Tatum knew his football, though. He was a wonderful defensive coach, and coach Wilkinson was a wonderful offensive coach.

During those first few practices [of 1946], there were a million prospects out there. You could say that the competition was keen.

I don't know what threw us together, but Darrell Royal became my best friend—and still is. Darrell was married and had a child then, and I would go to his house during two-a-days because he had a fan. Nobody had air-conditioning. We would lie down in front of that fan and go to sleep. He later named a son after me, David Wade Royal.

I will always love Darrell Royal, I promise you.

Darrell was a hot-rod safety in those days. He may not tell you how good he was because he is very modest, but let me tell you, he was a great one. Playing Texas was our yardstick of whether we were a good football team, and during one game, one of the Texas ends dropped a pass. Darrell picked up the ball and gently flipped it back to him.

"There," he said, "see if you can catch that one."

I almost died when he did that.

We opened that first season at Army, and Tatum got so upset because President Truman was late getting to the ballgame. They held the kickoff for 30 minutes waiting for him, and Tatum got to stuttering and shaking because he was so mad.

At halftime, he screamed at us in that Southern accent, "Liss-ssen, they even got the presss-ident on their side. Thoo-ooose dirty rats!"

My teammates used to mimic him quite a bit.

When he left for Maryland after that season, he asked me to transfer there, but I told him, "No, Coach, I can't go. I love it here."

I knew coach Wilkinson would become the head coach. He was the epitome of grace. He was an English major and spoke properly, and I already knew by then that Oklahoma was a great place to play football and get an education. So why would I leave?

I also knew this: Bud—it was never "Bud" for me back then. I always called him coach Wilkinson; Eddie Crowder and Billy Vessels called

Wade Walker was an All-American tackle on the 1949 national championship team and later returned to Norman as OU's athletic director for 16 years. *Photo courtesy of OU Athletics Media Relations.*

him Bud—was a great organizer and his teams were going to win. One philosophy he used to say was, "We will pour the pine to them for three quarters. It will be so fierce for three quarters that come the fourth quarter, they will give up. We *will* win the fourth quarter."

The worst I ever heard him say to a player was, "Son, it just looks like you don't want to play."

You think about that. How can you put it any better to motivate someone? You can't put that needle any deeper, can you?

"Son, it just looks like you don't want to play."

That was coach Wilkinson.

We were 21-point underdogs against Missouri in 1947, but we beat my old Navy coach Don Faurot's team 21–12. That was the beginning of Bud's career. After that game, it really took off.

We opened the next season by losing to Santa Clara—and then we never lost again. We ran out of gas in the fourth quarter that day against Santa Clara. We played in the Sugar Bowl against North Carolina and Choo Choo Justice that year. Choo Choo was a tailback, and I was a defensive tackle. One time after I knocked him down, he looked up at me and said, "I would rather be playing golf."

New Orleans was so good to us that week. Gomer Jones said that coach Wilkinson was worried about us getting into trouble that week, but I told him, "Gomer, you don't have to worry about us. This bunch will be ready."

That was true. We were old enough to know not to get our noses bloodied on Bourbon Street. We knew why we were there. We knew how to train, we knew how to knock the heck out of people. We knew how to study and we know how to go to school. We were a mature group.

It doesn't get any better than what we did in 1949: win all of our games. I was lucky, too, because I never got hurt playing football. I played 11 years: four in high school, three in the Navy, and four at Oklahoma.

Oklahoma was so good to me as a player. I got a Big Six ring in 1946 and gave that to my youngest son. I gave my Big Seven ring to my oldest son and a Big Eight ring to my middle son. My favorite ring was from our undefeated team of 1949, but I lost it when it popped out of a golf cart a few years ago. I figured a mower got it. I wanted to cry that day.

When Darrell and I graduated, we made a bond. The first one to get to be a head coach would bring the other as an assistant. Sure enough, he got the job at Mississippi State [in 1954] and he called me. At that time, we had always felt that if you made $10,000 you were really cutting it.

Darrell told me, “I can’t get you $10,000, but I can get you $9,500.”

“I’ll be there,” I said.

I was an assistant for Darrell and then after he left I became head coach and later athletic director. We stayed in Starkville for 16 years before I got fired. Then I returned to my alma mater as athletic director for 16 years there before I retired in 1986. How lucky could a guy be?

You have to put playing at Oklahoma in perspective. It was the greatest thing to happen to me other than my wife and five children. Another great thing was that my bride shared Oklahoma with me for my final two years as a player.

Oklahoma will always be the Alpha and Omega for me. When I was athletic director there, I once said, “Football is the biggest thing in Oklahoma” and the governor didn’t think it was very funny, but it is true. It is very true.

I think of my teammates almost every day. I think we have lost seven or eight of them in the past year. I can’t emphasize enough how dear those people are to me. I love them.

I love Oklahoma!

Wade Walker was an All-American tackle in 1949 during Oklahoma’s first national championship season. He is one of three OU players ever to be named all-conference four times. He later became head coach at Mississippi State 1956–1961 and returned to Oklahoma as athletic director 1970–1986.

| chapter two |

The Fifties

Eddie Crowder | Quarterback | 1950–1952

It's been more than 53 years since my last football game as an Oklahoma Sooner and rarely has a day gone by that didn't bring a memory of that unique and wonderful experience. An experience that has a lasting effect on your daily life for more than a half of a century must have some kind of mystique that others don't.

I believe that is true in my experience as a Sooner.

The relationships that were born in being Sooners together have led to some of the strongest friendships of my life. Two of them, Billy Vessels and Buck McPhail, were especially treasured, and I am deeply saddened that each has passed away.

First of all, I want to tell a few stories about them.

Before I called each play back then, we used an open huddle instead of the oval that most teams currently use. One reason Bud Wilkinson used this configuration was so the quarterback could see the faces of the other three running backs. If any of them looked less than fresh, we would call a play for one of the other backs.

The Notre Dame game at South Bend in 1952 was brutal and by the second quarter, I looked at the backs and all three were looking down at the ground rather than at me. It was obvious to me they were beat up already.

I remember thinking, "In this situation, no question, give it to Billy."

I called "23," and Billy hit the dive-play hole so quickly that it was a reach to get the ball to him. He accelerated through the hole and ran right past Notre Dame's secondary for a touchdown. He scored all three touchdowns that day, but the Irish came back in the fourth quarter to beat us 27–21. It was our only loss of the season, but I believe that performance earned the Heisman Trophy that year for Billy Vessels.

In the first quarter of that game, we ran a counter pass. It called for me to make a strong fake to Buck McPhail and to retreat as though I were watching him run up the middle with the ball. Then I would turn and hit Billy in the left flat. It worked perfectly. Notre Dame tackled Buck, and Billy took the pass 28 yards to a touchdown.

If something worked, we always came back to it. So in the fourth quarter, we called "30 pass" again. It looked like Billy was open, but I never saw Johnny Lattner lurking out of my view. He cut in front of Billy and intercepted the pass. [The next year, Johnny won the Heisman Trophy.]

Over the years, I have told the story of being the only quarterback in college football history to throw a touchdown pass to two Heisman Trophy winners in the same game. It's really a flawed story, because one of our guys pulled down Lattner at the 1-yard line and Neal Warden scored on the next play. But let the record stand that I am the only guy who completed a pass to a Heisman winner on each of the two teams in the same game.

To make the play-action pass work, you really had to have a fullback who was good at carrying out the fake. The fullback had to bend over the football so as it's withdrawn by the quarterback it is not seen by the defense. Then he had to run as though he had the ball, and nobody was ever better at this than Buck.

He was so convincing in carrying out the fake that he took explosive shots by defenders trying to tackle him. Buck was a devoted team player who made that sacrifice over and over again during his career. He also blocked as well as any Sooner back—before him or since.

And Buck had his moments carrying the ball, too. He is tied [with Jeff Frazier, 1995] for the longest run from scrimmage in Oklahoma history at 96 yards [against Kansas State, 1951]. He also rushed for 1,018 yards as a senior—uncommon for a fullback even then.

Buck was a fine man and as loyal and as dear of a friend as I have ever known.

Those are the friendships that last for more than 50 years, which brings me to another story of a friendship and treasured relationship. During my sophomore year, Claude Arnold was the starting quarterback. That could make for a competitive situation, I suppose, but it wasn't. Claude had been in the service before returning to Oklahoma, so he was more experienced and ready to play than I was. I looked up to him and learned from him.

That year, 1950, we were playing Texas A&M in Norman. I had taken a knee to the kidney so I had been in the hospital for a few days, but they released me on Saturday in time to watch the game from the press box. A&M had a great team that year, and the third quarter ended in a 21–21 tie before the Aggies took a seven-point lead in the fourth quarter. As the clock wound down, Claude drove us deep into A&M territory. With 3:36 remaining, he hit Billy Vessels for a 32-yard touchdown pass, but Jim Weatherall's kick that would have tied the game missed.

The defense stopped A&M, and the offense took over on its own 31-yard line with only 1:46 remaining. Claude hit four of five passes for 65 yards before Leon Heath scored on a four-yard run with only 37 seconds left as we won the game 34–28. As a young quarterback, that comeback left quite an impression on me.

Furthermore, I always believed Claude was the most underrated quarterback in Oklahoma history.

I can't summarize great memories and treasured relationships from Oklahoma without mentioning Bud Wilkinson. Of the many wonderful people I've had the opportunity to know in my life, Bud was one of a kind.

I remember the first day I arrived in Norman. I'd met Bud briefly earlier, but on my first day on campus, we arrived at his office at the same time. He greeted me with a sincerity, a warmth, and a humility that assured me that he really cared about me and loved me as an individual and not only as a football player. I was only 18, but that left an indelible imprint on me that has lasted all these years.

Bud had remarkable vision and insight.

Let me give you an example. Each day, he would spend time with the quarterbacks on a one-on-one basis. He would set up this checkerboard-like display with miniature football players that looked like little soldiers on a board that represented a football field.

He'd give you the game situation, the down and distance, and have you call the play. You'd get a result and go through the process all over again. During the week of a game, you'd go over at least 13 possessions with him—the average number of possessions per game.

One time during my junior year, as we prepared for Colorado, he told me that with our running game having great success heading into the game, he expected the defense to take some risks and commit their secondary to run support. Our play-action passes would be the ideal way to attack them, he predicted.

On our first possession of the game, sure enough, their defensive backs were positioned like linebackers—all were within five yards of the line of scrimmage. We threw four touchdown passes that day and won 55–14.

Eddie Crowder strikes his quarterbacking pose prior to his All-American season in 1952. *Photo courtesy of OU Athletics Media Relations.*

The next season before we played Texas, Bud had a meeting with the quarterbacks in his suite at the Worth Hotel in Fort Worth. He told us that he had a premonition the previous night that Texas would play us the same way that Colorado did the year earlier. So we would use plenty of play-action passes that day. He said it would be the same type of game. He was right, it was. Play-action passes worked all day, and we won 49–20.

The unique thing about Bud was that along with his talent and mind was a consistent demeanor and persona. Three years after finishing my education at Oklahoma, Bud invited me to join his staff by replacing Pete Elliott, who was leaving to become the head coach at Nebraska. It was then that I saw a practice situation that detailed how Bud was the ultimate teacher.

One day in the spring of 1958, Bud was conducting a drill to teach the fullbacks the cross-body block used to chop down the defensive end so we could run outside. He was ready to have Ronnie Hartline make the block just when the horn blew, indicating the end of practice. Whenever the horn blew, the entire team would assemble wherever coach Wilkinson was standing.

As we all approached him and his blocking drill this day, he told us to gather around while they finished practice with one last block. Another player would hold a dummy to simulate the defensive end. He would pull the dummy back from the oncoming fullback to simulate a realistic response by the defensive end in trying to avoid being blocked. As Ronnie approached the dummy that day, he had committed to throw the block and, as it was pulled away, he fell flat on his face without making any contact.

Just then, Bud ran over and said, "Ronnie, Ronnie . . . you have no idea how close you came to making the perfect block!"

He then told everyone, "As you approach the defensive end, you want to place your outside foot as close to him as possible so when he moves away you recoil off that foot and into him to make the block. Now Ronnie, let's try it one more time because I know you can do it."

Ronnie Hartline then made as great of a block as I ever saw.

That illustrates how great Bud was at teaching and communicating the game. Imagine what it did for Ronnie Hartline's confidence. He went on to become one of the Sooners' greatest fullbacks.

Those are a few of my memories of the plays, games, teammates—and Bud Wilkinson—which made my experience at Oklahoma so special.

What does it mean to be a Sooner? To answer that question, I had to ask myself, "What are the most important blessings and experiences that have molded my life?"

The first is my faith. The second is my family. The third is clearly the treasured years I spent as an Oklahoma Sooner.

Eddie Crowder was an All-American in 1952 and All–Big Seven in 1951 and 1952. He passed for 1,189 yards and 11 touchdowns, and rushed for 661 yards and eight touchdowns in his career. He was a member of OU's first national championship team in 1950 and then led the Sooners to two conference championships as the starting quarterback in 1951 and 1952. Crowder was an OU assistant coach 1956–1962 and later became head coach at Colorado.

J. D. Roberts | Guard | 1951–1953

I grew up on the east side of Dallas, rooting for Oklahoma, selling programs and hot dogs in the Cotton Bowl with my best friend, Eddie Joseph, when the Sooners played Texas. Eddie rooted for Texas, but he still was my best friend.

My dad was an auto mechanic, and mom was a homemaker. Dad was a big sports fan and, naturally, so was I. We lived on Worth Street, and I was like most kids, I loved all sports. I played baseball, softball, and football, and back in those days in Dallas we played in the parks. In the summer, you played a game against teams from other city parks. I was always sort of short and stocky, so football was my best sport.

I went to school at a Catholic school, which had grades one through eight. At Saint Edward's we played against other Catholic grade schools. Once I got out of grade school, we moved to Wiley, Texas, about 20 to 25 miles from Dallas, and I had to catch a ride to my high school, Jesuit High. Then I would hitchhike home.

I made varsity as a sophomore at Jesuit, but we didn't do that well. We might have won three games that year. The next year, we only had a couple of losses, and both games—by the scores of 7–0 and 13–7—could have gone the other way. Then we got a new coach, Don Rossi, who was a great football coach. The first two years I had been a blocking back in the single-wing. But one day I was walking in the hallway at school before my senior year, and coach Rossi stopped me.

"Are you a football player," he asked me.

I said something like, "I try to be."

"What position do you play?

I told him I was a blocking back.

"Not anymore," he told me. "You're now a guard."

That became my position for my senior year and for the next four years of college, too.

I was about 5'10" and 230 pounds, so I guess I was built to play guard back then. Anyway, that senior year we went undefeated.

I was working for a construction company owned by a Texas A&M graduate and I had decided to go to A&M. I also liked Notre Dame, but I figured it was just too far away. It wasn't as easy to travel to places like that in 1950.

My coach wasn't happy with my decision to go to A&M because he wanted me to go to Oklahoma. Toward the end of that August before my freshman year, he told me he was going up to Norman the next day and that I should ride along with him, even though I was set on going to A&M.

He had me meet with coach [Bud] Wilkinson, who just said something like, "If you come here and play well, you will have a nice career."

He talked me into being a Sooner right on the spot.

And guess what? I never came back to Dallas. I had my parents send me some clothes, and I stayed with my grandparents in Oklahoma City until fall practice started in Norman. I never even called the coaches at A&M. It surely wasn't the typical way to choose a college, I guess. I thought I was going up there for the weekend and I ended up staying the whole semester.

Guard J. D. Roberts was voted the nation's top lineman after the 1953 season. *Photo courtesy of OU Athletics Media Relations.*

Right from the start, I liked coach Wilkinson. He had a lot of class and he knew how to talk to you.

I did go back to Dallas when we played Texas in the Cotton Bowl, and as freshmen, we got to sit right behind our bench. I remember Billy Vessels made a great run toward the end of the game, and Jim Weatherall kicked the extra point, and we won 14–13. That 1950 team went on to win the national championship, and as freshmen, we were all proud of them.

When I came back for two-a-days in 1951, I was on the third unit. All I knew was I was trying to make the team. As it turned out, I was on the first team at right guard and was the backup middle guard on defense by the end of camp.

We played William & Mary in the opener that year, and I was going against a big old guy. I remember his name—pronounced "Creamcheck"—but don't ask me to spell it. I weighed 230 and he was all of that and probably 6'3" or 6'4". I jumped offside twice in a row early in that game and I thought I was going to be pulled at any minute—coach Wilkinson didn't like errors. I looked over at the sideline, but nobody was coming in for me. After that, I was fine, but I think I did jump off once more later on.

After that first game, I played fairly well against A&M and Texas. A&M had a great punter and kept us in a hole all night long. Back then, not throwing the ball any more than we did, it was tough to drive the ball 80 or 90 yards all on the ground, and we lost 14–7. Texas beat us 9–7. Playing in that first Texas game was such a tremendous thrill, just to think that two years earlier I was up in the stands selling hot dogs. We won the rest of them and finished 8–2 that season.

That next spring, the coaches told me they wanted me to play both ways the next season. They said, "It will be up to you to work at it this spring to get ready to start both ways."

I weighed about 218 that year, but I thought playing both ways would be fine. What the heck? You practice and work out both ways—you might as well play on the field both ways, I thought. I enjoyed it. And remember, back then if you were on offense, you played on the kick-receiving team. If you were on defense, you played on the kicking team. So I never came off the field.

We tied Colorado 21–21 in the opener and then won the next five games. We had a heck of an offensive football team. We had Texas down 28–0 in the first 10 minutes (of a 49–20 win). We scored 40 points or more in all five of those games before playing at Notre Dame. Two minutes before the half, I got into a complication with Notre Dame's guard, and the officials caught me swinging at him and threw me out of the game. We ended up losing 27–21, and I knew we should have beaten them that day.

That year was a lot of fun because we moved the ball pretty darned good in every game. It was a heck of a year with a really outstanding football team, but that Notre Dame loss was our only one. We finished 8–1–1, but I still don't know why we didn't get to a go to a bowl game.

I was back home in Dallas for the holidays. Texas was playing Tennessee in the Cotton Bowl, and I wanted to go to the game in the worst way. Texas was staying at the Melrose Hotel, so I went down there and ran into one of their coaches and asked him for a pass.

He said, "Just come sit on our bench."

So I did. I was a Sooner who actually sat on *Texas*' bench during that Cotton Bowl. And they kicked Tennessee's butt all day long.

The next year, we lost quite a few people from the 1952 team and had only seven or eight seniors. It was primarily sophomores. And we opened with Notre Dame in Norman. They had Johnny Lattner, who was one heck of a football player. He was a good offensive back, a good defensive back, and he punted. Lattner went on to win the Heisman Trophy and rightfully so. He deserved it. We had a chance to tie it at the end of the game, but we either overthrew a pass or dropped it, I can't remember, but I know our receiver was wide open and we ended up losing 28–21.

That was our last loss before the famous 47-game winning streak.

Then we went to Pittsburgh and tied 7–7. I can't explain that one. We should have had that game hands down. We scored right off the bat and then did everything wrong for the remainder of the game. We beat Texas 19–14, but had them down 19–7 late in the game when we fumbled. They scored to make it close, then made an onside kick and recovered it, but they were offside. They tried it again, but we got it and managed to run the clock out.

Since I had sat on their bench in the Cotton Bowl, I got to know some of the Texas guys. It was an extremely heated rivalry with them, but once the game was over, I got along with them. I always believed once the game was over, you shake hands and let it go.

We finished 9–1–1 that season and went to the Orange Bowl to play Maryland. It was the first bowl game for all of us. Quite a few guys on that team were married, and their wives had made the trip to the Orange Bowl. The night before the game, they always had the Orange Bowl parade and some of the guys asked me if I would say something to coach Wilkinson about maybe all of us going to the parade.

I told them, "I think everybody already knows the answer to that one."

I knew damn good and well that wasn't in the game plan, but I went up to coach Wilkinson anyway.

"Coach," I said, "I was asked to ask you . . . "

After dinner that night, coach Wilkinson got up and gave a little talk. He went through the whole season, from the Notre Dame game to the Pitt game to the end. He talked about how we had practiced hard, how we had played hard, how we didn't quit, how we got better as the season progressed. Then he came to the parade issue.

"I understand a lot of you want to go to the parade," he said. "All I can say is that if you think going to this parade will help us win this ballgame, I am all for it."

Then he gave all the reasons why it wouldn't. He said we could vote on it as a team, and he and his staff then left the room.

The captains said, "Let's vote. Raise your hands if you want to go to the parade."

Not one hand went up.

Maryland was a great team. If I had to rate Texas, Notre Dame, and Maryland one, two, and three, I couldn't. They were each great teams in their own way. We scored on "29 Quick" with Larry Grigg to beat Maryland 7–0 in that Orange Bowl.

As you can tell from the outcome of the parade issue, you could say we believed in coach Wilkinson. Before home games, we always stayed in Oklahoma City, and I always made it a point to go to an early mass on the mornings of our games. Saint Joseph's Cathedral was right down the street from the hotel, and I would walk the four blocks to mass that started at about 6:15 or 6:30.

One time during my junior year, coach Wilkinson, who always took a morning walk, saw me coming back into the hotel at about 7:00 a.m., so he sent [assistant coach] Gomer Jones to talk to me after our pregame meal.

"Jess," Gomer started, "coach Wilkinson saw you coming into the hotel around 7:00 a.m. Where were you?"

"Coach, I've been to church," I answered.

"What? You want me to believe that?" he said. "Where's the church?"

I told him where the church was and told him it was the truth.

After the game that day, Bud, who usually came around to all the lockers after a game to speak with every player one-on-one, stopped by my locker.

"You played a fine game, Jess," he said.

Then he said he was very sorry for quizzing me about where I had been that morning. That's the type of gentleman he was.

It was a great experience playing for coach Wilkinson. I had tremendous teammates: Billy Vessels, Buddy Leake, Buck McPhail, Larry Grigg, Jim Weatherall, Kurt Burris, Harry Moore, Eddie Crowder, and Gene Calame.

But no matter where I went after my OU days, this is the first thing people wanted to know: What is Bud Wilkinson like?

That always made me feel really good. He just had that ability to get the most out of all the players, whatever their potential was. Players respected him, no doubt about that. Not all of them loved him, but they all respected him.

One time my roommate was the starting guard one week and on the sixth team the next week because of a bad game. He went to see Coach one day to confront him about not playing. He came back to our room and I asked if he saw coach Wilkinson.

"Yeah, I saw the silver-tongued, gray-haired coach," he snapped.

"How'd it go?" I asked.

"Oh, the hell with it . . . ," he said. "Boomer Sooner!"

That's how good coach Wilkinson could make you feel. Oklahoma was my school, and Bud Wilkinson was my coach.

J. D. Roberts won the Outland Trophy and was named an All-American in 1953. He also was a unanimous selection as the National Lineman of the Year. He later joined the U.S. Marines, where he played football. He was an assistant coach at Oklahoma 1958–1959, Denver, Navy, Auburn, and Houston. He became the head coach of the NFL's New Orleans Saints 1970–1972. Roberts was inducted into the College Football Hall of Fame in 1993.

Prentice Gautt | Fullback | 1957–1959

Editor's note: Prentice Gautt was a star football player at Douglass High in Oklahoma City. He led his high school team to 43 consecutive wins and became the first black player in the state's all-star game. In 1956, he became a freshman at the University of Oklahoma and the first African American to play football for the Sooners. Prentice died March 17, 2005. The following was compiled from excerpts of several of his interviews.

When I was growing up, I never thought I would be able to go to the University of Oklahoma, let alone be a part of the structure of the NCAA. I was a kid who learned not to ask for a lot of things. When I got something, I was grateful for it.

The only thing that I knew was that I wanted to play football for Oklahoma and for Bud Wilkinson. I didn't think of it as being a pioneering kind of thing. I didn't go to Oklahoma for that reason.

People to whom I will be forever grateful believed I could make it both academically and athletically at the university. Once I got there, I had a lot of people telling me that I wasn't going to make it, either academically or athletically. I had to bust my fanny to make it all happen.

It seems to me that doors opened for me without my thinking about it. It seems I have been blessed all my life.

When I arrived as a freshman, some players had quit and I am sure there were others who felt like leaving, but they stayed and they deserve as much credit as I do.

Bud Wilkinson was a blessing to me. Without him, things would have been a lot different. His philosophies and his values really rubbed off on me. People knew this man as a football coach, but his essence transcended more than that for me. As I think back, he was a confidant, a father-figure, a person whom I never heard use abusive language. He treated all of his players the same way—with dignity.

The spring of my freshman year, he called me in one day after practice. I admit I was not putting out my best and he told me, "If you continue as you are, you are not going to make our traveling squad."

Prentice Gautt was the first African American to play football at Oklahoma, and he enjoyed a highly distinguished college and professional career on and off the field.

It almost shocked me. I know he had never told anyone that. It was like he wanted me to do well. He wanted me to improve. I would spend Wednesdays talking to him as if it were my time on the couch. Bud was so supportive of me. He didn't let me sink. He was constantly telling me, "You've got to be smart, you've got to work hard, you've got to be tough and you've got to be powerful."

In many ways, I saw myself as just another football player trying to make it at a great program. It was never about setting a trend or writing history. It was about football and school and teammates.

As grateful as I was for the chance to play, it was frustrating. It wasn't the people any more than it was the atmosphere at the time. I was fortunate I participated in athletics to take the pressure off. That's the way I dealt with my frustrations and my anger.

[Before the OU-Texas game in Dallas in 1957] I remember the team walking into the old President's Hotel in Fort Worth and me being ushered through the back door into a cab that took me to a house owned by a black family. At the time, I didn't see myself as a pioneer because I was too caught up in the excitement and the mystique of playing Texas. But now that I look back on it, I am pretty proud that I was the first. Going through those things was a knock at one's self-concept. It was difficult at that age to just say, "That's their problem, not yours." It was difficult, but I had supporters encouraging me, telling me, "Hey, you're bigger than that."

I am glad I went through the things I did when I was younger because they made me a better person. I had maybe five or six negative things happen to me, but I was at Oklahoma for four years. Just look at all the positive things that happened to me. That is what I always tried to do.

I've found that people who live in the past, emotionally, are usually very angry people, inwardly angry. People who live in the future are usually depressed people. You must live in the present. You must do your best at the time.

I was part of a gradual awakening, a gradual acceptance. I just happened to be at a place in time where I could be a part of the process.

[When informed in March 1999 that OU would name the school's athletic academic center "The Prentice Gautt Academic Center"] I was overwhelmed! It was overwhelming. That's all I could say when they told me. I'll always have a significant spot in my heart for Oklahoma because of all the things we experienced together.

As I think about it now, it still brings back so many emotions. Going to Oklahoma and hearing some of the cat-calls and some things about how I didn't belong there, to having that day when they acknowledged that the center had been named after me, that's a 180-degree turn from the things that I remember.

We're talking about a program that has consisted of so many great players over the years. Oklahoma football is rich with tradition that has been created by hundreds of players who have worked hard for a common goal and achieved greatness on so many levels.

I am proud to be a part of that, but I respect all of the players who came before me and who have come well after I moved on in life.

Prentice Gautt was a two-time All–Big Eight player and an Academic All-American. He was named MVP of the 1959 Orange Bowl victory over Syracuse in which he gained 94 yards on six carries, including a 42-yard touchdown. Gautt played eight seasons in the NFL, including seven with the St. Louis Cardinals. He later became an assistant football coach at Missouri, where he earned a doctorate degree and then joined the Big Eight Conference in 1979 as assistant commissioner. He also served as secretary-treasurer of the NCAA, and in 1996 he was named senior associate commissioner of the Big 12 Conference. In 1999 the Prentice Gautt Academic Center was dedicated at the University of Oklahoma. Four years later, he received an honorary doctorate degree from his alma mater.

Jerry Thompson | Guard/Tackle | 1957–1959

Luckily, I was born and raised in what is probably the Mecca of high school football in the state of Oklahoma—Ada. And I still live there today.

My parents were divorced when I was six years old, and we moved to Oklahoma City during the war, when Mom learned to be a beautician, and then we moved back to Ada when I was in the third grade. She set up a little beauty shop and worked hard to raise my brother and me.

I wasn't very big . . . weighed probably 135 pounds as a freshman but then I met a man named Ralph "Fireball" Evans, who was a candy distributor. "Fireball" also had been a professional weightlifter and he kept his weights in the back of a candy store there in Ada. I started lifting there and by the time I was a senior, I weighed 195. I am sure that we were the first high school players that ever lifted weights, thanks to "Fireball" Evans.

Coach Elvin George at Ada High mimicked everything that the Oklahoma Sooners did in those days and he certainly didn't believe in lifting weights. Neither did Bud Wilkinson. The thought back then was that it made you muscle-bound and slowed you down, but "Fireball" knew better. We would get in back of that candy store and lay on a big crate of Wrigley's chewing gum and do our bench-presses.

I was very fortunate that my brother, Ron, who was four and a half years older, had made all-state in football and earned a scholarship to Oklahoma. That was the start of me wanting to be a Sooner. We went to quite a few OU games when Eddie Crowder and Billy Vessels were the stars.

My dream was to follow my brother to Oklahoma and play for coach Wilkinson.

In my junior year at Ada, we went undefeated and won the mythical state championship, along with Muskogee. For some reason, they didn't have playoffs that year, so we had to settle for the mythical thing. In my senior year, we lost one game early but came back and won the rest of them to win the state championship on the field.

We didn't have classes then that divided the schools by size in Oklahoma. We were a school of probably 400 students and we played all the big schools. And over the years, Ada has won 19 state football championships.

I had been recruited by quite a few schools, but I just told most all of them that I was going to become a Sooner. But when it came down to the end of recruiting, for some reason, Oklahoma never offered me a scholarship. I was really upset about it. They signed two other players off of our team: Ben Wells, our fullback, and Billy Jack Moore, one of our guards.

Billy Jack and I were pretty much twins, the same size and body build. He and I were all-state and all I wanted to do was to go to Oklahoma with both of them, but I had no idea why they didn't want me. They knew about me through my brother, so I don't know why I slipped through the cracks. I know this: I didn't have the money to go up there and go to school on my own.

"Fireball" was an SMU grad and he wanted me to go down there to play football, but when coach George found out about Oklahoma not offering me a scholarship, he called coach Wilkinson. The next day, he came down to Ada to sign me.

I, like everyone else, was completely in awe of coach Wilkinson. He was a God-like figure, very much a gentleman and very intelligent. He always shook your hand and wanted to know how you were. As I knew him for the rest of his life and later coached with him, he never changed.

My first memory of arriving in Norman was moving into Jeff House where the players stayed. I had seen it all those years and I was so proud to finally have a room there, although it was really a little oversized closet. The one guy I wanted to meet when I got to Oklahoma was Bill Krisher, and one day when he came walking into my room, he scared me to death.

I remember coming out to practice for the first time in those old green jerseys, the sloppy pads and uniforms they gave the freshmen. There were about 130 of us and only about 30 were on scholarship. Of those, 13 stayed and ended up graduating. Among them were Prentice Gautt, Bobby Boyd, and Ed "Wahoo" McDaniel.

As most people in Oklahoma know, Prentice was the Sooners' first black player, and I'll always remember that incident when our freshmen team returned from a game at Tulsa. We stopped by a restaurant to eat and they had a nice dinner set up for all the players, but they wouldn't let Prentice eat in the restaurant with us.

[Freshman coach] Port Robertson stood up and told us all, "Boys, we're leaving."

We all marched out of there in unison. I think we ended up eating hamburgers on the way back to Norman.

I didn't know it until recently but when we played in Dallas against Texas every year, Prentice couldn't stay with us at the team hotel. He stayed with Jakie Sandefer somewhere else. Prentice was a great human being. He was a good student, very humble and very easy-going. I don't know anybody who didn't like Prentice Gautt. I saw Prentice three months before he passed away this year and I was very, very saddened by his death. He was a great Sooner.

That next spring, I was at guard and I was way down on the depth chart as most sophomores were, but by the end of spring practice, I had worked my way up and was named a starter for the alumni game. That game is when I got indoctrinated into Sooner football.

I played across the line of scrimmage that day from Stan West, who had been an All-Pro with the Rams. I think coach Wilkinson always asked all the pro guys to test the young guys who didn't have much experience, so Stan gave me a good headache. He slapped me around pretty good that day.

When I came back that fall for my sophomore year, I had moved over to tackle on the second unit. We had two units, but Bud called them "two first teams," and we played about the same amount of time.

When we went to Pittsburgh for the first game of the 1957 season, it was the first time I had ever flown on an airplane. I got sick—on the way out there and on the way back. A lot of us got sick.

I'll never forget the first guy I ever lined up against in a game—his name was Jim McCuster. Those big ol' coal miners were a lot larger than us country boys from Oklahoma. One time I fired off the line of scrimmage—and remember that we didn't have facemasks back then—and McCuster hit me in the face so hard that my nose was sticking out the side of my face. The next play, I thought I would get even with him. So I fired out and he hit me again and straightened it back up. He knocked me out cold. The next thing I remember I was waking up on the airplane and Bud was sitting next to me.

He asked, "How do you feel? Don't worry, it only hurts when you laugh."

Jerry Thompson was an All-American in his senior season and spent three seasons as an assistant coach at Oklahoma.

I must have looked awful, but I broke my nose a few more times after that. They used to call me "ski-jump nose," and it remains pretty flat against my face like a boxer's nose. Anyway, that was my introduction to college football. [Oklahoma won 26–0 in the 41st game of the 47-game winning streak.]

Of course the streak was going pretty good at that time, but you always remember the one you lost. That would be the Notre Dame game, which was tough on all of us. I don't remember many details from that day—November 16, 1957—but I remember Dick Lynch scoring that touchdown on a sweep to our left side. I can still see it.

After losing 7–0, you could have heard a pin drop in that stadium except for the Irishmen going crazy. We didn't leave the field right away because we were so stunned and our fans stayed, too. It was very traumatic to all of us.

The trip to Miami for the Orange Bowl was a great trip. I had never been out of Oklahoma except for our earlier games to Pittsburgh, Kansas State, Missouri, and Nebraska, but to go and swim in the ocean was something I had never experienced. I can say that football opens up the doors of life to you.

During the Christmas holidays before the trip, I had been working out in Ada and sprained my ankle. I wasn't able to do much and between the two-a-day practices in Coral Gables I stayed in the training room and tried to get my ankle in shape while other guys were at the beach. We beat Duke 48–21 in the Orange Bowl.

We had a very good team again in 1958, but Texas beat us by one point [15–14] and that was our only loss.

We always had a great defense, and I always believed the one man who never received enough credit was Gomer Jones. Gomer ran the defense while coach Wilkinson ran the offense. It was as if they were partners. Gomer also was my mentor because he was the line coach. He was so far ahead of other line coaches in the game of football at that time. He taught footwork and used boards to teach you your steps and we had sled drills—things that no other coaches were doing at the time. He was far, far ahead of the game.

We entered the 1959 season ranked No. 1 in the nation, but we probably weren't that good of a football team.

Most everybody has heard or read about the details leading up to our first game that season at Northwestern. Coach Wilkinson always liked to take us to nice places on the road, so we went to Chicago on that Thursday and ate at The Chez Paris. When we started eating the fruit salad, almost three quarters of the team got sick instantly. They were throwing up and laying all over the parking lot that night, but I never got sick for some reason. I was eating everyone else's fruit salad and their steaks, too. I always told everyone that they just poisoned the *good* players.

As it turned out, they had put some drug in the salad that was supposed to make you groggy for a few days. As we later found out, it was related to the bookies and gambling. Somebody wanted to make sure Oklahoma didn't play very well in that game. We had several guys in the hospital the night before the game.

The weather was awful for that game, too, but we would have had a hard time beating Northwestern, anyway. Ara Parseghian was their coach and they had a very good team, but we had guys pulling one direction when they should have been pulling another direction. To this day, I don't know what that drug was, but it worked. [Oklahoma lost 45–13.] When we got back home, Bud down-played the whole thing. He told us they had put a drug in our food, but that was all that was said about it. He didn't want to make too much stink about it.

Texas beat us and then Nebraska beat us, which was our first conference loss in 74 games. We had a 3–3 record and we never expected to lose any game at Oklahoma. We were surprised every time we lost a game, no matter whom we were playing.

Looking back, I can say we probably didn't have the talent on the entire football team as we had in the past. I don't know what causes those things, but maybe the talent pool in the state was down a little or recruiting fell off some. But I felt good about winning our last four games and when I walked off that field the final time, I was sad. I knew it was the last time I would ever be on that football field as a Sooner.

When Bud hired me to become an assistant coach in 1963, I got to see more of the man himself. I saw his family values and how he appreciated people and his concern for anybody with whom he came into contact.

After he hired me, one of the first things he told me was to quit calling him "coach."

He told me one day, "Start calling me 'Bud.' We are on the same level now. You are a coach, just like I am."

That was a hard thing to do at first. He had always been a coach to me.

Bud was close with President Kennedy, and it was a sad day for everyone when we were in Lincoln, Nebraska, and found out the president had been shot. Bud was absolutely torn up, I am sure, but he never showed it in public. We played the game the next day after Bobby Kennedy had reassured him that is the way the president would have wanted it.

It was great working as an assistant coach for him, and I later worked with him when he was head coach of the St. Louis Cardinals. When he decided to leave Oklahoma to run for the U.S. Senate, he wanted everybody to be taken care of before he made the announcement. That's just the kind of guy he was.

I wasn't shocked when he decided to retire and run for office. He had been on the President's Council on Physical Fitness and Sports, and when we went out socially, he insisted that we not talk about football. He would say, "Don't talk football. Talk politics, talk history, talk about anything, but don't talk about football."

What made Bud Wilkinson such a great coach? First of all, he was a very intelligent person. He was a student of the game, probably more so than anybody ever realized. And he was very innovative. He created some things that had never been done before. He was always looking at new ways to make the football team better.

When Bud left, I still had a job when they named Gomer Jones head coach. We were 6–4–1 that first year and then slipped to 3–7, and that was enough for the people at Oklahoma as far as Gomer was concerned. If only Gomer had just been Gomer, we would have been successful. He was one of the all-time great football coaches, but he tried to do a lot of the things that coach Wilkinson had done and he wasn't Bud Wilkinson.

I've had season tickets to Sooners games since I left college, and I stay in contact with many of my teammates to this day.

How can you not be proud to play athletics at one of the finest universities like Oklahoma? I am a Sooner through and through, born and bred.

I consider myself fortunate—fortunate to grow up in Ada, fortunate to play for and later coach for a man like Bud Wilkinson, and fortunate to be a member of the Sooners family.

Jerry Thompson, an All-American in 1959, was considered one of Oklahoma's finest two-way players. He also was All–Big Eight and Academic All–Big Eight in his senior season. He was drafted in the ninth round by the Buffalo Bills. He was an assistant coach at Oklahoma 1963–1965.

| chapter three |

The Sixties

Wayne Lee | Center/Linebacker |1960–1962

When I was a kid, I went to many of the Oklahoma Sooners' football games and I would pay a buck to sit in those general admission seats. That was during the famous 47-game winning streak.

We all went to those games with the thought, "Well, how much are we going to win by today?"

I was there when it all ended in a 7–0 loss to Notre Dame on November 16, 1957, and when that game and that streak was over, it was absolutely quiet. Nobody left the stadium and nobody said a word. Everyone just sat there in stunned silence. The fans couldn't comprehend that OU had finally lost a game. Neither could I.

To give you an idea of how much I loved Oklahoma football: after that game and while watching the movie Bambi were the last times I ever cried.

Until I was 12 years old, we lived in a house that was one house away from the grade school in Ada, a town of about 15,000 people in southeastern Oklahoma. We always played pickup games on that grade-school property and somebody always brought a ball, either an oblong one or a round one. Whatever season it was, we played it.

When I was younger, I loved basketball the best and didn't play organized football. I was always fooling around with the football—long-snapping it like a center would on punts—and I got pretty good at it.

So before my ninth-grade year the school team didn't have a center, and a couple of my friends approached me about coming out for football. I came out, made the team and got to start. Then I broke my leg in the fifth game of the season.

At Ada High School, I had the opportunity to play for Elvin George, who probably was the premiere high school coach in the state in the fifties and sixties. Coach George had a close relationship with Bud Wilkinson. As you can imagine, all of our drills and practices were very much like Oklahoma's. By the time I was a junior, I had really developed a passion for football and I was getting better and better.

In Ada, you played basketball for fun and football to win. It was that serious.

Over my three years in high school, we lost two games. We lost one during my sophomore year by two points, went undefeated during my junior year, and lost in the state finals during my senior year. When we took the field, it just never occurred to me that there was a chance of losing. I later learned in college, however, that you learn much more when you lose than you do when you win.

I always wanted to study architecture in college and I started to think about football, too. My parents, however, did not want me to continue football because they were not a big fan of me getting hurt. But they were fans of OU football. My parents had started buying season tickets to Sooners games in the late forties. When the great tradition of Oklahoma football really was born in the fifties under coach Wilkinson, I was there to see it.

My father's name was Bill and they called me "Little Bill" as a kid because my real name is William Wayne. But I didn't like "Little Bill" so I always went by my middle name as I grew up.

My mother was a great sports fan. She grew up in a small town in Oklahoma and played softball and basketball, so she would go outside and shoot goals with my brother and me. Even to this day, and she's in her late eighties, she is a very knowledgeable sports fan. She really knows the game of football. My father liked sports but had never played much. And the great thing is that neither one of them missed any of my games, high school or college, home or away.

All-American Wayne Lee (left, with cocaptain Leon Cross) was drafted by both professional football leagues in 1963, but decided that he would rather end his football career as an Oklahoma Sooner.

As a senior, I was 6'4" and 192 pounds, but skinny as a rail. I played center and linebacker and started lifting weights in coach George's program. His weight-lifting program was even better than OU's at that time.

I had visited Tulsa and Oklahoma State, but I knew if there was any chance to play football at Oklahoma, that's where I wanted to be. I had no interest in any other school. If you were from Oklahoma, and you were good enough, you would be a Sooner and that's just the way it was. All they had to do was open the door for me.

Later on, I decided I would attend OU no matter what, even if I didn't get a football scholarship. My mother made an agreement with me: if I wasn't third team or better by my sophomore year, I had to quit and concentrate on architecture. My parents were concerned that I would be so preoccupied with football that I wouldn't do well in school. Thank goodness I never had to make that decision.

I knew then that Bud Wilkinson was the kind of man from whom I could learn to play football and learn to be a man. He had such a high profile in the state at that time and he had such an overwhelming presence.

Coming from a small high school, the university's sheer size was overwhelming to me. As a freshman, you are a nobody. Then I went out onto the football field and there must have been 40 other freshmen on scholarship. So many of them were larger and faster than me.

There were times I wondered, "What in the world am I doing out here?" and, "How in the world can I compete at this level?"

I think I was a third-team center on the freshman team, but as time went on, only about a third of those players ever played a down at Oklahoma. Either injuries, grades, girlfriends back home, or some other reason led to attrition.

During two-a-days one day, Gomer Jones, one of coach Wilkinson's top assistants, came up to me and said, "Wayne, can I meet you at the dining hall after breakfast? There are some things I want you to work on."

Immediately, I thought, "What am I doing wrong?"

Then I thought, "Well, at least they must think I am worth saving."

So the next day, he spent an hour with me teaching me the steps I needed to take as a center. He taught me about the importance of inches and small things like how you pick up your right foot and how you move your feet to get into position to make the perfect block. We were a running offense, and the difference between making a block or not making a block was a matter of inches. Gomer Jones met with me three or four times with one-on-one sessions like that. I guess he saw something in me that I didn't see in myself.

I soon realized that it wasn't all about athletic talent. It was about understanding the game of football, preparation, and conditioning—all of the things that make you successful in life, as well. I moved higher and higher on the depth chart and by my sophomore year [the NCAA] had changed the playing rules on free substitution. You could substitute only one player as a free substitution. I was what they called "wild-carded," which means I would go in when we punted or kicked and then I would play defense at inside linebacker. When they kicked to us, I would go out of the game and the quarterback would come in for me.

In my first game, I played against this tackle for Northwestern, who was about 6'4" and 270 pounds. His name, and I'll never forget it, was

Fate Echols. I made a decision before that game that he would never hit me because I was going to use my speed to stay away from him. I always watched a lot of film then and it taught me about preparation. I learned right then how to study my opponent before the game, and I did really well that day against Fate Echols.

We were all shell-shocked by finishing 3–6–1 in my sophomore year. None of us ever thought about having a season like that when we arrived at Oklahoma. [It was the worst season in OU history, in terms of winning percentage until 1996's team finished 3–8.]

On the other hand, it was a very unique period in Oklahoma football history because of integration. As I look back, I am very honored to have participated in that change in our society. I had experienced this during high school when Ada had a scheduled game in Fort Smith, Arkansas. At that time, Arkansas was not integrated and they wouldn't let our African-American players play in that game. We had a vote on it, and all of our black players said, "Look, we'll ride on the bus with you and sit on the bench with you and support you, so go over there and kick their butts!"

We had to shuffle positions to cover for four starters that day and I played defensive end for the first time in my life. And we won 7–6. In high school, we also experienced this when we ate in restaurants after some road games. The restaurant staff would say to our black players, "You can eat here, but you have to eat in the kitchen." Sometimes, we would all get up and walk out as a team. We walked out of several restaurants back then.

As most Sooner fans know, Prentice Gautt was OU's Jackie Robinson. Prentice was a phenomenal person and football player. He was such a gentleman. He was a cadet colonel for the ROTC unit and an outstanding student.

In my senior year, we had a great player by the name of Eddie McQuarters. He played guard right beside me, and I had requested him to be my roommate on road games. Eddie wasn't a great student of the game, and I wanted to help him. If we saw a guard line up in the gap between us, we never had time to talk about it at the line of scrimmage. So I wanted him to know what I was going to do. I thought rooming with him and helping him was the right thing to do for all the right reasons, and we turned out to be great friends.

It was certainly an interesting period in OU history. We had a little tension because we had some players from West Texas who weren't used to integration, and when we played Southwest Conference teams, I heard several inappropriate things during pileups on the field.

A man I want to especially mention is Port Robertson, who had more to do with my career than maybe anyone else. Everyone at Oklahoma knew Port, the former wrestling coach who coached the freshman football team and was the chief disciplinarian. He ran the study hall and took care of the problem people. Port is the man who took all the renegade freshmen and gave them humility. He probably had more to do with the good graduation rates at OU than anybody, because he was responsible for you for about 270 days of the year. I never got into any trouble with Port, except maybe once which I will get into later, because he treated everybody like they were responsible—until they proved him wrong.

Port would say something like, "Mr. Lee, you little yardbird . . . what do you think you are doing not going to class?"

But I never missed class so I never had any problems with Port. One time a few of the guys came to our room—I roomed with Charles Mayhue—and they had a few beers and got to playing with one of our barbells in there. We were having too much fun and they could hear that barbell banging against the floor. Finally, the dorm counselor came in and told us to stop. The noise continued and he had to come back. This time he told us, "You guys are to see coach Robertson tomorrow morning at 7:30!"

We had to run 25 sets of stadium steps, and Port was there to blow the whistle. You had to run them in less than 15 seconds and if you didn't, they didn't count. When we got there that morning, Port told us, "You guys of all people? Didn't the dorm counselor warn you about not making too much noise? Why didn't you listen?"

That session was ugly. Guys were leaping over each other to touch the wall and make it in 15 seconds. They were throwing up. I am telling you, those stadium steps were work! I did about five of them before I had to go to class. I was supposed to be back at 4 p.m. to finish them and I asked Port, "What am I going to do? I have a lab class from 1:00 till 5:00?"

He looked at me and said, "Wayne, you don't have to run anymore, but I couldn't very well not make you run this morning."

Port knew I wasn't a trouble-maker.

When I would return to Oklahoma after my playing days, Port Robertson was the one person I most wanted to see. He was a phenomenal man, a friend to anybody who ever played football at OU. And I miss him very much.

My junior year was very unusual. We started off 0–5 and there were two reasons for it, in my opinion. First, I think Bud was getting a little tired of coaching. Second, I think OU had gotten a little casual in recruiting. There just wasn't the talent on campus there had been in the fifties. The newspapers, the alumni, and the players were in shock after that 0–5 start. We were losing sleep and losing weight because we were frustrated.

But then Bud predicted publicly we would win our final five games, and Gomer Jones called a bunch of us together for a meeting. He told us, "Listen, it's obvious you are not having fun and this is just a game. You've got to go out there and enjoy it and not worry about losing."

After we had defeated Kansas State and Missouri to break the losing streak, we faced a huge game against Army at Yankee Stadium. It was the first time any of us had been to a city like New York. We stayed in the Roosevelt Hotel near Times Square and we had to bus through Harlem to get to Yankee Stadium for practice. When we would pass through there, there would be people standing on the side of the street holding signs supporting the Sooners.

Coach Wilkinson and the coaching staff always had two or three trick plays ready for every game. Sometimes we used them, sometimes we didn't. This time we used one that helped us win the game. The coaching staff had noticed that Army's defense usually huddled in a tight huddle, away from the line of scrimmage. We had warned the referees ahead of time that we might do this. If a play ended on the right hash mark, we had designed a play where we would have several players remain on the left hash mark. We would get set quickly and pick the ball up in a casual way, instead of the normal center-snap, and just hand it to the quarterback. The quarterback would throw it to Mike McClellan who remained on the left hash.

We ran the play perfectly, and Mike scored a touchdown before the Army defense knew what hit them. We won the game 14–8.

That was the most successful of any trick play during my time at OU.

After that game, we were in the locker room celebrating when coach Wilkinson walked in with all these envelopes. He handed each one of us an envelope that included two $10 bills.

"Go out and have fun tonight," he told us. "The plane leaves tomorrow at 10:00 a.m. Be on it!"

We had groups of players all over New York City that night. Some of us just rode the subways because we had never seen subways before. Some went to Times Square. Some went Uptown, some went Downtown. I can still picture all of us drifting back to the hotel in different groups about midnight, telling each other what we had seen and what we had done.

The Army team happened to be staying on the same floor. When we got back there, I saw all of these Army players and OU players sitting out in the hallway on the floor just talking and having fun together. I think we stayed up all night swapping stories and talking with each other. It was just an example of what the great spirit of college sports is all about.

The next week, we fell behind Nebraska 14–0 at the half. Bud came into the locker room and after we had been re-taped and settled in for his halftime talk, we realized he was going to chew us up one end and down the other.

He stood in front of the chalkboard, turned and looked at us, turned back to the chalkboard, turned back to us . . . and he didn't say anything the entire time.

Finally, he just said, "I really don't have anything to say to you."

And he walked out.

He couldn't have made a better speech than what he did. We were self-motivated guys and we hadn't played well and we knew it. It was our job to go out and play the best we could and we had let him down. We flew out of that locker room and came back and won the game 21–14.

And then we beat Oklahoma State to win the final five games and finish 5–5, just like coach Wilkinson had predicted we would.

That Nebraska story leads me to coach Wilkinson's motivational techniques. He was such a gentleman that you never heard him curse. But if you did hear him say a bad word, and his bad words were really not that bad, you knew you had better shape up. He would never criticize you in front of your peers, and I give him a lot of credit for that. It was always in a one-on-one basis. But that Nebraska game is a lesson that your life is about your will and your commitment to action. Ultimately, what you become and what you are is about your will and your personal action, isn't it?

Coach Wilkinson always had great stories. He told them before games and they all had great meaning and were so compelling. We never heard the same one twice.

The bird story was his most-famous story, and all the players loved it. It went something like this: this old man lived in the hills of Arkansas and he was noted as being a very wise man who advised his neighbors on everything. On Saturday mornings, everybody would gather around his cabin to listen to his advice and wisdom. There was a young man who grew up in the valley who wanted to prove his superiority by embarrassing the old man somehow. He thought, "What in the world can I do to fool this man and raise my own self-esteem?"

He came up with this idea to capture a baby bird and cup it in his hands. Then he would ask the old man if the bird was dead or alive. If he said it was alive, the young man would crush it and let it fall to the ground. If he said it was dead, the young man would open his hands and let the baby bird fly away. He thought he had a full-proof plan to prove the old wise man wrong. A big crowd gathered around the old man that next Saturday and the boy tried to get his attention. The boy went through the question of whether it was alive or dead but the old wise man didn't say anything. The boy was getting irritated.

Finally, the old man said, "Young man, it's as you will it."

That's what Bud would always say to us. "It's as you will it."

What he meant was, "I have prepared you, I have taught you our scheme and our game plan and now today's game will be won or lost . . . as you will it."

And that was just like the Nebraska game of 1961.

Another one of his stories I really liked was of Ben Hogan. At one of the major tournaments, Bud sat next to Ben at the head table and after dinner, it seemed that Ben wasn't paying attention to the speaker. Ben had his head bowed down and his hands under the table. This went on for a while and coach Wilkinson thought that maybe Ben Hogan was feeling ill.

Finally, Bud asked him, "Mister Hogan, are you OK?"

Ben Hogan answered, "Yes, I am fine. You see, everyone in this room will play that golf course tomorrow and they all have had a practice round. Right now, I am playing that course through my mind and I am on the 16th hole with a club in my hands."

He had his hands under the table the whole time going through his club selection and the course, hole-by hole, shot-by-shot, so he would be prepared the next day.

Coach Wilkinson taught us that story because it illustrated the power of mental preparation.

Then there was the one about the man from an Eastern bloc country. He didn't have a car and he had to walk about five miles to work every day. Along the street in which he walked was a series of trees. One morning as he walked to work, he had decided to see how many trees he could pass without breathing. The first day he walked by three trees while holding his breath. The next day, he walked by four. Pretty soon he was walking by 10 or 12 trees while holding his breath.

He thought to himself, "I could pass more trees by running than I could by walking."

So he started jogging. Over the next six months, he made himself into a distance runner by doing this and he eventually became the Olympic marathon champion. But it all started with one small step.

And that lesson was that you have to begin somewhere with a small step and keep improving yourself along the way.

Which is exactly what we did for my senior year, 1962.

We had rebounded from 3–6–1 to 5–5 and now it was time to take the next step.

Coach Wilkinson came to us before the season and told us about a player who had superior talent but had been problematic in other areas. He had a meeting with Leon Cross and me, the cocaptains, and told us, "Listen, this player wants to play for us but he can be a problem. Do you want him or do you want to stiff-arm him?"

We talked and decided we had the leadership to deal with a problem like this. We could handle Joe Don Looney. That season, Joe Don made some phenomenal plays and led the nation in punting, too. [Looney rushed for 856 yards, scored 10 touchdowns, and averaged 42.4 yards per punt.] He had just amazing strength and speed.

We started 1–2, losing to Notre Dame and Texas again—we should have beaten them both—but then we won seven straight games for an 8–2 record.

When it came time to play in the Orange Bowl against Alabama, there had been a history between Bud and Bear Bryant. Bear had beaten him while at Kentucky [in the 1951 Sugar Bowl] and Bud really wanted to beat Bear badly. Our preparations were more demanding than in any game we had ever played and I really think our legs were burned out when we went into that game. We were facing Joe Namath and we never saw anybody throw it like Joe could.

Right before the game, President Kennedy walked into our locker room. Here we were trying to get ready for the most important game we had ever played and in walks the president of the United States. As everyone knew, he and Bud were good friends. The president came around to everyone and introduced himself and some of us were standing there in a T-shirt and jock strap. It was an emotional experience, but at the same time, it was a huge distraction.

That pregame coin flip was one for the books, too. President Kennedy was to flip the coin, but they didn't want him on the field for security reasons, so they held the coin flip up in the stands. Unfortunately, we lost to Alabama 17–0.

When I look back on my time at Oklahoma, sure it would have been great to go undefeated those three years, but I got to play more than I ever expected and learned more than I ever dreamed of.

All these years later, if I ever needed something in my life, I know there are about 30 guys I could call and they would do anything for me. And I would do the same for any one of them. Those relationships were born with blood, sweat, tears, and experiences together.

When I try to describe the feeling, I am not sure "tradition" is the right word. Oklahoma football is a way of life. As a young man who grew up watching it, and having heroes like Billy Vessels, Eddie Crowder, and Jerry Tubbs, it took on a life of its own for me.

And then evolving into a player myself and to come back after a few down times to have a very successful senior year . . . all I can say is it doesn't get any better than that.

I was drafted by both the AFL and NFL, but I had no interest in playing professional football. Playing the game at Oklahoma was enough for me. And I just knew the professional leagues could never compare to that.

Wayne Lee was an All-American and a cocaptain of OU in 1962. He also was an Academic All-American. As one of the last two-way stars for Oklahoma, along with teammate Leon Cross, Lee was considered one of the Sooners' best blockers and was also one of the team's leading tacklers.

Jim Grisham | Fullback/Linebacker | 1962–1964

When I was five years old my parents, Clarence and Lucille, moved the family from Houston to a 21-square-mile farm in Swisher County, Texas. The winters brought snow and cold and the summers brought hot weather and dust storms from the South.

All of the family members would pitch in to plant, water, and harvest the crops. My brother, Eddie, who was two years older, and I would get off the school bus and pick cotton until dark. We also were responsible for feeding 1,500 head of cattle with 90- to 100-pound bales of alfalfa. The crops depended on irrigation, so we would get out of bed between 1:00 and 2:00 a.m. to change the positions of the irrigation pipes. We all had to learn how to drive cars, jeeps, tractors, combines, and trucks at an early age. When you are young, however, you never think how all that regimental hard work and constant exercise will benefit you later in life.

In 1948 we moved to Olney, Texas, a town with a population of less than 4,000. When I was 12, I would ride my bicycle downtown before school to sweep floors and clean windows at three stores. After school, practice of whatever sport I was playing, and a quick meal, I would bike back downtown to operate the projectors at the local theater while doing my homework. During the summer months, I would manage the skating rink. I received my drivers' license when I was 14, so I could make the 12-mile trip to the drive-in theater because the downtown theater had only one matinee on weekends.

Playing varsity football was a unique experience for me. I switched positions every year because we had a fantastic fullback named Harold Philipp, who was one year ahead of me in school. Harold eventually signed to play with the University of Texas and had a great career.

I was skilled enough and had the size to play quarterback, end, and halfback while waiting on the fullback position to open. When Harold finally left for Austin, I was in hog heaven because he had the position I had wanted all along.

The Olney Cubs made it to the state semifinals during my last two years in high school, which was not bad for a team that suited up only 18 players for each game. There was no such thing as getting hurt or coming out of the game with that team.

I remember Dad said he would take me deer-hunting with him in Marble Falls, Texas, if I scored two touchdowns in the upcoming quarterfinal game. In that game, the guys opened holes that you could drive a truck through. In the first half alone, I scored four touchdowns with runs of 56, 38, 41, and 52 yards—twice what it took to earn a great day of deer-hunting with my father. I had finished my senior year with 21 touchdowns and just over a mile rushing, making all-state.

We had six players from my senior class earn football scholarships. One day my dad asked me where I wanted to go to college. I knew he wanted me to get an engineering degree, so I told him I would look for a top school that would let me major in engineering and play football. I knew that the only way I could go to college was to get a scholarship. I had graduated in the top 10 percent of my class and was named to the National Honor Society, so I knew my grades would help me.

After recruiting calls started coming in, I began to realize that it would be difficult to find a college where I could do both. Most of the recruiting interviews were conducted over the telephone because I did not want to waste their time or mine. I did take a trip to TCU when the Fort Worth Fat Stock Show held their annual event and I had entered a 220-pound Spotted-Poland-China hog. I placed second in show with "Reserved Grand Champion" and slept comfortably that night in the athletic dorm instead of in the foul-smelling hog barn.

My second recruiting trip was recommended by Glenn Atchley, an Olney native who had graduated with an engineering degree from Oklahoma. He wanted me to see his alma mater. We toured the Oklahoma campus, meeting several of the football players and interviewing with the engineering department. Before we left, I dropped off some film of my games and a copy of my grades at the coaches' office.

Within a week, Bud Wilkinson made his first trip to Olney to see what I thought of the school and to see if I had any questions. I told him

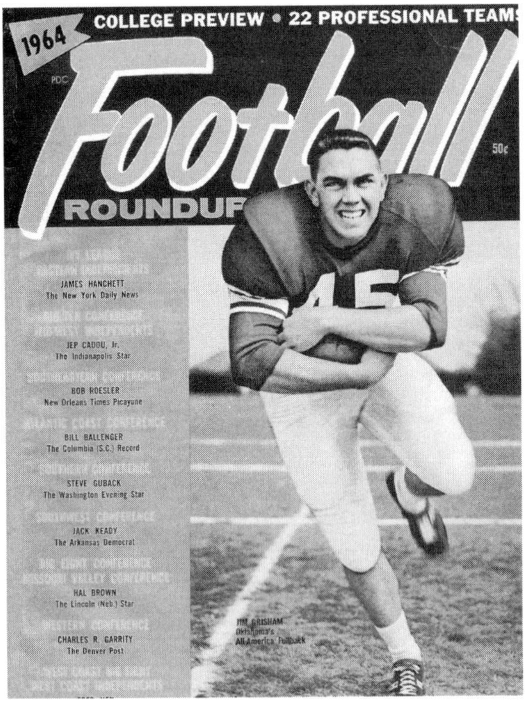

Jim Grisham, an All-American at fullback as a junior in 1963, was the cover boy for a preseason magazine leading into the 1964 campaign.

I was impressed, but I just wanted to know if I could major in engineering and play football. He told me, "After seeing your grades and films of your games, you can do both. You can get an engineering degree and become an All-American."

From that conversation, I was beginning to learn what it means to be a Sooner. Over the next few years, I also would learn what a great man Bud Wilkinson was.

Next to my relationship with coach Wilkinson, I want to give thanks to Port Robertson, our academic counselor and chief disciplinarian. All freshmen were required to attend study hall every evening except Friday. Tutors were available to answer questions but not do the work for the athletes. We had access to the tutors and were encouraged to seek their help. With all the math classes in the engineering program, I took full advantage of their help.

Our 1961 freshman year was mainly a challenge to determine who really wanted to play football at Oklahoma, as coaches tried to match players with different positions to optimize their talents. The year ended with me on the third team as fullback and linebacker.

Frankly, playing for the Sooners had become more important than being an engineer. The tradition and history of football at Oklahoma makes it one of the top programs in the country and I had decided to give 100 percent effort and to sacrifice whatever it took to be a part of it.

The two-a-day practices of the 1962 season proved to be very productive since we reported to training in good condition and ready to work and I worked my way up to first-team at linebacker.

In our 1962 season-opener, our sophomore-studded team beat Syracuse 7–3 on a 60-yard run by Joe Don Looney on his first career carry for Oklahoma, with only 2:20 remaining in the game.

Notre Dame came to Norman and beat us 13–7 and the following week Texas beat us 9–6 at the Cotton Bowl in Dallas. After three weeks at linebacker, I had been awarded the "Ug" award two times as OU's defensive player of the week, but we had a 1–2 record.

Coach Wilkinson asked me to prepare to play more offense than in the previous year, so I polished up on my blocking and faking skills. We then won seven games in a row and won the Big Eight championship before accepting an offer to play Alabama and Bear Bryant in the Orange Bowl. Alabama, led by Joe Namath, blanked us 17–0.

After my sophomore season, Clay Cooper, an assistant at Missouri, had told the media, "Grisham doesn't tackle 'em, he gores 'em."

For a few of those summers, a group of us would go to Lake Tahoe to work construction jobs to build stamina. The thin air in the 12,000-foot mountains helped us perform in a location such as Colorado. Leon Cross was the designated coach to keep the players under control and "the mother hen" did a good job at it.

We opened the 1963 season with a seasoned team of juniors anticipating a great year. We beat Clemson 31–14 before facing the No.1 Southern California Trojans in a record heat wave in Los Angeles [it was 100 degrees]. In a see-saw battle, we finally prevailed 17–12 and grabbed the top-ranking for ourselves.

That set up a No. 1 versus No. 2 showdown with Texas, but we were soundly defeated 28–7 after a lackluster effort on our part. We then won five consecutive conference games before playing Nebraska. We arrived in Lincoln on a day the country will never forget, November 22, 1963, and we soon heard of President Kennedy's assassination in Dallas. Coach Wilkinson, who was close with the Kennedy family, felt that the game should be played as scheduled, and the Cornhuskers beat us the next day 29–20.

For the Oklahoma State game, my parents flew in from Reno, Nevada, to see me play for the only time in person during my career. It also was coach Wilkinson's final game. We were trailing Oklahoma State 10–7 in the second half, but I didn't want to disappoint my parents.

On our way to a 34–10 victory, which sent Bud out in style, I gained 218 yards and scored four touchdowns.

We opened Gomer Jones' first season as head coach with a 13–3 victory at Maryland before losing the next three games. Southern California blew us out 40–14 with their overpowering running game behind the great Mike Garrett. After Nebraska came to Norman and beat us 17–7, we won the final regular-season game over Oklahoma State 21–16 in Stillwater before playing in the Gator Bowl, where we lost to Florida State 36–19.

My time at Oklahoma had come and gone.

What does it mean to be a Sooner? To me, it means dedication, trust, fellowship, sacrifice, honesty, and sharing.

As I write this, I am recovering from surgery to replace a faulty heart valve, which apparently had been defective since birth. So that puts it into perspective for me: I was fortunate to have survived playing football for so many years and to have had such a fulfilling experience.

I realize now more than ever how special it was to play for the Oklahoma Sooners.

Jim Grisham was one of Oklahoma's greatest two-way players. He was an All-American in 1963 and was named All–Big Eight in 1962, 1963, and 1964. He was one of the few Sooners ever named the Big Eight's Defensive Player of the Week and Back of the Week during his career. In Bud Wilkinson's final game at OU, Grisham rushed for a then school-record 218 yards and four touchdowns in a 34–10 win over Oklahoma State. He finished his career with 2,404 yards rushing and 18 touchdowns.

Carl McAdams | Center/Linebacker | 1963–1965

I had two idols when I grew up in White Deer, Texas—Johnny Unitas and his main receiver with the Colts, Raymond Berry.

White Deer was a town of about 1,500 people in the Texas Panhandle, between Amarillo and Tampa. Everybody always talked about how the wind blew there. It could be the coldest place in the world to some people in the winter because of the way the wind whipped, but it helped me play football.

I didn't have any brothers to play with [I had three sisters], so I had to play football with myself. I could throw the football up in the air and let the wind bring it back to me and then catch my own passes. That way, I could be both Johnny U. and Raymond Berry.

I was little when I was a high school freshman: about 5'6" and 120 pounds when our team won the state championship. By the time I was a junior, I started basketball season as the point guard and finished it playing the post. That gives you an idea of the growth spurt I was going through.

By the time I graduated, I was 6'4" and 190, and it was a wonder that I could walk and chew gum at the same time.

My dad owned a motel, a used-car lot, and a furniture store in White Deer, and he was a big sports fan. He always said if he had somebody who would have pushed him when he was younger he could have been a major-league baseball player.

Growing up, I had a sister living in Oklahoma City so Dad and I would drive up there and go to a few Oklahoma games. I was very conscious of the Sooners' 47-game winning streak and I thought Bud Wilkinson was the only coach who could do something like that, so I wanted to be a part of his team.

Jim Weatherall, one of Oklahoma's All-Americans from the early fifties, also was from White Deer and his father called Bud during my senior year to tell him about me. When coach Wilkinson came to my home to recruit me, I had never seen such a distinguished man in my life. The first time I saw him it looked like he had a halo around his head. My high school coach came over to the house to meet him and he brought some film from one of our games. I was playing tailback at that time and I had broken loose and ran about 50 yards, but I got caught from behind on the 3-yard line and I fumbled! We got beat in that game 3–0.

Before coach Wilkinson left that day, he offered me a scholarship and I naturally accepted it. But after he left, I asked my coach, "Why did you bring *that* film? I got caught from behind and I fumbled . . . "

"Relax," he said. "They don't want you as a running back. They want you as a linebacker."

I had played every single position in high school but center, so I thought I would play whatever they wanted me to.

That next summer I had come down with pneumonia and had a heart murmur, so the doctor wouldn't release me for practice when I got to Norman. Thank goodness I missed those first six weeks of practices. I don't know how the players stood it. We had about a hundred freshmen out there, and I guess they wanted to weed out a lot of them because it was hard conditioning and pushing that seven-man sled up and down the field. It was scary just watching it.

I hadn't lifted any weights and I looked pretty skinny at the time. I was running to get equipment for everybody just to help contribute, so some of the players thought I was a manager. I had been passed over when the good equipment was handed out, and when I did get my helmet, it looked as if it was held over from the forties.

When I finally was cleared to practice, they put me in at linebacker and one of our recruits, Larry Shields, took a handoff and I met him at the line of scrimmage. I hit him pretty hard and busted my helmet. When the coaches saw that I had busted my helmet they were pretty impressed, but I never told them it was one of those old helmets from way back.

Some of my greatest memories and biggest disappointments come from my sophomore year, 1963. In that first game, against Clemson, I came running down our ramp to the field and the first step I took, my feet went out from under me. I crawled the rest of the way down that ramp on my hands and knees. I was so excited for that first game . . . I had never seen so many people in one place.

We played at Southern Cal that year, and they were ranked No. 1 in the nation; we were No. 3. I remember coach Wilkinson put in the greatest game plan. We had this one trick play where the tight end would take a step back off of the line of scrimmage and throw up his hands and say, "Hold it, hold it, hold it."

That was designed to get the defense to relax and then we would run a play behind it.

So we got down to their 3-yard line and called this play. But instead of one of our tight ends doing it, both of them did it. We got a five-yard penalty but we still beat them 17–12, and it remains one of my biggest thrills.

We entered the Texas game No. 1, and Texas was No. 2. It was the first time I had ever even seen the OU-Texas game and I was playing in it. It was a sight to behold, even though we lost 28–7.

Later when we were playing Nebraska, I was playing on the punt-return team and I was the guy off the line of scrimmage who had to block their first person down to keep him off of the receiver. They had this big tackle named Bob Brown . . . the biggest man I had ever seen. So

Bob came running down the field and I was fixing to wipe him out. A few moments later, I picked myself up off the ground and Bob was about 20 yards downfield. I didn't look for Bob Brown anymore.

We finished 8–2 that year and got invited to a bowl, but coach Wilkinson thought it was a "secondary" bowl and didn't want to go. As I look back on it now, I figure he was getting ready for his next career and didn't want to play in that game. Soon afterwards, he announced

Carl McAdams was a two-time All-American who went to the NFL and even earned a Super Bowl ring with the 1968 New York Jets. *Photo courtesy of OU Athletics Media Relations.*

he was leaving as head coach. I sure hated to see him go, but I was just thrilled to death they named Gomer Jones head coach, because I really liked him.

The other person I got to know really well in four years was Port Robertson. He was the disciplinary coach there and I had to see him every Monday morning for one reason or another. I guess you could say I was mischievous. I never did anything major, just little things.

Port once told me, "See that corner over there? I would rather see a rattlesnake in that corner than you. You know why? Because I know what that rattlesnake is going to do."

Port was a military man and he ran a tough ship. He would give us a little break in study hall and we would all go to the OU Club to play some pool. But at a certain time, we had to be back sitting in our desks. A bell would ring, signaling the time we had to be back. The pool tables were only about 20 yards from our chairs in that study hall, but we had to go through a door to get there.

One time the bell rang and we took off running. Port was standing behind that door and as we all ran through there, he whopped one kid over the head with his keys. The kid dropped to the floor like he had been shot. It turned out to be one of Port's counselors whom he had hired. That was the last we saw of that counselor.

My junior year we dropped to a 6–4–1 record.

Southern Cal got back at us the next year. They came out with this spread offense and just passed us silly. I kept trying to cheat outside further and further to cover their spread offense and then they would run Mike Garrett up the middle on us. We had no chance of stopping them that day [in a 40-14 loss].

Gale Sayers ran the opening kickoff back for a touchdown for Kansas a few weeks later, but we held him to under 30 yards rushing. We were leading and they ran a reverse for a touchdown on the final play and then got the two-point conversion to beat us 15–14. We did beat Nebraska 17–7 to knock them out of the national championship, which felt very good. It was the best game we had played all year.

Before the Gator Bowl, we had six seniors who had signed with agents and were ineligible to play, not that it would have mattered. Steve

Tensi and Fred Biletnikoff wore us out in that game. [Florida State beat Oklahoma 36–19.]

In 1965, we lost our quarterback, Tommy Pannell, who broke an ankle during two-a-days and we never could get situated at quarterback. We played three different quarterbacks and we had a young offensive line and a young defensive line.

I remember at halftime of our game against Texas, which we lost 19–0, we hadn't hardly made a first down. My sister told me later that as the bands were playing at halftime, there were tears running down my dad's face.

She asked, "What's the matter with you?"

"I'll be damned," Dad said. "Even their band is even better than ours!"

Never beating Texas was a big void in my career and it remains a big void today. I came from the state of Texas and was named Lineman of the Week against them twice, but we never beat them.

I sprained an ankle against Iowa State and then missed the Missouri game that year. I played the final two games with a pretty severe sprain. We finished 3–7 that season, and I am still hurt by that today. I went to Oklahoma looking to have another 47-game winning streak and we didn't come close to that. I don't go back to reunions because of that 3–7 record. It really stayed with me.

That season, and one similar later on when John Blake was coach, were the worst seasons in Oklahoma football history, at least dating back to the pre-Wilkinson days. I hated to see that for Gomer Jones. He never deserved it. I loved him to death and he gave his heart and soul to OU. I hated that we didn't win more games for him. We had some outstanding players in 1964, but we never got our team chemistry right. I don't know why, really, because Gomer didn't change much from coach Wilkinson's way of running things. We had good game plans. We had good discipline. We would just always get a penalty at the wrong time or have a fumble at the wrong time.

I felt very proud later on that sophomores and freshmen from 1965 got to go down and play in that Orange Bowl a few years later [in 1967].

I always felt that if you looked hard enough at any negative, something positive comes from it.

That terrible season of 3–7 ultimately brought Jim MacKenzie and all those great assistant coaches to Oklahoma. And one of them was Barry Switzer. It's the same as how those losing teams in the nineties ultimately brought Bob Stoops to Oklahoma. So you have to look for the positive when the negative happens.

When I hear the word "Oklahoma," I think football. We have so much tradition there, and every Oklahoma kid and a whole lot of Texas kids want to be a part of it.

I did, too, and I am thankful for that opportunity. It's just a shame we had to have a 3–7 record every 30 years or so, but someday I look for us to have another 47-game winning streak.

Carl McAdams, a center and linebacker, was named Big Eight Lineman of the Year in 1965. He was an All-American in 1964 and 1965 and cocaptain of the 1965 team. He was also MVP of the East-West Shrine game and the Hula Bowl. He was drafted in the third round of the 1966 NFL draft by the New York Jets, for whom he played three seasons.

Granville Liggins | Nose Guard | 1965–1967

Sports meant everything to me while I was growing up in Tulsa in the fifties and sixties.

I competed in track and field, throwing the shot put and discus, I wrestled and I played football. I never even gave a thought to playing football in college one day, but when I got to Booker T. Washington High School, I had a few coaches who saw some potential in me.

Booker T. had a very good program and a great head coach, Art Williams. It was still during segregation, so Booker T. was an all-black school.

I don't want to be heavy here, but I want to be honest and candid about growing up. There were actually times during the sixties when I was ashamed to be black because there was such a negative connotation to it.

I'll never forget one day during my senior year. It was November 23, 1963, and I was sitting in botany class, which coach Williams taught. It was around noon when the voice came on the school PA system to announce that President Kennedy had been shot. Coach Williams started to cry right there in front of the class. You know, football coaches are not supposed to cry, so that gives you an idea of what kind of impact that day had on us.

It was just like September 11, 2001. You remember where you were when it happened.

When I was a senior, I was being recruited by schools such as Notre Dame, USC, Michigan, Michigan State, Indiana, Oklahoma, and Oklahoma State. When a university representative came to your school, he didn't come to see you. He went straight to the office to check out your grades.

I knew I always wanted to play at Oklahoma because I grew up watching Bud Wilkinson's Sunday morning TV show. He would have

Granville Liggins, a two-time All-American lineman, played for three coaches in three seasons. *Photo courtesy of OU Athletics Media Relations.*

that chalkboard with those magnets and he would show how a play worked. I never missed watching his show.

Plus, I wanted to stay near my mother, who was a single mom raising three children.

So what happened? I signed my letter of intent to be a Sooner, and Bud Wilkinson left the university. I never got to play for him. Bud Wilkinson was OU to me, so I was shocked, but the Sooners were my destiny no matter who was the coach.

Gomer Jones became the head coach, and I spent 1964 as a freshman whom the varsity used as a blocking dummy. I will never forget sitting in those stands while Oklahoma was playing Kansas and seeing the great Gale Sayers run back a kickoff 93 yards for a touchdown. I am telling you, that run was totally awesome, even if it was against my school.

I didn't do a whole lot my sophomore year, but I became a starter as a junior when Jim MacKenzie became head coach. Jim was a great coach who had a presence about him. He was a quiet-spoken man who wasn't overpowering. He had brought this young guy named Barry Switzer with him from Arkansas as his offensive line coach.

One game I remember during that season was against Notre Dame, which averaged about 250 pounds on their offensive line. Our defensive line was a three-man front with me at nose guard. I was about 205 or 210 pounds, and our ends weren't much bigger. We were hanging with Notre Dame for about a quarter because they were trying to run wide and we were fast. We would chase them down.

At one point, their coaches in the press box must have asked, "Why are we running away from them? Let's run at them."

They started running right at us and they killed us. [OU lost 38–0.]

I was having a pretty good year when the Oklahoma PR guy came to me one day and said, "We can't use Granville for your name."

I said, "But that's my name."

He said that I needed a nickname, so he suggested "the Chocolate Cheetah."

"I don't like that."

"Well," he said, "they called Joe Louis 'the Brown Bomber.'"

"That may be fine for Joe Louis," I told him, "but I don't like 'the Chocolate Cheetah.'"

Then he asked, "How about 'Granny' Liggins?"

For some reason, that name stuck with me. I didn't love it, but I got used to it over the years. When I left Oklahoma and started playing in the Canadian Football League, I was hoping that name wouldn't follow me to Canada. But the day after I signed my first contract, I saw the headline in the newspaper in Canada: "Granny Liggins Signs Contract."

One day during the summer when I was a junior, I had a job at the Tulsa Paper Company and I walked into this local grill with two other guys I worked with. We each ordered lunch before the manager came out and told me I couldn't eat in the restaurant because I was black. The other two guys sat down and ate while I had to take my sandwich and eat it while walking back to the plant.

I was shocked and devastated. That is something you never forget.

Now don't you think that while we were playing Notre Dame and I was sacking the quarterback, those people who had asked me to leave the restaurant were the same people cheering me on the football field?

Of course they were.

But that was the era. It was 1966 and it was a rough time to be black, but the one thing I can say is that I am not upset about it today. I really am not. When you travel and meet people and see the real world, you learn to see people as people. If I don't like you, it's not because you are white, red, green, or yellow.

I am not the sharpest knife in the drawer, but I realized even then that my athletic ability could help me make friends and make it easier for me. I never felt much attitude from the white players, but there probably was a little tension behind the scenes. I must say that today's black athletes are living the life of Riley. I just hope they realize it.

When I was at Oklahoma, I think there were only a few black players on the team: me, Ben Hart, James Ray Jackson, and Eddie Hinton. I have to thank Prentice Gautt for paving the way for myself and many to follow. My biggest regret is that I never met Prentice, but I wish I had. I knew of him and all the great things he did, and I was truly saddened by his death.

That was one reason I always loved coach Switzer. He had grown up in Arkansas and he embraced black athletes. I sensed his tolerance, his sensitivity, his dedication, and his excitement about coaching.

It was devastating to the entire team after the 1966 season when Jim MacKenzie died of a heart attack. Chuck Fairbanks replaced him for my senior season, meaning I had three head coaches in three seasons at Oklahoma.

We lost to Texas 9–7 during my senior season, although I don't remember too many details from the game. Maybe I have blocked them out because they were too painful, but that was our only loss of the season. We would have won a national championship with a few more points against Texas.

We went down to the Orange Bowl and beat Tennessee, which was ranked No. 2 at the time. I went out of the game in the third quarter with a knee injury, and my mom told me later that she almost rushed the field to be with me. I am glad she didn't. That was my final game as a Sooner.

Playing defense was my salvation because I was quick enough to get into the backfield and get to the quarterback. Quickness was what I was all about because I wasn't overly big. One of my high school coaches had taught me to watch the center's hands. I learned that when you see them tense up, you take off because you know he is about to snap the football.

I was fortunate to receive great coaching along the way. I always loved coach Switzer and still talk to him once in a while. I want to mention my defensive line coach. Pat James was indeed the driving force behind my success at Oklahoma. He truly provided me with the knowledge and motivation to be successful.

My wife and I went to a game a few years ago in Norman after coach Switzer had arranged for the 1968 Orange Bowl champions to be honored. The focal point though, was to surprise coach James—and he was surprised. Sadly, he died the following year.

Playing at Oklahoma was a huge, huge ride for me. I will always cherish it as long as I live. I am wearing my OU Club ring right now and I always wear my Orange Bowl watch. My wife bought me a license plate that reads "XSOONR," and I wear my Oklahoma football T-shirt when I am gardening.

Today, I live in the suburbs of Toronto. I played five years for the Calgary Stampeders and five years with the Toronto Argonauts. When I retired from football in 1978, I had been in Canada so long and I loved it here, so I decided to stay. I became a Canadian citizen nine or ten years ago, but I still get back to Oklahoma to visit friends and family.

Like my mother always told me, once a Sooner, always a Sooner!

Granville Liggins was an All-American in 1966 and 1967. He also was named UPI's Lineman of the Year in 1967 and finished seventh in the Heisman Trophy balloting. He played 10 seasons in the Canadian Football League.

Steve Zabel | Tight end/Defensive end | 1967–1969

I'll never forget my first organized football game as a seven-year-old playing for the North Denver Hawks. It had snowed the night before, and they used this jeep with a plow to clear the foot of snow off the field. I was on the sidelines that day shivering—I never made it into the game—when one of the mothers saw me and said, "Hey, go sit over there in that Jeep and warm up."

So I spent my first football game watching from the warmth of a Jeep.

One day after one of my games, my stepfather took me home and we went out into the yard. He threw a dollar bill on the ground and told me, "If you can tackle me in the next 10 minutes, you can have that dollar."

Mom was up on that porch screaming at Dad, and I was trying everything to get him down.

I never did tackle him, but after a lot of effort, he said, "I wanted to teach you that you can really get after it in football and get thrown around pretty good and you won't get hurt."

Then he gave me the dollar.

That little lesson really helped me later on. I called him Dad and he was a real outdoors type of guy who taught me everything I know about hunting and fishing, but he was very tough on me.

My mother and real father were divorced when I was in kindergarten, and Mom and I had moved from St. Paul, Minnesota, to an Indian reservation north of Lincoln, Nebraska. Once Mom remarried, we moved to Lakewood, Colorado, in 1954.

I have three half-brothers and one sister, who is 18 months younger than me. My mom once put me on a bus when I was a young boy to go see my real father in Salt Lake City. I remember the feeling of independence in doing that.

I can characterize my childhood as a pretty cool time. I was generally happy and I knew the value of hard work from an early age. I took on a morning paper route for the *Rocky Mountain News* and I worked sweeping up after school at Lake Junior High School, making 90 cents an hour. If I collected all of my money on the paper route, I made 30 bucks a month.

Our eighth-grade football team, the Hawks, finished 12–0, but I'll bet that if I saw our two running backs from that team, they are the same size today as they were then. The next year we moved north of Denver, and I went to Merritt Hutton High in Thornton, Colorado.

I met a coach by the name of Max Wilsey, who taught me how to run, and I have to give him a lot of credit. I then won the state high-jump championship and the state pentathlon championship, which consisted of the 100-yard dash, high hurdles, discus, high jump, and the mile-run.

In football, we went to the state playoffs during my sophomore year. I returned a blocked punt for a touchdown and received my first football notoriety. I remember one game when the starter got hurt, I was in the game, and they called a pass play. I had no idea what to do, but I went out, caught it, and scored a touchdown. As I got to the sideline, the head coach grabbed me and asked, "What were you supposed to do on that play? You were supposed to stay in and block! . . . Good catch."

I think we won three games my junior year and four during my senior year because our school had gone up one class. Statistically, I had a pretty good year as a senior, but after one game near the end of the season, we had beaten our arch rivals. I went out with some teammates. At the time, the legal drinking age in Colorado was 18 and we drank some beers. One of the cheerleaders with us turned us in to the coaches the next Monday, and the coach confronted me about it. I told the truth. He kicked me off the team, and I missed the final game of the season as well as half of the basketball season.

Maybe that was the best thing that ever happened to me, however, because if that wouldn't have happened, I may have wound up playing basketball at Colorado.

At that time, I was a better basketball player than football player and I had been offered a scholarship to Colorado. I really believe that if that suspension hadn't happened, that's where I would have gone to school.

The Air Force Academy also wanted me, but I hadn't taken the SAT yet and I needed a 650 score on the math and 650 on the verbal, so I ended up at the New Mexico Military Institute.

I worked in heavy construction that summer and got into really good shape. Once I got to New Mexico, I was the second-fastest guy on the team. I was 6'3" and up to about 190 pounds. I played split end, which was great because we threw the ball on just about every play. I caught somewhere around 50 passes and scored 12 touchdowns. We finished 6–3 that season.

All of a sudden, several schools took an interest in me. I visited New Mexico and Houston. Now Colorado wanted me, too. The Air Force Academy still wanted me, and I almost ended up there, but in the 11th hour, I had an opportunity to visit Oklahoma.

It happened in a quirky way, I guess. They had hired a new coach named Leon Cross, a former OU All-American who had come in from West Point. He had been recruiting my roommate, Rick Mason, to go to West Point. When he was looking at the film, he asked Rick, "By the way, who's your split end there?"

Rick said, "Well, it just so happens that's my roommate."

Leon invited both of us to come up to OU for the spring game of 1967 to check out the university. I remember watching a spring scrimmage before the game and there was a pile-up right in front of where I was standing. One running back had been speared, held up, and then pounded. The kid got dusted badly and then he got up and looked directly at me.

"What are you looking at?" he shouted.

Then I went into the training room before the spring game, I noticed they just had a swagger about them, a confidence that I had never seen before. I ran into Barry Switzer, and he pulled me close and said, "If

Steve Zabel, an All-American tight end, was one of the few players in the modern era of college football to play both ways. *Photo courtesy of OU Athletics Media Relations.*

you come here, you can start next year and we'll go out and win some championships."

That's all it took.

Jim MacKenzie had flown out to Roswell to visit with me, and I really liked the guy. Later that spring, Don Boyce, an assistant at New Mexico Military, who later coached at Oklahoma, came into my room and told me Jim had just died.

He asked, "Will this make a difference in your decision to go to Oklahoma?"

It didn't. I was set on going there and as it turned out I was the first player Chuck Fairbanks ever signed at Oklahoma.

When I arrived in Oklahoma City that summer, I got a job working construction but I didn't have a car. I arrived with two pair of jeans, six white T-shirts, and a pair of desert boots. That was it.

One day I went out to get some food at the Sooner Superette. I bought two bags of groceries that they put in brown paper bags before I walked six blocks back to my apartment. It was so hot that day that the bags disintegrated by the time I got home and I had to make a few trips back to pick up my groceries.

I thought, "Oh my gosh, what did I get myself into? It is so HOT here!"

I had never felt heat like that before.

That summer the coaches sent us a series of workouts . . . so many 440s, stadium steps, up-downs, grass drills, sprints, etc., and you had to sign this card verifying you had done all of this work and send it back to the coaches each week. I had been working out and was in great shape. When we reported to camp, I did really well in the physical fitness endurance test they put us through.

I know I was pretty dedicated to becoming a good football player at Oklahoma. In camp, my first blocking assignment was to block this guy named Granville Liggins. Little did I know he was the best defensive player on the team. He was the epitome of a nose guard, but I had no idea who he was. I held my own right away while the coaches were screaming at Granville. I think I opened some eyes that day. And by the way, I always believed that Granville was the best defensive player ever to play at Oklahoma.

I was introduced to our offensive line coach, Carl "Buck" Nystrom, who remains in my mind as the toughest SOB who ever lived.

We had a board drill where you went head-to-head with another lineman, and one day Buck was angry that the scout-team linemen weren't giving the effort needed. Buck turned his cap around and got down and took us all on in that drill. I was first in line and I just didn't want to get embarrassed by Buck, but I didn't want to hurt him, either. He was an assistant coach and he was probably 5'10" and about 180. The final guy through the line was Bob Kalsu, who was about 6'5" and 230. He hit Buck and picked him up and planted him.

Later that night, Ken Mendenhall and I went out for some ice cream and ran into Buck and his two-year-old son.

Buck lifted his shirt and said, "Look what you SOBs did to me today."

He had a huge helmet mark on him, and it was Bob's. Man, Buck was the best. When he retired after my junior year, we all cried.

He had told me during my sophomore year, "Zabel, if you listen to me and do the things I tell you to do, I will make you a first-round draft choice."

Since I mentioned Bob Kalsu, I have to say that that guy was larger than life. During my sophomore year, Bob was a senior and our acknowledged offensive leader. He was drafted by Buffalo and was a starter by the end of his rookie year. When he was asked to fulfill his military obligation, as everyone in Oklahoma knows, he did just that even though he could have declined to do so. He went to Vietnam and died on that hill. He is revered in Oklahoma and for good reason. I'll never forget him.

That first game of my sophomore season, we beat Washington State 21–0, and I caught a touchdown pass on the first pass that Bobby Warmack threw that season.

Because we had Steve Owens and Ron Shotts at tailback, Mike Harper at fullback, and Eddie Hinton in the backfield, too, we knew what we were going to do offensively: run off tackle, run off tackle, and run off tackle. When we would catch that free safety creeping up to stop it, we would play-action and throw it.

We won at Missouri 7–0 on a day that Gordon Wheeler, our punter, pinned them inside their 5-yard line about three or four times. It was scoreless when we threw deep, and the ball was tipped up into the air. I caught it on the dead run and got tackled on the 6-yard line. We scored on the next play, and that's how we won the game.

After that game, I was watching film with the receivers. I was four rooms away from where the offensive line was watching film, but I could hear Buck Nystrom screaming, "Zabel! That sucks! Zabel! That sucks!"

Apparently, I didn't block very well that day, so thank God I caught that one pass.

Our coaches were really tough on us. During that season, we would come out of film sessions and ask each other, "Did we win that game? I thought we won that game?"

After we beat Colorado 23–0 that year, quite a few players went out and celebrated that night, and I was part of it. On Monday morning, I ran into coach Fairbanks as I was going to class.

"What time did you get in Saturday night?" he asked me.

I started to stutter and he snapped, "Don't lie to me! I know you didn't come in until 2:00 in the morning."

Knowing that I didn't come home at all, I thought that sounded pretty good, so I just said, "You're right, Coach."

It was early November and very cold and coach Fairbanks told all of us that we had to get up and run that Tuesday morning—at 5:00 a.m.! We figured that he wouldn't come out to run us but that hc would send some assistant. Then out of the dark comes this yellow, four-door Olds 88 that coach Fairbanks drove. He yelled at us to get over to the stadium, but the gates were locked, so we started climbing the fence. Then he told us to climb down and run all the way around the stadium to the other entrance. As we jogged, he was chasing us in that car, honking his horn and screaming, "Sprint! Run!"

As we ran that morning, I could tell he was there watching us the entire time because I could see the glow of his cigarette in the dark in the southeast ramp of the stadium. By 8:00 a.m. only two of us were left—me and Bruce Stensrud. We had one more sprint to run, and I beat Bruce by about 20 yards. As I ran up the ramp and ran by coach Fairbanks, I felt so good. I wouldn't quit. I couldn't quit. That remains one of the greatest days of my life.

We had played and we had paid and we were all scared to death of Chuck Fairbanks.

The Kansas game remains a highlight in my career. We were down 10–7 with about three minutes to go and we were on our own 4-yard line in the north end zone.

Bobby Warmack, the "Wicked Worm," got us in the huddle and told us, "Let's go boys! We can do this!"

I caught a pass for about 11 yards, then Steve Owens ran left, right, and up the middle a few times. We converted on fourth down twice on that drive. With about a minute to go, we were on Nebraska's 30-yard line when we called a play-action pass, and I ran right by the safety who was coming up to take on Owens. I caught it and scored, and they say about 100,000 oranges were thrown onto the field at that moment. I can still picture Pepper Rodgers, the Kansas coach, throwing oranges back into the crowd. We had clinched an Orange Bowl berth with that 14–10 win.

We beat Nebraska and Oklahoma State and then Tennessee in the Orange Bowl to finish 10–1. If not for that 9–7 loss to Texas when we missed a field goal near the end, we would have been national champions.

Those Orange Bowl practices were the most difficult practices of the year. We needed every ounce of that preparation we had to beat Tennessee. And at the end, I remember praying that their field-goal kicker would miss the kick. He did, and we won. It was a great game.

The funny thing was, a year earlier, I was back in Denver and I went out to dinner with a former girlfriend. As we waited for a table in this restaurant, the Orange Bowl was on TV and I was thinking, "Man, it would be unbelievable to play in that game."

The very next year I was there playing in it for Oklahoma. That is still amazing to me.

To this day, when Oklahoma fans recognize me, they say one of two things. They will say, "You were guy who caught the pass against Kansas," or they will say, "You were the last guy to play both ways for OU."

Going into my junior year, I broke my foot on the first day of two-a-day practices, but I still tried to practice. It turned out I had a stress fracture. I wasn't full speed but played in the opener at Notre Dame and caught two touchdown passes as we led 21–14 at the half. We didn't score another point [in a 45–21 loss] that day.

Then we lost to Texas 26–20 after leading them 20–19 with 1:20 remaining. After beating Iowa State and losing to Colorado, we were 2–3 at the time when coach Fairbanks called me into his office.

"We've already proven that we can't out-score our opponents," he said, "so I want you to switch to defense."

I had played a stand-up defensive end some in high school, so I had a little experience at it. The Oklahoma coaches wanted me now to use my speed coming off the corner and my athletic ability to rush the passer, so I played defensive end for the rest of the season and also played on about 50 percent of our offensive plays. I had always considered myself a team player and I agreed to make the switch to defense to help the team.

In that first game on defense, I had two sacks against Lynn Dickey of Kansas State. And I also punted that season. It was great fun being on the field all that time. I was in tremendous shape and I always felt I could handle the workload. I just didn't think about it. I never really got tired, either. I played 10 years of pro football, but it was in that junior season when I was in the best shape of my life.

At the end of that season, we played SMU in the Bluebonnet Bowl, and I tore my knee up trying to block a punt. The fullback cut me. After the operation, I started rehabbing and lifting weights, and my legs got very strong.

On the Fourth of July during a softball game, I pulled my hamstring. Nobody had told me that I had to work on my hamstrings. It turns out that my quadriceps were so strong from all the work I had done after surgery that my hamstrings couldn't compensate.

Before the 1969 season, all of the offensive linemen started to talk together about blocking our butts off to help Steve Owens win the Heisman Trophy.

Most of us seniors thought Mickey Ripley, a junior, should start the season as the starting quarterback, but coach Fairbanks talked to us about starting a sophomore named Jack Mildren. We beat Wisconsin 48–21 to open the season, and Steve Owens had a big day.

On the first drive against Pittsburgh the next week, we put together a long touchdown drive of about 13 plays. It was very hot that day, about 100 degrees on the field. The next time we got the ball, I was dreading another long drive in that heat, but on the first play, Jack broke it for an 80-yard touchdown run and I thought to myself, "Thank God."

Suddenly, I was a huge Jack Mildren fan.

It wasn't a great year, since we would win one week and lose the next. We were playing a lot of sophomores, including two offensive tackles. With Byron Bigby and Bob Kalsu a few years earlier, we had two tough tackles. Now our sophomore tackles were very inexperienced. We had another sophomore who fumbled two punts inside our 5-yard line in the loss to Texas.

After that game, we had a film session on Sunday, and coach Fairbanks' first words were, "Zabel! Stand up. You're an embarrassment to this team. You played a horseshit game, and I would advise you to quit!"

As I started to walk out of the room, he said, "Sit down!"

When everybody else went out to run after the film session, coach Fairbanks said, "Not you, Zabel. Sit down!"

So we sat there and watched the film, play-by-play. The best thing he said was, "That's horseshit."

Then he asked me if I had anything to say.

I told him that the way he treated me in front of the team wasn't right. I said something like, "It's tough blocking next to those sophomore tackles."

Three days later, I was walking to lunch when coach Fairbanks came up and put his arm around me and said, "You know what, Zabel? You're right—those sophomores aren't worth a shit right now. So I moved Ken Mendenhall to tackle. That will solve the problem."

It did. Ken was a great player who later played 11 years in the NFL.

As for coach Fairbanks, I thought he was a terrific coach. I respected him. I feared him. To this day, I don't think he's received the credit he is due for building OU football into what is. He was very, very organized and he knew his football. I was proud that he thought enough of me to trade for me later when he coached New England.

For some reason after that season, we voted not to go to a bowl game. I guess we were embarrassed with a 6–4 season and just didn't want to go to a lesser bowl. Looking back on it, I am shocked that the university allowed us to do that.

We took a lot of pride in Steve Owens' 100-yard rushing streak [18 games].

There is something to be said for playing football at Oklahoma, which is one of the top football programs ever. When I look back on it, I can say that what I am now is a result of playing at Oklahoma. I met the love of my life, my wife Susan, and we had three kids and a granddaughter.

Granville Liggins once said that he had two goals in life—to play at Oklahoma and to play pro football—and everything else after that is a bonus. That's kind of how I feel about it.

The tradition and heritage of Oklahoma—to be mentioned today in the same vein as Steve Owens, Granville Liggins, Joe Washington, and all of those other great players—I can't express what it means to me. I am just thankful for all of it.

Steve Zabel is considered one of the most versatile players in Oklahoma history. He was an All-American in 1969 and named Academic All–Big Eight three years. He also punted 58 times for a 38.8-yard average in 1968. He finished his career with 64 receptions for 885 yards and eight touchdowns. He was the sixth pick by the Philadelphia Eagles in the 1970 NFL draft. He also played for New England and Baltimore.

Steve Owens | Running back | 1967–1969

I grew up in Miami, Oklahoma, up in the northeastern corner of the state near the Missouri border. Mickey Mantle was raised in Commerce, which was only a mile away, so he became my first hero [we became friends later on], and I naturally grew up loving sports. I played them all. If it was football season, I played football. If it was baseball season, I played baseball.

And I became an Oklahoma Sooners fan when I was very young.

I still can remember that in the ninth or 10th grade when I worked at a shoe store, I would hide in the storeroom on Saturday afternoons with this little transistor radio. Nobody could find me while I listened to the Sooners play, and I can still hear Bob Barry's voice.

When I got to high school, I used to come down to Norman to see a game every season, paying a dollar and sitting near the south end zone.

I knew one thing for certain: I wanted to come to OU to play football if I ever had the chance.

My father was a wonderful guy. His name was Olen, but everybody called him "Peanut"—he was about 5'6" but stocky. He had a fourth-grade education but he worked his tail off. He was a truck driver and trying to feed nine kids—seven boys and two girls—so he didn't have time for sports. Dad grew up during some difficult, very tough times and he worked as hard as he did because he just wanted all of us to be happy. My mom, Cherry, went to all of my games. She was so dedicated to all of us. She was truly a great mother.

When I was in high school, we were the Miami Wardogs and we had a very good program. I started all three years and began to be recruited some by my junior year. I played running back and the rover-type of linebacker on defense and I started to get a bunch of letters from colleges. As a senior, I was the Player of the Year in Oklahoma and the state champion in track in the high hurdles, high jump, and broad jump.

By then, I was being recruited by Texas, Notre Dame, Nebraska, Kansas, and Missouri, to name a few. I remember being up at Nebraska for the OU-Nebraska game in 1966, and Bud Wilkinson was the TV commentator for that game. He was on the sideline before the game when somebody introduced me to him.

He looked at me and said, "What are you doing on *this* sideline?" He wondered why I was at Nebraska. And I remember Nebraska beat the Sooners that day.

As far as my future, it all came down to Arkansas and Oklahoma.

Jim MacKenzie was Frank Broyles' top assistant at Arkansas, and I got to know him very well during the recruiting process. It just so happened that during my senior season, OU was having its worst season since coach Wilkinson had left. The Sooners finished 3–7 and they weren't playing like the teams I grew up listening to on the radio.

Jim would tell me, "You need to come to Arkansas because Oklahoma will be rebuilding for a while."

I had thought about all of what Jim told me. I thought that despite my dream of being a Sooner that maybe the best thing was to go to Arkansas.

But then Gomer Jones was out at Oklahoma and guess who they hired as head coach? That's right, Jim MacKenzie.

Jim came to my house and asked me, "Remember all that stuff I told you about coming to Arkansas? You need to forget all of that and follow your dreams of becoming a Sooner!"

Of course, I followed his instructions. I became an Oklahoma Sooner.

My brothers drove me to Norman when I first arrived, because freshmen were not allowed to have cars. As we drove into town, we took a wrong turn and drove into the entrance of this big building where some older people were outside in heavy coats.

I thought, "Is this the university?"

It turned out we were at a mental institution. One of my brothers looked at me and said, "I think we're in the wrong place." We still laugh about that to this day.

When I checked in, I went from being a star to just another player. We had about 50 or 60 freshmen on scholarship alone back then, and that year was difficult for me. My girlfriend was back home going to school and I was away from my family for the first time.

One day I called home and said, "Dad, I think I will come back to Miami and go to junior college."

He asked me, "Where are you going to stay?"

"Well, I thought I would stay with you all," I told him.

"Son, we don't have any room here," he said. "You need to stay in Norman."

That was the best advice he ever gave me. So what could I do? I toughed it out and stayed in Norman.

I think I had a great feel for coach MacKenzie. He was double-tough, and that first year he and his new staff really wanted to find out who wanted to play football at Oklahoma. We did a fourth-quarter drill that was the toughest thing I ever went through, physically and mentally. It was an hour-long drill of constant motion.

I'll never forget that one day Jim came out with his suit and tie on while we were finishing that drill. He walked around for about five minutes and then called everybody up and told us, "Start this thing over—I don't like the way you are doing it."

One day somebody came running into my dorm room and said coach MacKenzie had just died of a heart attack. I just sat there in shock. The Sooners had turned it around to finish 6–4 that year, had beaten Texas for the first time in nine years, and coach MacKenzie had been Big Eight Coach of the Year.

And then all of a sudden, he was gone.

To this day, I have no doubt that he would have been a great coach, and Oklahoma would have become a consistent winner under him.

That summer I worked very hard to prepare for my sophomore season, and I married Barbara that summer. I was in great shape by the time camp started. One day we were running the goal line offense against the first team and I scored just about every time I carried it.

Chuck Fairbanks, whom they had promoted to head coach, said something like, "This is the type of guy we need carrying the football."

I didn't start the first two games but I had over 100 yards in one [129 yards in a 35–0 win over Maryland] and close to 100 in the other. Against Texas, we were trailing 9–7, and I broke a sprint draw and ran about 40 yards. I thought I was going to score, but this guy caught me at about the 20-yard line. Mike Vachon, who had kicked four field goals in the win over Texas a year earlier, missed a short field goal, and that was the way the game ended. It was his fourth miss of the day.

We out-played them, out-rushed them, and we were a better team that day, but we still lost. That was as bad as I felt in my entire career. As it turned out, if we would have won that game, we probably would have won the national title. I still think about that game to this very day. That was a tough loss.

After that game [15 carries for 106 yards], they put a first-team jersey in my locker—that's how I found out I would become a co-starter with Ron Shotts, who was a great player.

We rolled on during that season and won the rest of them to head to the Orange Bowl against Tennessee, which had a great team. Really, not many people thought we would win that game since Tennessee was loaded. We jumped out to lead 19–0 at the half, and they came storming back. It went down to the wire with us leading 26–24 when we had a fourth-and-one at midfield. They called on me to get the yard, but

Steve Owens is remembered as one of the finest players in Oklahoma history. Among his feats at running back was his 18-game streak of 100-yard games.

Tennessee sent Jack "Hacksaw" Reynolds on a blitz and I never got back to the line of scrimmage.

I was on the sideline as Tennessee worked its way into field-goal position, feeling terrible about not getting that yard. As they lined up for a field goal, I couldn't even watch, so I just turned my back on the game and looked up at all the Oklahoma fans to see their reaction. They went crazy after the kick, and that's how I knew we won the ballgame.

That 1967 team was a very good team, finishing 10–1, but we did it because of the way the guys felt for Jim MacKenzie. We all dedicated that season to him. Looking back, I can say that team was a special team, and we played for the memory of coach MacKenzie.

I loved coach Fairbanks, too. He was tough, a Michigan State guy who was extremely organized and he had a great football mind. He was all business. Everything he did was to the T. That really was a very good staff, with Barry Switzer, Galen Hall, Pat James, and Larry Lacewell as a few of his assistants. All of those guys were great coaches and great people.

Heading into my junior year, our expectations were very high because we had so many good players back. We went to Notre Dame to open the season, and I had never seen guys as big as that. We always felt like quickness and speed were our edge, but Notre Dame was so much bigger—and they had the same speed as we did.

They beat us [45–21], and a few weeks later we lost to Texas again. They drove 80 yards in the final minutes to beat us 26–20. After a tough loss at Colorado, we came back strong and won five in a row and beat Nebraska 47–0. At that time, we were playing great football and had tied Kansas for the Big Eight Championship.

They went to the Orange Bowl while we went to Houston for the Astro-Bluebonnet Bowl, which we lost to SMU 28–27.

In my senior season we lost to Texas again after we jumped to a 14–0 lead, but they came back to beat us 27–17. We never beat Texas in my career and that's something that is tough for me to think about all these years.

We got humiliated a couple of times that season. Kansas State took 40 years of frustration out on us [59–21] but they had a pretty good quarterback in Lynn Dickey. We got pretty banged up on defense at times that season and by the end of it, we heard the coaches were in trouble. We had finished 7–4 the year before and now we were 5–4 heading into the Oklahoma State game.

On that Monday they were to announce the Heisman Trophy winner. The way it was set up back then was for the finalists to be sitting by the phone at a pre-arranged time and they would call the winner. So on that Monday, Barbara and I were in the student union and the call was supposed to be made at 11:00. Well, about 10 minutes past 11:00, I told her, "Let's go. I have some things to do and then I have to get ready for practice."

Just then, somebody hollered down from upstairs where they had a wire-service hookup, "Hey, Steve, you just won the Heisman!"

And that's how I found out.

As I walked from the student union over to the locker room, I guess word had started to get around campus, because people were shouting at me and calling my name.

My dad was in Dallas that day and he had pulled into a truck-stop and called Mom. "Did the boy win that there trophy?" he asked her.

Like I said, there was some talk that if we didn't beat OSU, that they might fire the staff. The captains got together and said, "Look, these coaches are great coaches, we got to go win this game for them." We realized the worst thing for the future of this program would be if these coaches weren't here.

At that time, I was exhausted from the Heisman and I knew the week after the game I would be traveling to New York for the ceremony.

We were behind late in the Oklahoma State game and coming off of our goal line. I had carried the ball 25 times in the third quarter alone. Can you imagine that today—25 carries in one quarter? Anyway, Oklahoma State had a pretty good defense that year with two first-round draft choices and a second-round draft choice on that side of the ball.

So we start to drive off the goal line, slowly making our way out of there, and I ran a sweep for my sixth straight carry. Now I am starting to get worn down. I was so tired that I told Jack Mildren to call a timeout. He went to the sideline and got on the headphones to the coaches upstairs and well . . . Jack likes to tell the story about what coach Switzer said.

The basis of his message was to "tell that SOB that he could rest after the game, but he's not done carrying the football yet."

We had momentum, and Barry didn't like it at all that we had called timeout. He threw in a few choice words for Jack and me. So I ran six more times—12 straight total—to score, and we beat Oklahoma State 28–27 in the final game.

The offense was built around me and it was a basic ball-control type of offense. We just knew we could wear defenses down in the second half. It was a burden at times, but any running back loves getting the ball as much as I did.

Reporters used to ask me all the time, "How can you carry the ball 55 times in one game?"

"Easy," I would say. "Coach Switzer makes me carry it 100 times a day during practice."

I was conditioned for it. Coach Switzer made sure of that. Fortunately, I never had any major injuries, just a deep thigh bruise coming out of camp my junior year.

After the Oklahoma State game, I flew to New York for the Heisman ceremony and took my parents. That remains the best part of it for me. My parents had never flown before and they saw things they had never seen before. My dad never forgot that trip.

The ceremony was on a Thursday night, and I remember meeting Tom Seaver of the Mets. They had just won the World Series that year. And I met Howard Cosell and Doc Blanchard and so many other celebrities. I just couldn't believe this was happening to me. You could never prepare yourself for something like that.

On Friday, I appeared on *The Tonight Show Starring Johnny Carson*. As I sat in the green room waiting to go on the show, Muhammad Ali was in there with me. Someone stuck there head inside the door and said, "Mister Owens, you have a call from the President of the United States."

An aide to President Nixon was calling to see if I would ride with him aboard Air Force One down to the Arkansas-Texas game. So the next day we flew down to Fayetteville aboard Air Force One and I got to spend time on board with the President. He gave me some horseshoe cuff-links, which I still have, and I gave him a Heisman memento.

The funny thing is that after the game, Barbara and I rode back to Norman with some friends in an old, beat-up Chevy. We arrived on Air Force One and departed in a clunker. We still laugh about that.

I wouldn't trade the experience of winning the Heisman for anything. The guys I have met and become friends with—Doak Walker, Glenn Davis, Paul Hornung, Archie Griffin, John David Crow—I could go on and on but they are all special people.

And of course, in our OU family, I have been close to Billy Sims for a long time, and we welcomed Jason White into the club recently. Billy Vessels [OU's 1952 Heisman winner] was such a great man. When they had an appreciation day for me in Miami after the Heisman, Billy flew there from Florida for it and he became a close friend of mine.

But the Heisman wasn't possible without my teammates. I have to say that the relationship I had with my teammates was so special to me. I could go on and on about these guys when people always ask me about the Heisman. If it weren't for the guys I played with, I never would have won the Heisman Trophy.

One story I love to tell came from the 1969 game against Colorado. I had rushed for more than 100 yards in 13 straight games, and we were leading late in the game. I was under 100 yards, and we had the game won, so I looked at Jack in the huddle and told him, "Just run out the clock. Fall on the ball. This streak isn't that important."

That's when guard Billy Elfstrom looked at me and said, "It might not be important to you, but it's important to us!"

So we ran a few more plays and I got my 100 yards. That streak was stopped at 18 in a row by Nebraska later that year.

What can I say about my teammates? They mean the world to me. Guys like Mike Harper, a fullback who blocked for me on every one of my carries. I named my son after him. Guys like Steve Zabel, Ken Mendenhall, Billy Elfstrom, Bobby Warmack, Jack Mildren, Eddie Hinton—I wish I could mention them all.

Dad died in 1985, and Mom is in her eighties now. I am so thankful that I had them as parents. That's another reason the Heisman means so much to me—it gave them a chance to see some things and to enjoy something they wouldn't have otherwise had the chance to do.

As far as coach Switzer goes, all you need to know about him is one thing: all the players who played for him love him. And he loved us. I consider him a best friend. I respect him so much. He made me a better player. He would not accept me being complacent and he really pushed me during my senior year. I always appreciated the fact that he never eased up on me.

Before games, he used to tell me what was expected of me and he had a special way of getting you inspired. What he went through here in 1989 was very tough on him, and the picture painted of Barry was not the real Barry that I know. I felt so bad for him at the time and I was proud to stand up and support him. That whole thing took its toll on him. He's human, but he's still a legend in Oklahoma.

When I think of Oklahoma's tradition, sometimes people don't appreciate what we have until it's gone. The importance of this program and its impact on these people in this state is tremendous, so when we had those difficult 10 years after coach Switzer left, it gave us all resolve to get it back where it should be.

When I grew up, Oklahoma was all about winning. I always had great respect for our tradition. There was a standard set here, a standard of excellence. When you talk about being a Sooner, what does it mean? It means all of those things: championships, All-Americans, and winning, but there is much more to it. I have such great feelings for this university and being a Sooner. It's emotional for me. Regardless if you played in the forties, fifties, or sixties through today, we all have that common thread running through us.

It is truly something special.

I have to sum it up by saying that my dreams came true. I reflect back to when I was in that storeroom listening to Oklahoma football games and for me to take that journey through OU while all my goals and dreams became a reality. How do I put that into words?

It was the four greatest years of my life. Being a Sooner became a part of me.

Like the song says, "I am a Sooner born and Sooner bred and when I die, I'll be Sooner dead."

Steve Owens, the recipient of the 1969 Heisman Trophy and a two-time All-American, holds five OU records, including the most 100-yard rushing games (23). He finished his career with 4,041 rushing yards and 57 touchdowns. In his senior season, he rushed for 1,523 yards and 23 touchdowns. He also was named All–Big Eight in each of his three seasons. One of the greatest workhorses in college football history, Owens holds OU's top-seven positions in rushing attempts per game, including his record 55-carry performance against Oklahoma State in 1969—Owens' final game in a Sooners uniform. He also was a team captain in 1969. He played six seasons with the Detroit Lions. Owens was inducted into the College Football Hall of Fame in 1991.

| chapter four |

The Seventies

Jack Mildren | Quarterback | 1969–1971

I was born in Kingsville, Texas, the oldest of three brothers. Dad was a high school coach when I was born, and by the time I became a football player, he had gone on to other things. When I was in the first grade, we moved to Abilene and that became a very good move for my future. We played sports all the time, and I soon discovered that track was a very big deal in Abilene. Abilene Christian had some track stars go to the Olympics in the past, and the track program had garnered the interest of all the local kids.

In football, Abilene High had won some 50-odd games in a row in the fifties, so the sport was king around town. I remember in grade school when I first started playing, they had some interesting rules, such as if you played in the first quarter, you couldn't play in the second. None of the kids liked it, but it gave all the kids a good chance to play.

As I look back on it now, it was a typical Southern childhood and a nice way to grow up.

I ran the second leg of the mile relay team that won the state championship in my sophomore year and I also ran the hurdles, so I guess I was relatively fast. I also enjoyed basketball quite a bit.

I went to Cooper High, which was the new school on the south side of town. When I entered Cooper, they had not been very good in the past, but they hired a new coach by the name of Merrill Green. He had played at Oklahoma and he was a really interesting guy. I give him a lot of credit because he had the guts to start sophomores.

I started my first game there even though we had two seniors at quarterback. We had three sophomores in the backfield at one time, and coach Green would joke that "the game had better end by 9:00, or their mothers will make me send them home for bed time."

We won only two games that year, but we were averaging 12,000 to 14,000 fans per game. As I said, football was big in Abilene.

In my junior year, we lost only one game—to San Angelo which was coached by Emory Bellard, who later became head coach at Texas A&M. They went on to win the state championship that year.

I had a pretty good year, and we had a junior-dominated team with guys like Kenny Stephens at tailback and Jon Harrison catching passes.

The next year nobody knew how good we could be, but we were all seniors so we had big expectations. We won 13 games in a row before meeting Austin Reagan in the state championship game.

We led 19–7 at the half playing at TCU's stadium on a crummy, drizzly day in December. Somehow, I don't know how, we lost that game 20–19. That still bothers me a little all these years later. Our hearts were broken. I was all-state and so was Jon, but it didn't matter that day. It's funny how games like that stick with you.

That summer, I had visited some colleges to get an honest look at them without the bands playing, without the cheerleaders cheering, and without the stands full of fans.

My brother Richard was a big TCU fan, which was the closest campus to home. I had been to the SMU campus more than any other, and the Ponies were good then, too. A lot of my friends went to Texas Tech, which was 150 miles from Abilene. Gene Stallings was at A&M then, and they had just won the Southwest Conference championship, but the University of Texas was, and still is, the preeminent university in Texas. And I liked Arkansas and coach Broyles, so I had a lot of choices to choose from.

Unbeknownst to me, my high school coach had allowed OU coaches into our locker room, but I didn't know then that the SWC coaches couldn't come in. The SWC had a rule then that coaches could have only two meetings with recruits, but Oklahoma didn't have those restrictions. So coach Royal came to see me twice and coach Fairbanks came about 50 times. That was the only year they had that rule because the SWC coaches had complained it hampered their recruiting efforts.

It was a fun time. When I visited Houston, I got to see the famous basketball game between UCLA and Lew Alcindor and Houston and Elvin Hayes. The highlight was Johnny Unitas calling me once on behalf of Baylor, but I wasn't going to Baylor. After Alabama and Texas A&M played in the Cotton Bowl, Bear Bryant called me. Then Oklahoma was playing in the Orange Bowl [in a 26–24 win over Tennessee] in coach Fairbanks' first year, and he also called me right after the game.

My family got to know Barry Switzer very well during the recruiting process. He was Chuck's offensive coordinator at the time and he visited us often. We liked him. He likes to tell that story of us pulling up to a stoplight in Abilene and getting out of the car to go over some plays in the Oklahoma playbook. It's true—we actually did that as traffic whizzed by. He had noticed on film how I sometimes cut the tailback off, so he wanted to show me the right way to take the steps. We're lucky we didn't get hit by a car.

We didn't have a dishwasher back then so it was our job to wash dishes for Mom, but Barry always washed dishes at the house when he had dinner with us. You can imagine how my brothers loved him for that.

Dad was my devil's advocate during recruiting. If I offered an opinion on something, he would be the contrarian to make me think about it. Mom just wanted me to be happy wherever I went. I put all the pluses and minuses down on each school, and it came down to Oklahoma and Arkansas in the end.

I just felt that Oklahoma was the better choice of the two, so I made my first call to coach Broyles to tell him the bad news before I called Barry to tell him the good news.

I get to campus in the fall of 1968 and you can imagine the welcome I got. Here was this kid, who *Sports Illustrated* already had written a story about during the recruiting process, and yet I was only a freshman.

We had a very talented freshman class and we were winning our freshman games pretty easily while the varsity started 1–2 that year.

The school newspaper wrote some article about how the freshman team should play the varsity schedule so Oklahoma could win more games. So as you can imagine, there was not a lot of love between the varsity floors and the freshman floor in the dorm. Hey, we didn't write the story, right?

At that time, coach Fairbanks always named "big brothers" for us, an upperclassman who would take a younger player under his wing. Chuck named Steve Owens as my big brother. Even before he won the Heisman Trophy, Steve Owens was a great guy. And he remained a great guy after he won it. So he helped shut up some of the upperclassmen who had given me a hard time.

Our job as freshmen was to get the varsity ready for their next game. One week on the scout team I would get to be Terry Hanratty of Notre Dame and the next week I would be James Street of Texas.

On Monday nights we would scrimmage toward the end of practice. "Finesse" is not a word you would use to describe those scrimmages. We would have those goal line sessions where they lasted so long that we finished them in the dark. I would come to the line of scrimmage and try to count the guys on defense in the dark and I would see 13 or 14 players. They always wanted to send a message to the freshmen. It wasn't too much fun, I know that.

Jack Mildren, considered the "father of the wishbone," guided one of the most explosive offenses in college football history—the 1971 Sooners, who averaged 557 yards per game. *Photo courtesy of OU Athletics Media Relations.*

The varsity would leave on Fridays and spend the night in Oklahoma City before games. While the freshmen would still be practicing, [assistant coaches] Buck Nystrom and Pat James would be there in their suits and ties waiting for the bus to be ready to leave. They would be yelling and screaming at us. Buck would get into my face and say, "You'll never do this or never do that."

Finally, coach Fairbanks would come over and tell them, "Let's go. We're leaving."

I guess they just had extra time on their hands and had to come over to yell at somebody.

Speaking of that, I'll always remember Port Robertson. He was the quintessential man's man and he ran the study hall with an iron first. You learned never to be late for study hall. He would call you "Peehead" and knock you on the head with that big ring of his. He scared us and intimidated us, but he is a guy who helped so many Oklahoma players get through school. Port died a few years ago, but he is a legend around Oklahoma. Everybody has a Port Robertson story.

That next spring of 1969, Mickey Ripley and Mike Jones were the returning quarterbacks with me after Bobby Warmack had graduated. I was running second behind Mickey, but I could read. All the sports writers were saying I would take over eventually. It wasn't a pleasant situation for Mickey, I am sure. And Mike Jones certainly had as good a spring as anybody.

Eventually, I was named the starter, and we opened the season at Wisconsin on a day in which Owens carried 30 or more times and we won 48–21. The first pass I ever threw was a touchdown to Joe Killingsworth that day.

We beat Pittsburgh in the next game when it was hotter than all get out in Norman. We jumped ahead of Texas 14–0 and ended up losing 27–17 after I made a couple of crummy decisions in the fourth quarter.

That year became an up-and-down year. That's the way sophomores play. But the one thing stands out about that season: Steve Owens was consistently great.

We ended the season trailing Oklahoma State at the end of the game and we just ran Steve over and over again. He was gasping for breath and was tired after we crossed midfield, so I called timeout. I went over to the sideline, and Barry Switzer just ripped into me big-time.

"What did you call timeout for?" he screamed at me.

"Owens is tired," I told him.

"You tell the big guy he can rest in the spring, we need to go score right now," he said, except he threw in a few "bleep, bleep, bleep" words to get his point across.

I got back to the huddle and told Steve, "Barry says 'bleep, bleep, bleep and you can rest in the spring!'"

We scored, Steve carried 55 times that day, and we won the game 28–27.

Chuck Fairbanks turned down a bowl game after that 6–4 season—I think it was to the Liberty—telling us something like, "You guys don't deserve it." It was the only year we didn't go to a bowl.

We lost three first-round draft choices: Steve Owens, Steve Zabel, and Jim Files, but we had plenty of young talent returning.

We had been in the I-formation, of course, and that next spring we switched to the Houston veer. We used split backs and we were going to throw it more. It sounded good to me and I was excited about it. We moved up and down the field during the spring.

We beat SMU and Wisconsin to open the season and then the bottom dropped out and we lost to Oregon State 23–14. We were called to a meeting the next day, two weeks before the Texas game, and told we were switching offenses to the wishbone. It takes a lot of courage to switch offenses in the middle of a season. I think about it now and the coaches' jobs were on the line.

We got thumped pretty well [41–9] by Texas and it was a miserable day. We headed back to Norman with a 2–2 record and not much confidence.

Only Barry Switzer, in his usual style, could see some good signs. He pointed out all the glass-is-half-full stuff, and we went back to work. We beat Colorado 23–15 and we were adjusting as we went in front of 75,000 fans. We continued to work on it in practice and watched a lot of film of Texas' wishbone and we improved every week. After we lost to Kansas State, we won three in a row.

I never thought Barry was given enough credit for the teaching that went on during that time. We finished the season by beating Oklahoma State 66–6 and we could have scored 100 points if we had wanted. Maybe that was the first time the light came on for all of us. All of a sudden, running the wishbone and moving the ball was easy for us.

As it turned out, it was the right thing to do. I didn't agree with it at first and I took it personally that we had made the change to the wishbone. We started out very simple with it and we became very complex. It got to the point that I would pitch the ball without looking, knowing the guy would be there. We even added one more wrinkle: if the quarterback turned up the field, the running back turned up with him and that resulted in pitches downfield. That was a lethal weapon with guys like Greg Pruitt and Joe Wylie.

The coaching staff, in my opinion, never has been given enough credit for teaching this offense to us. They really did a great job.

As we started the 1971 season, we felt we could move the ball on anybody, and we did. I would put that offense up against anybody's offense. We had a three-game run, against USC, Texas, and then Colorado, which ended up No. 3 and had beaten Ohio State and LSU on the road. We beat all three of them and clearly had a lot of confidence.

As the season progressed, Nebraska was never far from our thoughts. We weren't fools. We could read the newspapers. Just think about this: we went to Kansas State and their quarterback, Dennis Morrison, passed for 400 yards and four touchdowns, and we won by 47 points [75–28]. We scored on 11 of 12 possessions that day, totaled more than 700 yards. Greg Pruitt had 294 yards on 19 carries [an OU single-game rushing record]. It was another game in which we could have scored 100 if we wanted to.

We were on a real roll by the time Nebraska came around. Our closest game had been a win by 13 points over a great USC team.

We had the No. 1 offense; Nebraska had the No. 1 defense.

Games like the Game of the Century are why we all came to play at Oklahoma.

Heading into that game, I don't remember the game plan being any different. We were going to do the same thing we had always done—run the triple option and make decisions after the ball was snapped.

All the hype that led up to it was fun. It was the perfect setting. The game was the only game on TV, and it was Thanksgiving, so everybody around the country would be watching. It was colder than all get out that day.

At halftime, we were up 17–14 and we had controlled the ball. We had driven the length of the field three times. Then the game went back and forth. They took the lead and we would come right back. I had thrown two touchdown passes to [Jon] Harrison. I know the Nebraska secondary guys like to talk over the years about them being confused in their coverages, but the facts are that Jon beat them like a drum that day.

The one pass I would like to have back is the one late in the game when I overthrew Jon. Once they went ahead for the final time, time became a problem and we ran out of it at the end of the game. Being a senior, I realized that my college dream of winning the national championship would not be realized. It was fresh and raw at that point and it hurt.

Life has its ups and downs. You never forget how the game turned out, but it wasn't life or death. I know the score of it just like I know the score of that high school championship game we lost. I just don't want to be defined by it. I have never been embarrassed by the fact we lost to Nebraska that day. That game has a life of its own now and it has stood the test of time. I never thought that would happen.

It's ironic that at a school that has so many big victories, so much time is spent talking about a game we didn't win. I can't explain that.

The next week we beat Oklahoma State [58–14] and I really don't know how we got ourselves ready to play. It was just methodical, I guess.

I went to New York for some awards banquet after that and I roomed with Johnny Musso of Alabama, who had to play Nebraska in the Orange Bowl. We got to joking around at some function and Johnny said, "We are going to kill Nebraska."

I said something like, "Well, we're going to beat Auburn by 60 points [in the Sugar Bowl]."

That was my first experience of getting quoted out of context. We were just having fun and those comments appeared in the newspapers. Did I have some egg on my face? Yes.

We really didn't know much about Auburn, other than they had been hammered by Alabama. What helped us is that we got to see on film how they would line up against the wishbone because that is the offense Alabama used. We led 31–0 at the half, and Greg Pruitt was giving me a hard time because I had scored three touchdowns.

That game was great [a 40–22 win], but it was anti-climactic for sure. It was still hard to overlook not winning the big one. And Nebraska just hammered Alabama to win the national championship. The Big Eight finished 1-2-3 in the nation that year with Colorado No. 3. That was pretty impressive. I haven't thought back much to what a nice accomplishment that was, beating Auburn like we did.

I still say that 1971 offense of ours was as good as any. Look at the numbers: Oklahoma averaged a school-record 556.8 yards per game, 7.6 yards per play, and 44.5 points per game. It was a great, great offense.

I couldn't have picked a better place to play college football or go to school, for a lot of reasons. I got my degree in four years. I had plenty of ups and downs, but I don't regret it for a second. It turned out much better than I ever could have expected. I consider myself an Oklahoma Sooner for life.

Jack Mildren, an All-American in 1971, completed 170 of 358 career passes for 3,092 yards and 24 touchdowns. He rushed for 1,289 yards and 20 touchdowns in 1971, and 2,025 yards and 32 touchdowns in his career. He owns the OU record for pass efficiency in one season (199.52 in 1971). He also was an Academic All-American and a member of the GTE Academic All-American Hall of Fame. He was drafted in the second round by the Baltimore Colts. He also served as Oklahoma's Lieutenant Governor 1990–1994.

Tom Brahaney | Center | 1970–1972

Growing up in Midland, Texas, my granddad wanted me to play baseball and I was a pretty good little-league player. As a 12-year-old, my team played for the city championship, and I hit two home runs in the game. In fact, I hit a lot of home runs that season. One of my earliest memories is of my granddad coming over to the back door of our house to give me a little cash for each home run.

I liked baseball and I liked the cash, but what I really loved was playing football.

Therefore, I made the choice to focus on playing football during junior high and high school. In West Texas, football is king and most of the town turned out for a Friday night football game. My high school team, however, Midland High, was not a great team by any means.

In fact, we won only three games during my senior year. Still, there were schools interested in recruiting me, and I narrowed the choice to Texas and Oklahoma. My dad probably wanted me to go to the University of Texas because he had been a great basketball player at Texas during the early forties, playing on their first Final Four team.

But he let me make my own decision and really didn't pressure me at all. I did get some pressure from some local UT alumni, however. We were getting ready for the district track meet [I threw the shot put and discus], when some local businessmen showed up at practice to talk to me. At first, I thought it was neat, but it got really distracting having these guys hang around.

I finally decided on OU, which really surprised a lot of people in my hometown. At that district track meet in San Angelo, Texas, we had to introduce ourselves to the members of the competing teams. There was another shot-putter who was telling everyone that he was a linebacker recruit headed to Texas.

He told me, "I'll see you in two years on the floor of the Cotton Bowl."

"Nice to meet you," I replied. "I'll be looking for you."

In August, I reported with the other freshmen, who were ineligible for varsity in those days. That was OK with me because our freshman team was the best team I had ever been on. We were undefeated, beating Tulsa, Texas Tech, Kansas, and Oklahoma State. We had a phenomenal team with Joe Wylie, Leon Crosswhite, Greg Pruitt, Dave Robertson, and Dan Ruster.

Oklahoma had recruited several centers, and some of those recruits changed positions. The coaches gave almost everyone a chance on offense and defense, but when the coaches took one look at me on defense, they said, "You stay on offense!"

Our freshman coaches, Don Jimerson and Jerry Pettibone, tried to instill in us a strong dislike of Oklahoma State football. Before that game, Jimerson threw a fit, telling us that we weren't ready to play and that Sweeny Grade School could beat us. He was trying to get us mad and motivate us to beat OSU. His strategy worked.

Coach Pettibone had put in some gadget plays, and each worked perfectly. On one play near the goal line, Robertson was at quarterback and Wylie at halfback. Dave started his snap-count when Joe yelled out, "Wait a minute! Wait a minute, Dave!"

When he hit the word "Dave," I snapped the ball and we easily ran in for the touchdown because all of their defensive linemen had raised up out of their stances to see what our problem was. The play worked perfectly.

I started my sophomore year as the backup center. We were running the Houston Veer at the time. We beat SMU 28–11 and Wisconsin 21–7, but we didn't look very good in doing it. We lost to Oregon State 23–14, and there were "Fire Chuck Fairbanks" and "Chuck Chuck" signs all around campus.

Offensive coordinator Barry Switzer called me into his office and told me that I could be a much better player than I had been showing and he wanted me to start displaying some leadership. That motivated me, and when we came back from an open week, I had determined that I would do what coach Switzer had asked.

The coaches had also decided to switch to the wishbone as we prepared for Texas. I remember they called Bob Barry, the radio broadcaster, to come down to watch practice so he would know what was going on, but it was a secret to everyone else.

Texas had a great team and it didn't matter what kind of offense we tried to run. We played so badly in the second half that I got to play with our second-team line. Texas was running a defense where two linebackers lined up in the middle somewhat over the guards and center.

Remember that linebacker recruit from the high school district track meet I had mentioned? Well, here it was two years later and I was playing on the floor of the Cotton Bowl, but I didn't have any idea if one of those back-up linebackers was the guy from the high school meet. So I played as if I was facing him on every play. I would fire out into one of them and drive them 10 yards downfield. I guess the coaches thought I played pretty well, because on the next Monday, before the Colorado game, I was named the starting center.

There were other changes, too. Dean Unruh was the new starting left tackle and Leon Crosswhite was the new starting fullback. We were so fired up, we upset Colorado 23–15 on their home turf. I remember hitting a middle linebacker so hard that he fell backward. Dean was running downfield and yelled, "That's a great block."

That was the game when Dean and I started head-butting each other before player introductions. Other players, like our good friend Vic Kearney, joined in, and soon the entire team was doing it. All of that emotion worked in our favor. Not only did we win that day, but Leon and Joe Wylie each rushed for more than 100 yards.

The next week Kansas State came in and knocked us back down to earth. Lynn Dickey threw for more than 300 yards to beat us 19–14. Some of their fans were so obnoxious that day that I promised myself I would do all I could to see that Kansas State never beat OU again.

When we played Iowa State the next week, we fell behind 21–0. I remember making a blocking call at the goal line that worked perfectly before an end-around pass from Willie Franklin to Albert Chandler got us back into the game. That turned into an thrilling 29–28 win.

I had to sit out the Missouri game with a staph infection in my elbow. Our left guard, Darryl Emmert, was playing over their great defensive tackle Rocky Wallace. Someone on the sideline asked, "Emmert, how are you blocking Wallace?"

He said, "Block him? I'm out there just trying to protect myself."

The next week, against Kansas, their great running back John Riggins had 178 yards and left his mark on Steve O'Shaughnessy, one of our cornerbacks. Early in the game, Steve came chasing up the field to try to tackle Riggins, who ran over him, badly cutting his face. That made Osh really mad! He got the last laugh, intercepting a pass in the end zone to preserve a 28–24 win. I still kid Osh about the great hit he put on John Riggins.

Even though Nebraska had a great team that would end up winning the national championship that year, we played very well against them, losing only 28–21.

We ended the 1970 season with a tremendous win over Oklahoma State 66–6, with more than 500 yards rushing in a game that earned us

Center Tom Brahaney played for two Sooners teams that finished second in the nation, and bolstered one of the nation's most prolific offenses of all time. *Photo courtesy of OU Athletics Media Relations.*

an invitation to play in the Astro-Bluebonnet Bowl in Houston against Alabama.

Playing in that game was a real experience. When coach Bear Bryant walked by our table at the banquet, we were all in awe. We rushed for over 300 yards, and Greg Pruitt had two long touchdowns, but it took Bruce Derr's 42-yard field goal to tie it 24–24.

After turning the season around, finishing 7–4–1 after changing the offense, we all felt we would be better in 1971.

When we arrived for workouts in August, Barry Switzer had studied and perfected the wishbone blocking schemes. He had plans to counter defenses, get the ball pitched outside, run inside, or have quarterback Jack Mildren keep it.

When the season opened, Nebraska was ranked No. 1 and we were No. 10. We opened the season at home on a cold rainy day against SMU. Our defense played extremely well that day as we shut them out 30–0.

We went to Pittsburgh next, and our offense was unstoppable, rolling up more than 400 yards rushing in a 55–29 win. I remember getting the last block on Joe Wylie's kickoff return for a touchdown. Then came USC. I have to say that their defensive line was huge. They looked like dinosaurs to me, but we rushed for more than 500 yards, and Greg Pruitt's "Hello-Goodbye" T-shirt was born that day.

Pruitt had over 200 yards and three touchdowns. On one pitch-out on the option, I think he changed directions in mid-air, came down running full speed, and scored. This was one of the greatest moves I have ever seen in all of my football years. We won 33–20 and interestingly we had zero yards passing.

Pruitt put together another 200-yard, three-touchdown game, and Mildren added 111 yards and two touchdowns as we whipped a very good Texas team 48–27.

After the Texas game, we were getting ready to play Colorado when coach Fairbanks called us together on the field one day. He told us that the AP had just announced their rankings and we were now ranked No. 2, right behind Nebraska. Everybody yelled.

We were pumped up for the Colorado game and won 45–17. Pruitt came close to another 200-yard game, and we had nearly 500 yards rushing and 670 total yards. Our offense was really rolling at that point, but we were about to set some serious records in the next game.

We all remembered how Kansas State had beat us the year before in Norman and how some of their fans rubbed it in a little too much. Kansas State would line up with an extra defensive player on one side, a position called a "monster man" or "rover." Thus, they were always overloaded to one side, so when Jack came to the line, he would locate the "monster" and audible to the other side. That helped Pruitt run for 294 yards, and our total offense accounted for a school-record 785 yards in a 75–28 win.

Iowa State didn't present many problems either, but Missouri was a different story. Missouri always played us tough. They had some very tough defensive linemen. They loved to forearm you in the face regardless of whether or not they made the tackle. We struggled with them, like we usually did, before winning 20–3.

We scored seven touchdowns against Kansas in the first half the next week.

People always want to know what it was like getting ready for the Game of the Century. To be honest, I don't remember too much out of the ordinary. There were a lot of journalists covering the game, but they mostly wanted to talk to the coaches or to Mildren and Pruitt.

It was a cold, gray day. I came out early to snap for the kickers and saw ABC producer Terry Jastrow, who also was from Midland. Terry wanted a picture for TV, so he lined me up against Rich Glover, the Nebraska nose guard and they took a picture of us. It was strange to speak to the guy you are about to knock heads with before the game, but we wished each other good luck.

Before the game, coach Switzer told me to try some false-influence blocks. For example, if the play was designed to go to the right, I would hit him on the left and he would play across the block the wrong way. I tried this on Glover's first two or three tackles before giving it up.

I think Nebraska had the ball first, and my high school teammate, Steve Aycock, made the first three tackles, forcing them to punt. Then we ran three and punted. I snapped to the punter, and my job was to run to Johnny Rodgers while the others on the coverage team were supposed to fan out five yards apart. I ran to where I thought Rodgers would catch the ball, but he was long gone. He was so fast that for me to have caught him he would have had to run into me! I later saw my picture in *Sports Illustrated*, standing on my left leg as Rodgers was already running up the opposite sideline. Even after his famous punt return, the game was far from over.

There was no doubt that Glover was the best defensive lineman in the country. After the game was over, there was a lot of press saying that

I was whipped badly throughout the game, but I didn't feel that way. I've been whipped before and it hurts physically when you are beat up play after play, but I don't remember feeling any unusual amount of pain during the game or even after the game. The mental anguish of losing was another matter.

I have thought about that game a lot over the years. I know I was guilty of terrible technique on all of the outside option plays as I tried to cut off Rich. I did lose my feet quite a bit. I now know that I should have just stayed up high and run with him, whichever side he wanted to go, but that's not the way we thought at the time. Nebraska completely shut down our outside option game that day, forcing our running backs back inside where there was nowhere to run. It is true that Rich was in on a lot of tackles, but we seemed to run up the middle OK, particularly on Mildren's quarterback counters.

Jack made some great throws and Jon Harrison made great touchdown catches. After we took the lead 31–28, I remember Dean, who played a great game, telling me, "We have them now!"

But we all know what happened: Nebraska drove the ball the length of the field to win 35–31. It was a crushing loss and the only time in my entire football career that I thought maybe my granddad had been right, maybe I should have played baseball.

I always thought that the mark of a great team is the way it rebounds from a defeat like the one we had to Nebraska. At Oklahoma State, our option once again worked well as we gained more than 600 yards and won 58–14. The only thing I remember was Pruitt and I having to rush to the Stillwater airport after the game to catch a flight with Steve O'Shaughnessy's father, who dropped us off at Will Rogers Airport. We had a close connection to go to Miami for the Kodak All-American awards.

The next week, Pruitt and I went to NBC's studio in New York for Bob Hope's All-American show. That was really a big thrill. They lined us up behind a wall on the set and then we had to jog down a ramp and smile, say our name and our school. Bob Hope delivered some corny joke that he read off a cue card, the audience would laugh and you would move off to the side.

From there, we went to the Sugar Bowl in New Orleans to play Auburn, which had a fine team led by Heisman Trophy winner Pat Sullivan. Since it was Mildren's last game, he wanted to go out in style, scoring three touchdowns in a 40–22 win.

I have to say that Jack Mildren's leadership and execution of the wishbone made it fun to be part of the offense. We had great backs and had so many yards rushing each game. [OU averaged 469.6 rushing, 556.8 total yards in 1971.] I once heard coach Switzer say that record probably will never be broken.

At the start of the 1972 season, Greg Pruitt and I were selected to be the cocaptains of the team. We knew we had a good team and another chance at the national championship. Dave Robertson was taking over as quarterback, and we planned to take advantage of some great freshmen talent, particularly Joe Washington and Tinker Owens. In fact, I heard coach Switzer talk about the first time he and coach Fairbanks saw "Little Joe" Washington run 80 yards for a touchdown in a scrimmage against our first-team defense. They just looked at each other and didn't say a word, but they thought, "Did we just see what we think we saw?"

Our defense was also full of talented linemen like Derland Moore, Ray Hamilton, Lucious Selmon, Gary Baccus, and Vic Kearney.

When the polls came out at the beginning of the season, we were ranked No. 6.

We beat Utah State 49–0 to start the season, and our second game with Oregon was similar. We held future NFL quarterback Dan Fouts to 106 yards passing. He told me years later that he got sick of hearing "Boomer Sooner" since it was played after each touchdown. We scored 10 touchdowns in a 68–3 win.

Clemson had to kick a field goal with two seconds left in the game to avoid being shut out, 52–3. Tim Welch filled in for injured Leon Crosswhite, who had a big game, but we had to make fun of him anyway. Texas had a player, Steve Wooster, and when he would make a good run, the fans would chant, "Woo-Woo!" So when Tim made a good run, we would yell from the bench, "Wee-Wee!"

We were getting ready for the next game, Texas, and I began to give Derland Moore a hard time. I told him that Texas was going to block him all over the field. Was I ever wrong. He blocked a quick kick, and Lucious Selmon covered it for a touchdown. Derland also recovered a tipped pitch out for a touchdown as we beat Texas 27–0.

We knew we were going to have a problem with Colorado when their coach, Eddie Crowder, accused one of our former players, Steve O'Shaughnessy, who was now in graduate school at Colorado, of spying on their practices.

Those of us who knew Steve knew that was impossible. The only thing he was interested in on the Colorado practice field was the cheerleaders, but nothing ever came of the accusations. As it turned out, however, we could have used some help that day. Colorado's defense played great, and we had a hard time making many yards. We led at halftime 7–0. In the third quarter, they scored on a long run, but missed the extra point.

On our next possession, I personally gave CU all the momentum they needed, making the worst mistake of my college career. I snapped the ball over the punter Joe Wylie's head, and they scored soon after that. Back in the huddle, Greg Pruitt was pleading for the coaches to give him the ball more and he finally did score with a minute left in the game, but we lost 20–14.

I felt terrible. Our national championship hopes were dashed and everyone was upset. Coach Fairbanks yelled at everyone during our Monday practice, coming up with very unflattering names for each of us. Those who were All-Americans or All–Big Eight players got the worst of it. It is a day I will never forget, certainly not the way I thought I would celebrate my 21st birthday.

We were still a really good team and got ourselves motivated for our next game against Kansas State, which we won 52–0. Leon Crosswhite was healthy again. Every once in a while, Leon would run full speed into my back, but he did this to all the linemen.

We told him, "Run around us, not through us."

He would say, "If you would just block the defensive linemen out of my way, there wouldn't be a problem."

Before the Kansas game, Dave Robertson and I were in coach Fairbanks' office when the Orange Bowl called informing him that they were going to take Nebraska to play Notre Dame. He said only "Yes," "No," and, "Good-bye."

After we beat Kansas 31–7, in which Pruitt hurt his ankle, we went to Nebraska to play the only team we had never beaten. It was Nebraska coach Bob Devaney's last home game. Pruitt couldn't play much and it hurt his Heisman chances.

Nebraska scored in the first quarter after a turnover and again after another turnover in the third quarter for a 14–0 lead. Our kicker, Rick Fulcher, had missed two field goals in the first half.

Tinker Owens caught a long pass, and Joe Washington scored a touchdown. Grant Burget, who had replaced Pruitt, was a sophomore. He told me later that I told him that he better not fumble, in not-so-polite terms. I don't remember doing that. Tinker caught another long pass to set up Grant's game-tying touchdown.

Then, Derland Moore forced a fumble that Lucious Selmon recovered. It set up Fulcher from the same distance in which he had missed earlier. This time it went straight through for a 17–14 win. One of the happiest guys on our team was right guard Ken Jones, who was from Omaha.

Ken would always work so hard in practice that he would start wheezing, so offensive line coach Bill Michael would tell him to go to the sidelines and "take a knee" to catch his breath. From then on, we called him "Take a Knee" Jones. Sometimes when he was hyperventilating, we thought we saw a sly smile on his face like he was planning it all along.

We were a very happy team flying back home, where there were thousands of fans waiting for us. We knew we would be Big Eight champs if we could beat Oklahoma State the next week. We had a 24–0 halftime lead on a couple of touchdown passes from Robertson to Al Chandler and Tinker Owens. We pulled away for a 38–15 win and we were Big Eight champions.

During our game, Ohio State had beaten Michigan, and Auburn had beaten Alabama, so we still had a chance for a national championship if USC would lose to Ohio State in the Rose Bowl.

Pruitt and I were invited back to the Bob Hope show. This time, after the taping, we wandered around the different studios at NBC and

I got to sit in Johnny Carson's and Ed McMahon's chairs. The next day, we were invited to the Downtown Athletic Club for the announcement of the Heisman Trophy winner. Greg was a disappointing second to Johnny Rodgers of Nebraska.

From there, it was on to our second Sugar Bowl of 1972. The first one, at the end of the 1971 season, was played January 1. This one would be played December 31.

The team buses were to leave at 5:30 for the ride to old Tulane Stadium, but there was a handful of players not yet on the bus. Being late was one thing that made coach Fairbanks extremely mad. Sure enough, he instructed the bus driver to leave. The missing were a handful of redshirt freshmen that would suit up but certainly not play—and Greg Pruitt.

As it turned out, they were riding down the elevator at the Marriott in the French Quarter, but someone had pushed all the buttons on the elevator, so the elevator stopped at every floor. The freshmen were very nervous about running late but figured with Pruitt in the elevator, everything would be OK. When they finally got outside and saw that the buses had left, the freshmen really got scared and wondered how they would get to the stadium.

Fortunately for them, alumni buses were nearby. You can only think how excited these alumni were when they got to ride to the game with Greg Pruitt. Coach Fairbanks, however, was not amused and yelled at everyone, especially Pruitt. He even held him out of the game for a short time.

We fumbled five times, but still won 14–0. Their defense was tough, but ours was tougher.

That was my last game as a Sooner, so it was a sad time. We didn't get the upset we wanted in the Rose Bowl, so we ended up No. 2 for the second year in a row.

Not being a part of a national championship team never changed my opinion that Oklahoma was a great place to go to school and to play football. I met a lot of great players and coaches. I still meet with many of them at the annual alumni weekend each spring.

Playing football at Oklahoma also helped prepare me for a pro football career, especially in the running game, but I had to work on my pass-blocking.

You are not guaranteed that you will win a championship when you decide to become an Oklahoma Sooner, but Oklahoma has always been thought of as one of the top football programs in the country. If things go right, you might be a part of a championship team. Seven Sooners teams have discovered that feeling.

Still, it will always make me somewhat sad to think that if a play or two had gone differently, we would have had two more national championships in our illustrious history.

Tom Brahaney was an All-American in 1971 and 1972. He also was a Lombardi Award finalist and a team cocaptain in 1972. He played nine seasons with the St. Louis Cardinals.

Joe Washington | Running Back | 1972–1975

You know how a lot of kids say that they can't wait to grow up? I never said that. I was the happiest little kid in all of Texas. My brother Kenneth [I always called him "Kim"] and I had it made in the shade. For starters, our dad was a football coach. During football season, we spent all of our spare time with him. He had keys to the gym and he ran the swimming pool in the summers. I am telling you, it doesn't get any better than that.

I can truly say that I knew back then just how great we had it.

I was born in Crockett, Texas, and moved later to Bay City. My dad, Joe Sr., had played football at Prairie View as a running back and defensive back. When he was coaching, Kim and I were the water boys. We called ourselves "trainers," but everybody else called us water boys. We would go out and wipe players' faces with the towels and we taped some ankles. We made all the trips and all the practices.

During halftimes of his games, we would run to the Coke machines before the players got there and then pick the two best seats on the benches right up front to listen to Dad's halftime speech.

The great thing was, Dad never objected. He wanted us there. We got run over about three times every day, especially me because I was always in the way, but it was exactly where I wanted to be.

I would fly out to the football field as soon as class was over. You couldn't stop me, but some people tried. One day in the first grade my teacher wouldn't let me go. I guess she figured I was in the way out there. I couldn't believe it, so I sat there crying. She took me to Mr. Fisher and told him not to let me go to Dad's practice, but as soon as he turned his back, I bolted out of there to the practice field. They told my dad about it, and the very next day I was on the field with him. I know he must have told them that it was OK, that he wanted me out there.

We would ride to the away games with Mom, but I would always sit right next to Dad on the bus trip back home. Even when I started playing for him later in high school I didn't sit back in the back with other players. I sat right up front next to Dad.

One thing about being a coach's son: you were well-rounded in the game of football. I probably forgot more football by the time I was 15 than most people learn in a lifetime. I participated in the Punt, Pass & Kick competition when it was still segregated, and I won my division. I remember the first-place prize was a Baltimore Colts' jacket. Kim always pretended to be Johnny Unitas and I pretended to be Lenny Moore.

Let me tell you, I didn't take that jacket off very often. I wore it everywhere. One time I was at a basketball game and I had left it in Dad's office. After I got it back, instead of walking in front of the bleachers—you know how kids are, not wanting to walk in front of all those other kids—I walked behind the bleachers. I caught my sleeve on one of those bleachers and I heard this rip. It was like somebody had ripped my heart out. I had torn it!

In my sixth-grade year, we moved to Port Arthur. In the ninth grade, all I thought about was playing varsity for Dad's team. One day, I was scrimmaging with the junior varsity and Dad called me over to the varsity's practice.

"Junior," he said. "Do you think you can run against these guys?" (He always called me "Junior," "June," or "Junebug.")

"Shoot yeah!" I told him.

Then he sent me back to the JV practice. I wondered to myself, "What was all that about?"

He called me back a little later, but this time I had my helmet.

He said, "You loose?"

I nodded.

"OK, hop in there."

I hopped in the huddle and I can honestly say that was the first time my knees ever knocked. I remember it like yesterday. I got the ball and took off like a jackrabbit. Once I got that football, I wasn't nervous one bit. I was ripping and running. I could hear all of the other coaches saying, "Who is this kid?"

Finally, I could hear them saying to each other, "Hey that's Little Joe . . . that's Joe Junior." They realized I was that little kid who had been hanging around practice for a few years.

Dad never got mad at me much, but I do remember one time. When he said "son of a bitch," you knew he was pissed. During my freshman year, I was a receiver and I was supposed to run a post route. I ran across the middle and the pass hit me in the hands and I dropped it. I really got hit hard, knocking the wind out of me.

I was lying on the ground, groaning and moaning. I took my helmet off, thinking I could get more air, but you really can't. You just have to wait for it to come back. Dad came over there and called me every name in the world.

He switched me to running back as a sophomore. I was a pretty good inside runner even then. I was able to cut and change directions and make people miss.

My brother and I had always dreamed of playing in the same backfield, and the greatest thrill for me, still to this day, is being a senior when he was a sophomore starter at quarterback at Port Arthur Lincoln. We had dreamed of playing together for our dad and it came true.

I have to say, Kim was ahead of his time. He was two years younger than me and yet he was like a big brother. They used to call him "Cool Kenny" Washington, because he was so in control. He was only a sophomore in high school, but he was more like a seasoned college senior. He stepped right into the huddle and took charge.

On the first play we ever ran together—it was a rainy day—we fumbled the handoff! We got it back, but we just looked at each other and grinned. It was something we had waited for our whole lives and what did we do? We fumbled.

My biggest disappointment is not winning a state championship for Dad. Kim broke his wrist that year, I broke my leg, and Dad broke his hip in a car accident. It wasn't a good year.

When it came time to visit colleges, I think I went about everywhere. There was no limit back then. I went to Texas, UCLA, Michigan, all the schools in the Big Eight, all the schools in the Southwest Conference. I canceled some trips after my trip to Michigan State when they had 23 inches of snow.

LSU was in the running early on. I visited there on the day they upset Notre Dame. After the game, pandemonium broke out and I was down there on the field because I wanted to talk to Ara [Parseghian] about my visit to Notre Dame.

All of a sudden, I heard this loud "pop" as I was walking through the end zone. It was on my shoulder and something knocked me down.

Running back Joe Washington starred on two national championship teams for the Sooners and dominated the national sports pages in 1974 and 1975. He was voted into the College Football Hall of Fame's Class of 2005. *Photo courtesy of OU Athletics Media Relations.*

I told somebody I had been shot and they brought a stretcher out there for me. It turned out that I was hit by a falling goalpost. I took that as a sign: "Don't go to LSU."

As a kid, I had always wanted to go to Texas. I loved watching *The Darrell Royal Show*. When they played "The Eyes of Texas Are Upon You," I would put my hand over my chest and dream about playing at Texas.

So I narrowed it down to Houston, Texas, and Oklahoma, which was one of my final visits. When I visited Norman, it was on one of the most beautiful days I had ever witnessed. It was spring and there was a warm breeze flowing and the flowers were in bloom. Greg Pruitt and [assistant coach] Wendell Mosley picked me up at the airport. Wendell had played against Dad in college and coached against him in the high school ranks. [We later became really close.]

At Texas, I thought the campus was too spread out for me. Plus, they were wearing black shoes at the time while Oklahoma was wearing white. I had finally got the nerve to wear white shoes during my senior year because I thought you looked faster in them.

I also knew Texas played in the Southwest Conference against other Texas schools and I would be on a bus all the time going to games. I didn't want to do that. I wanted to fly some place.

One day after my visit to OU, Greg Pruitt called me and asked, "Where are you going?"

How am I going to tell Greg Pruitt that I was not coming to Oklahoma? He wanted me to come there and play in the same backfield with him and I was going to room with him on the road trips.

Also, Wendell Mosley told me, "Oklahoma has to be OK, because we have 'OK' on the license plates." I thought he was kidding, but once I put everything together, the choice was pretty easy.

When I got to Norman, I checked into my room at the Washington House [I thought that was pretty cool—a dorm named after me] and then I looked at the depth chart and saw I was the on the 12th team. It didn't bother me too much because they were 15-deep at some positions.

I just thought, "Damn, they got this many guys?"

I knew I would do whatever it took to get on the field. I would return punts and kickoffs, whatever. I am a coach's son, so I would do anything.

We practiced three times a day in that hot sun on that artificial turf. That turf was so hot, my shoes started to melt. I admit that I missed home. I missed my mom and dad, my brother and my sister.

I didn't have too much interaction with Chuck Fairbanks. On the recruiting trip, he would stare at me with that funny-looking eye and I wondered what he thought of me. I had more contact with Galen Hall, who was handling the receivers. The first time Barry Switzer ever said anything to me was after the Kansas game that year.

I had gone into one of the bathroom stalls in the dressing room and painted my shoes silver, but Jack Baer, the equipment manager, smelled that paint.

"What do I smell?" I could hear him asking everyone. "Is that paint?"

I first wore those shoes in the Kansas game, where I had a pretty good game. I ran well and made some blocks, but nobody said a thing about my shoes. So we were sitting in the film room after that game and Barry was clicking the film back and forth.

All of a sudden, he asked, "Little Joe! What are those goddamn things on your feet?"

"Those are my silver shoes, Coach."

"Oh, OK," he said.

That was the only thing he ever said about it. I knew then that I would always get along with him. A couple of years later, people were giving him a hard time about players being undisciplined and for letting me wear silvers shoes and all that crap.

It was before the Colorado game and we were on the field when he told me how people gave him crap about my shoes.

I said, "What do you want me to do, Coach?"

He told me, "Just put a couple of hundred on them today, will you?"

Sure enough, I rushed for 211 yards that day.

People always talked about my shoes, but the idea came to my brother first. We had broke out our white shoes for homecoming during my senior year and we both thought they looked sharp. We had put gold shoestrings in them. When I decided to wear silver at Oklahoma, my brother told me to put red shoestrings in them because silver and red go together. We tried it and they looked fantastic and I knew that summer that's what I would do. But I waited about half the season before I broke them out. I never practiced in them, either.

When coach Fairbanks left after my freshman year and Switzer was named head coach, for whatever reason, I knew it was a good thing for me. I knew I had a fan in Barry. He won me over from that first time during the film session when he didn't have a problem with my shoes. As a coach's kid, that told me a whole lot. I knew he was a player's coach.

We tied USC 7–7 in his second game and we should have beaten them about 40–0 that night. We really didn't know how good we were then. Let me tell you, we were *really* good. We had Rod Shoate, the Selmons, guys in the secondary who would knock your head off . . . that defense was just starting to be its nasty self.

People ask about the punt return in that game. It was right before halftime, and what I do recall about it is that it was supposed to be a left return. They kicked it to my right, and I fielded it at about the 37-yard line and I probably forgot which way the wall was supposed to be set up. I started retreating to give the guys a chance to set up the wall. We always thought we had a chance to score on punt returns because we worked so much on them in practice. I always believed if I could get by one guy, I would make some big yardage. But as I continued retreating, I wasn't seeing the wall.

Dad was on the sideline for that game and he was probably thinking, "What the hell is Junior doing?"

I always had two mouthpieces: one in my mouth and one dangling from my face mask. Well, when I retreated back to about the 10, I stiff-armed one guy but he pulled my mouthpiece and my head went down when he did that. I then cut back to the right and ducked one guy and started to see some daylight, but I got caught from behind. I think I gained three yards on it.

One of the highlights was during my junior year when I was a co–National Player of the Week when we played Baylor [156 yards rushing]. The other co-player was my brother. He was the starting quarterback at North Texas as a freshman and he had a great game against SMU. I don't think that had ever been done before.

We were always close-knit. My family would drive up to Norman after Dad's Friday night games so they could see me play Saturday afternoon. Then we would drive down to see my brother play that night in Dallas.

Not being on TV and not going to bowls for those two years because of the probation probably affected me a great deal, at least it did in 1974 as far as the Heisman was concerned. At the time, you really don't think about those things much. But you would have loved to be introduced by Chris Schenkel on TV or had Keith Jackson call your name.

It is important, me coming from Texas, to say that we never lost to Texas. Some people hold it against you that you left Texas in the first place. But once we started beating the tar out of Texas every year, it looked like I made the right choice.

People in Texas probably thought I went to Oklahoma because Oklahoma bought me a car or something. Heck, Dad bought me the only car I had—and then he sent me the payment book!

I had a lot of feelings for coach Switzer. He allowed me to baby-sit his kids, and they loved me and I loved them. They reminded me of my family. That was neat for me. I respected him a great deal, the way he treated me as a person and a player. Some coaches, for whatever reason feel they must handle every kid the same way. That doesn't always work. He knew I would never do anything to make him look bad. There was not a lot said between us because I wasn't a kid who talked a lot at that age, but I always felt good about our relationship.

My senior year things became a little strained because I got hurt [bruised heal]. It started early on in the season, and by the Texas game I had to wear padding in my shoe. It was painful. I played in quite a bit of pain that whole season, but you start feeling that you are letting your teammates down. In the Kansas State game I fumbled a couple of times and some people talked about possibly benching me.

I think we fumbled about nine times, losing seven, in that loss to Kansas. I was disappointed they didn't come to me more to try to pull that game out. That day was a real downer.

With the Missouri game on the line [OU trailing 27–20], they pitched it to me and I didn't have to do anything but follow great blocking to score on that long [70 yards] run to cut their lead to one point. We knew we were going for two points for the win. I remember taking the pitch and thinking, "I am getting into the end zone no matter what happens."

Losing two games in a row would have been devastating to us, so I knew I had to score to win the game. I did a skip jump, like a triple-jumper would, because I was on the wrong foot to make a cut. But I did get in! Even though Missouri probably thought I wasn't in. That was a big game [a 28–27 win] for us.

I was still beat up for the Orange Bowl. I do remember being outside the locker room when somebody told us that [No. 1] Ohio State had lost in the Rose Bowl, meaning we had a chance at the national championship. That night, Michigan was playing a defense to stop me on the pitch. I almost got caught in the end zone for a safety on one running play and almost broke it 98 yards. It was great to win that one [14–6].

I have my national championship rings on a shelf in my trophy case. As I walk by them sometimes I think of all the great players I played with and all the great times I had at Oklahoma.

The new coach and the new athletic director have brought the old family back to Oklahoma the way it should be. The program was down for a while, but now it is back to where it should be, and Switzer is still the man there as he should be.

The people, the community, the university, the coaches, and the players . . . they all mean so much to me. I was fortunate enough to come to the University of Oklahoma. There is not a price on earth to get me to go anywhere else if we could go back in time and do it all over again.

The way we talk about Oklahoma and our tradition, I relate it to walking into a haunted house. On the walls, you see all those pictures of the people who lived in the house. But at Oklahoma, we are talking about a castle. The pictures of the people on the wall built the castle—not at one time, but over years in stages, stone-by-stone.

I guess it was pretty doggone big. It is something that I appreciate to this day. It is a time I enjoyed, and I am very grateful for it

Knowing that you are part of that tradition that still exists today, you realize that you are one of the ghosts on those walls. When I first got there as a freshman, I wanted to be one of those guys whose picture was on that wall. Now, as I get closer to the other side, I am even more proud that I am.

Joe Washington was an All-American in 1974 and 1975. He finished with 4,071 rushing yards (now second on OU's career list), with 39 rushing touchdowns and one receiving touchdown. He was All–Big Eight in three seasons and he also finished third in the 1974 Heisman Trophy balloting. He had 19 100-yard rushing games. He played in the NFL for 10 seasons with San Diego, Baltimore, Washington, and Atlanta.

Tinker Owens | Receiver | 1972–1975

Many people always asked me about being Steve Owens' little brother and how that affected me as I grew up. Let me say this: Steve not only was a great football player, but he was a great basketball player and a track star in high school, so he left a tough legacy to follow, but following him was a positive for me. And most of all, he is a great brother.

I saw how hard he worked and what he had accomplished through that hard work. I learned to stay after practice and work more because that is what he always did. Our father was a hard-worker, a truck driver for about 35 years. Mom had 11 kids, nine that lived. I am the next to the youngest, and Steve is almost seven years older than me. There is almost a 20-year gap between our oldest brother and our youngest.

Steve was our idol—he got all the accolades, but we knew he deserved them. He took care of the younger ones like me because he was not only older, but he was bigger than the rest of us. Four of us younger brothers would have to gang up on him to take him on. That is the only way we could fight him, but there was, and is, a lot of love between us.

My real name is Charles Wayne. When I was four or five years old, I loved watching the TV show *Pinky Lee*. I couldn't say it, they tell me, but I could say "Tinky," so one of my sisters started calling me "Tinky" and that evolved into "Tinker." It stuck. Hey, I thought Tinker was definitely better than Pinky or Tinky. I like it better than Charles.

Most people don't know this, but Steve isn't really a Steve. His real name is Loren Everett, but one of our sisters started calling him "Little Steve" when he was a kid and that stuck.

I remember the day they announced Steve won the Heisman Trophy because they let us go home from school early that day. They announced it on the loudspeaker at school and I didn't know much about the Heisman, but I liked getting out of school early.

I was always proud to be Steve Owens' "little" brother.

And I was *little*.

I weighed 125 pounds as a sophomore at Miami High, where we went from winning one game during my sophomore year to losing only one game during my senior year. We also won the state basketball championship with a 27–0 record (I was pretty good at stealing the ball and making lay-ups).

In football, I played safety and wingback, and I punted and returned kickoffs. I weighed about 155 as a senior, and when Oklahoma started recruiting me, people said it was only because I was Steve's little brother. I knew I wasn't a big bruising back like my brother, but I also knew I had some athletic ability. I didn't have blazing speed, but it got where nobody could outrun me.

I almost signed with Arkansas. When I visited there with my girlfriend, who now is my wife of more than 30 years (Terri, thanks for everything!), we attended a basketball game. Afterwards, we went to a party at a Holiday Inn and there was some drinking going on. I liked to have a drink once in a while, and this big old Arkansas player decided he didn't like me because I was Steve Owens' brother. I was standing on this bed in this hotel room, and he was standing on the floor and he still was just as tall as I was. I was glad his teammates were there, because they kept him from kicking my ass. Later, Frank Broyles threw that guy off the team.

Anyway, I considered going there until Steve found out about it. He said if I went to Arkansas, *he* would kick my tail.

He probably would have, so I signed with OU. The truth is, I always wanted to go to Oklahoma. Steve went there, and I grew up listening to them on the radio when he played. I knew I wanted to be a Sooner, too, but Chuck Fairbanks really didn't want me. Leon Cross had to talk him into offering me a scholarship.

I signed as a running back and planned on spending a year on the freshman team. They would take the running backs, receivers, and quarterbacks of the freshman team to run patterns against the varsity during practice. When we would walk from our freshman practice into the stadium, the varsity players would be chanting "fresh meat, fresh meat" just like at a prison.

I was 17 when I came to OU—I didn't turn 18 until that October—and I weighed about 160 dripping wet, so you can imagine how I felt. You're right: I was scared to death.

On that Tuesday after the opener against Utah State, we had those passing drills against the varsity, and I caught three touchdowns against them. Fairbanks was up in his tower watching it, and when they blew the horn, the freshmen were supposed to be done for the day. We didn't get a Gatorade and a popsicle like the varsity guys did, so I started to head to the locker room.

Fairbanks hollered down from his tower, "Tinker Owens, go get a Gatorade and popsicle."

So I did.

Then I started to walk out of the stadium when he hollered at me again, "Tinker Owens, stay out with the team."

So I did.

After that practice, Galen Hall, the receivers coach told me, "Coach Fairbanks wants to talk to you about playing for the varsity."

I was in shock, but I said, "If I am not going to play, I would rather stay with the freshman team."

At that time, we were pretty thin at receiver, and Fairbanks said, "I think you may get some playing time."

Against Oregon the next week, John Carroll, one of our receivers, hurt his knee, and all of a sudden Fairbanks is screaming, "Tinker Owens, get in the game!"

At first, I couldn't find my helmet. After I found it and got into the game, we ran a running play on the first play. The next play was a pass to me near the sideline and as I turned—Dave Robertson was our quarterback that year—I saw the ball very clearly. It was out a ways and I had to dive. So I dove and caught the ball on about a 10-yard out pattern. The announcers didn't know who it was because they didn't have a number 11 in their programs.

That brings up another story about how I got my number. Jack Baer was our equipment manager. He was a gruff old guy, and when I was told that previous week to go get a number from him, I asked him, "What are my choices?"

He said, "Eleven or some big number like 63 or 67."

I knew I couldn't wear a 63 or a 67, so I said, "I guess I'll take 11."

People always thought I took that number because of Jack Mildren, but that's how it really happened.

And that's how I ended up on varsity as a freshman.

Before that first Texas game, we walked down that ramp, and Texas guys were to my left jawing at us. I wasn't jawing back because this time I was scared to death of an opponent. Then they shot that big cannon and I thought I lost it. It scared the you-know-what out of me. I looked over and saw that big steer, Bevo, standing there. It was an amazing sight, but once the first play of the game is over, you forget all of that.

John Carroll got hurt again and I ended up as MVP of the Nebraska game [a 17–14 win] and MVP of the Sugar Bowl [14–0 win over Penn State]. Our defense was so good that Penn State wouldn't have scored on us even if John Cappeletti had played that game. That was the game in which Greg Pruitt had missed the bus to the stadium and when he got there, Fairbanks had removed his uniform from his locker, but he ended up playing in the game.

I had a decent freshman year [22 receptions, three touchdowns], but I really wasn't given a job. I had to earn it. I had proven I could do it on my own merits and not because of Steve. I knew I had the athletic ability, but I didn't have a lot of confidence when I walked onto campus. I had never been away from home, and the pressure of two-a-days that fall was pretty tough. Somehow I had made it through all that and survived.

Following that season, Fairbanks left for the NFL, and we had a new head coach. Everybody knew Barry since he had been on the staff for a long time. His personality was just the opposite of Fairbanks, and all the players loved him. He would BS with you and joke with you. Fairbanks was always up in his tower away from the players. We were all pretty happy with Oklahoma's choice to make Barry Switzer the new head coach.

That was the first of our two probation years. Before the 1973 season, Switzer addressed the probation issue by telling us, "I've been to 11 bowl games in 13 seasons. I've been around a lot of success and a lot of great players. Bowl games and playing on TV are fine incentives. But I'll tell you what, people, the greatest reward in football is winning. That's the most important goal there is. That's why they have scoreboards. So when they put us on probation, they made one mistake. They didn't tell us we wouldn't win the Big Eight championship. And nobody said we couldn't win the national championship.

"Men, that is our challenge."

In the second game, we doubled USC in about every statistic but the one on the scoreboard. [OU outgained USC 339–161 and in first downs 18–9.] It was a great game, as great as a 7–7 tie can be, but we really outplayed them. It was disappointing we didn't win that game. We won all of the rest of them. We couldn't win the national title, but that's the way it was and it was accepted by us. There was nothing we could do about it.

In the next game, at home against Miami, Steve Davis and I had hooked up on a long touchdown pass [52 yards] and we started to have more confidence in the passing game.

We beat Texas 52–13 in a game where we threw it deep pretty well. Jimmy Helms, one of our assistant coaches, had come from Texas, and he told our coaches how Texas' defense would read run or pass. The safeties would key on the offensive linemen, so we would make it appear we had called a running play and that was the reason I was so wide open all day. I caught a halfback pass for a touchdown [63 yards] from Joe Washington and another on a post pattern where I was so wide open . . . those are the hard ones. [Owens caught five passes for 163 yards.]

We scored early and often and beat a great Texas team that year. I am proud to say we never lost to Texas, never lost to Nebraska, and never lost to Oklahoma State. Not many guys who played at the University of Oklahoma can say that. That Texas game was kind of a hate deal. It goes

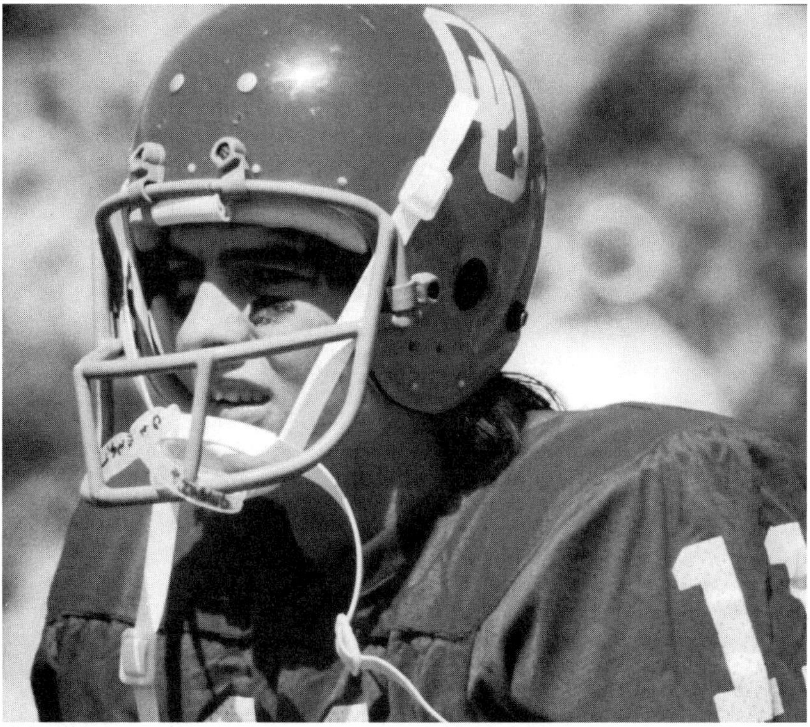

Tinker Owens successfully emerged from the shadow of older brother Steve while at OU, earning All-American status twice in a brilliant four-year career. *Photo courtesy of OU Athletics Media Relations.*

way beyond the football game. Oklahoma and Texas are forever battling over something. It starts in high school with the Oil Bowl.

The Oklahoma State game was a state rivalry. It's always been there and will always be there. The Nebraska game was with a lot more respect for each other.

That 1974 team was by far the best team during my time at Oklahoma. We knew we couldn't go to a bowl game, but we could win all of our games and win the national championship. We had only one really close game that year, a 16–13 win over Texas.

In 1975, we lost to Kansas [23–3] and could have lost the next game at Missouri. We had so many turnovers that day against Kansas, there was no way we were going to win the game. Our punter, Jimmy Littrell, had been having problems so coach Switzer told us one day, "Anybody who ever punted in high school, come out and practice some punts."

Joe Washington walked out and so did a few other guys. I walked out and ended up winning the job. On my first punt that year against Pittsburgh, I hit one high, and it turned over just like it is supposed to and went 45 yards. After that, it was all downhill. I don't know what I averaged [37.05 yards on 59 punts]. We really didn't have a good snapper and I was catching many of them off the ground and kicking it on one step just to get rid of it. In that loss to Kansas, I think I got hit by 12 guys, not 11, on one play. I think their entire team hit me and one of our guys fell on me. That was the start of a bad day. And I dropped a pass, the only drop I think I ever had.

Joe Washington told me once, "I knew that was going to be a bad day when you dropped a pass."

We won another national championship in my senior year, although we backed into it when Ohio State lost to UCLA in the Rose Bowl. I made a long catch down the middle in that Orange Bowl against Michigan, and then they put Billy Brooks in, and he ran a reverse for a touchdown on the next play. Our defense just pummeled Michigan in that game [a 14–6 win].

When it was all over, I knew I wouldn't trade anything for my experience of playing at OU. We won two national championships, back-to-back, had a 42–2–1 record, and went to two bowl games. It would have been nice to go to four, but we couldn't change anything about the probation.

We all felt terrible for Barry the way it ended for him, because we all respected and liked him so much. Here's a little story to tell you how he treats his players. On New Year's Eve day a few years ago, he called me up and said, "Where are you?"

I told him, "I am at the bank downtown."

"Stay right there," he said. "I'll be right down."

So he came walking into the bank and he handed me this glass case, inside it was a game ticket from the 1972 Sugar Bowl. It was an unused ticket that had the date, price [$7.50], and teams printed on it.

He told me, "Thirty years ago today, you were MVP of the Sugar Bowl. I want you to have this."

Somebody had given him two of them and he saved one for me. That's the kind of relationship he has with his players. It didn't end after we were done playing and he was done coaching. He would help me with anything, and I would do the same for him.

I felt so fortunate to be part of this great tradition at Oklahoma. I played with great players. I played for great coaches. It is almost like it didn't happen, that it was a dream. A dream come true. But people really make a bigger deal out of it than I make of it. An athlete's an athlete. They put us on a pedestal, but I never looked at it that way. I am just an ordinary guy. The way I look at it, I was just fortunate. I got a great education and, if it weren't for sports, I wouldn't have had an education.

So you can understand why the Oklahoma program means everything to me.

Tinker Owens, a two-time All-American, finished his career with 70 receptions for 1,619 yards (sixth-best in OU history) and 11 touchdowns. He also rushed for three touchdowns. He is the only player ever to lead OU in receiving in four consecutive seasons. He was MVP of the 1973 Sugar Bowl (played December 31, 1972) with five receptions for 132 yards and one touchdown. He played six seasons with the New Orleans Saints.

Lee Roy Selmon | Defensive tackle | 1972–1975

The Selmon family was raised on a farm about seven miles outside of Eufaula, Oklahoma, a small town of about 2,500 people. It was a typical upbringing, similar to everyone who lived in that community.

I was the youngest of nine children with five brothers, some of whom you know, and three sisters. My parents were farmers and very hard workers. They went about life the right way and encouraged us to do likewise. They taught us to be the best people we could be, having good character and using truthfulness to get along in life. They emphasized education, wanting us to go beyond high school if we could. They also encouraged us to develop a relationship with the Lord. That was important to all of us.

It was a fun childhood. I enjoyed my brothers and sisters a lot—and still do. We were close then and we are still very close.

Dad did the farming and share-cropping and Mom managed the house. With nine children, as you can imagine, that was a handful. As I look back, I realize the sacrifice they both made for all of us. They poured all of their resources into raising us and meeting our needs instead of buying things for themselves. They were very loving parents and they were always there for us. They weren't the type of parents who told you what you always wanted to hear, either. They told us what was right and what would help us in the long run.

Depending on your behavior, they would either encourage you, praise you, or discipline you. They had consequences if you acted badly, but we never got into much trouble. We knew who was in control of that household. Mom would handle most of the discipline, but if it ever got to Dad's level, you knew you were in for it.

When we were young, we were always rassling or tussling with each other, playing baseball or basketball. The truth is, football was one of our least-favorite sports. None of us understood the game. I thought it was rather unusual for guys to be running into each other over and over again.

But Paul Bell, who was the high school coach in Eufaula, also was an instructor in the PE class and one day he was teaching some kids how to lift weights. He saw that my brother Lucious was a pretty strong kid and he saw some potential in him, so he talked him into going out for the junior high football team. While Lucious was reluctant, he convinced him to give it a try.

He tried it and came home and told Dewey and me how much he liked it. Dewey and I just figured he must have got hit in the head on the first day of practice if he liked football. So we then started to have backyard games, and it was always Dewey and I versus Lucious. We could never beat him because he was three years older.

Dewey and I were always very close, as everyone knows. He was 11 months older than me, but we always attended the same class. What happened was that he was born in November and I was born the following

October. He didn't meet the deadline to start school and I started a little early for my age, so we were always in the same class.

When Dewey and I got ready to play eighth-grade football, Lucious tried to tell us how to get ready so we wouldn't be totally blind. He told us to get in shape, so we went out and ran up and down the road a little bit.

On that first day of practice, they didn't even have any footballs on the field. All we did that day was conditioning drills and I never got so tired in my life.

"Do I want to do this?" I wondered.

I was ready to give it up, but Dewey went back the next day, so I tagged along. It got a little better each day, and we learned the game gradually. By my sophomore year, we were having fun playing the game. That season, Lucious was a senior and he had a wonderful senior class. We lost one game and fell short of the state playoffs.

Lucious had a great year playing both ways, at fullback and linebacker, and suddenly schools were interested in recruiting him. That's when we discovered, "You mean people want you to come to their college for football? You can really go to school that way?"

It was a surprise to all of us, and to my mom and dad especially, but they were happy about it as you could imagine.

That's when we started to notice all of the college coaches in our living room. Larry Lacewell of Oklahoma spent a lot of time at our house. Eddie Crowder of Colorado came, too. We were excited. We had never experienced anything like that before. We didn't watch a lot of TV at the time, so we weren't experts on college football by any means. The only game I really remember watching was the 1966 tie between Michigan State and Notre Dame.

After Lucious decided on Oklahoma, Dewey and I faced a challenging year as juniors without him and his class. During one practice, Coach moved me into the backfield on a whim.

"Let's put you back there, hand it off to you, and see what happens," he said.

I was a pretty big kid with some decent balance and some toughness, so I didn't fall down when that first person hit me. It worked well and he moved me there for good, while I still played defensive tackle. I was a pretty big running back. I think we won six games that year because we had lost a good senior class.

After my junior year, colleges began contacting me and Dewey. We knew there was interest from Oklahoma because, when they were recruiting Lucious, they asked, "Who are *those* guys?"

There was no doubt that Dewey and I wanted to go to a school together. We really did. We have been together our whole lives and we wanted to stay together. It was just understood. Dewey is a tremendous brother and he was always right there for me. We took classes together and did about everything together. He is a doer—a very smart guy.

I thank God for him every day, as I do for all my family.

People always asked if we were twins. In fact, it worked to our advantage at times. When we got our first car, for example, I was driving one night and a highway patrolman pulled us over. Dewey had his license, but I didn't have mine.

I was very scared, so I told Dewey, "Give me your license. Quick!"

Lee Roy Selmon, shown here against Nebraska, is widely regarded as one of the greatest defensive linemen in college football history.
Photo courtesy of OU Athletics Media Relations.

There were no pictures on licenses back then, thankfully. It worked. We had a tail-light out and that is why he pulled us over.

Anyway, we would go on a recruiting visit, walk away and do our own evaluation, and then compare. We always had the same thoughts. We didn't take that many visits because our top choice always was Oklahoma, but we took a few just to compare other places.

To his credit, Lucious left us alone during our decision-making process. He wanted us to come to Oklahoma, but he respected us enough to make our decision. We wanted to join him there, and I think he knew that.

Dewey and I decided we would room together at OU, too. It was just like being at home. That summer, we worked out with Lucious and his roommate, Clyde Powers, who was like a member of our family, and those two prepared us for OU as much as possible. On that first day in Norman, they took us around campus and showed us the buildings—"this class is here, that class is there"—those type of things. That really helped. Dewey and I even took the same classes as freshmen, but we never skipped a class or had one do the work for the other. We may have fooled our way out of a traffic ticket, but we both went to all of our classes. Our parents had ingrained that into us.

Lucious also helped us avoid the usual freshman initiation. The upperclassmen always surprised the freshmen by capturing them and taking them to that duck pond for a little swim. They would always wait until the weather turned cold, too, but Lucious tipped us off to when it was going to happen.

That night, Dewey and I drove around, but Derland Moore was chasing us in his car. We said, "As long as we keep moving, he won't be able to get us."

And they never got us. I think they were going to try again some other night, but Lucious told them they missed their chance and there wouldn't be another.

It was the first year [1972] that freshmen were eligible to play, but I wasn't worried about playing. We were worried with just making the freshmen team so we could keep our scholarships. After a couple weeks of practice, I guess they saw something in us, because they let us know we would be on the traveling squad, backing up Derland Moore and Raymond Hamilton on the defensive line.

I remember coming out of that tunnel the first time and running onto the field. It was unbelievable. You see those 70,000 people and I was thinking to myself, "Wow, please don't trip over myself and fall down in front of all these people!"

By the fourth quarter, we were ahead so much [in a 49–0 win over Utah State] that we got into the game. It was exciting. I don't know if I made any tackles, but I was out there. That first year really was a growing experience for us. We had great players on that team and great leadership. I even got in on a few series against Penn State in the Sugar Bowl [a 14–0 OU win].

When we got word that coach Fairbanks was leaving [for the NFL's Patriots], the curiosity hit us: Who would the next coach be? What would his philosophy be?

We were really excited when we learned that Barry Switzer would be the next coach. I hadn't dealt with him much, since I played on defense, but I knew I liked him. He was certainly a players' coach. As we got to know him, we all loved him.

Just before we were to return to Norman for practices [before the 1973 season], I had some discomfort in my chest and didn't know what it was. Dewey, Lucious, and I were back home visiting Mom and Dad for a few days, and I could tell things weren't right with me.

I went to see a doctor in Eufaula and he said, "You need to get him back to Norman and into the hospital *now*."

Lucious drove me to the hospital and they started tests the next day. I had pericarditis [an inflammation/infection of the lining surrounding the heart]. I had to treat it with complete rest. I was in the hospital for a couple of weeks and then they moved me into the infirmary for a couple of weeks. Throughout that entire time, I had thoughts that I would be redshirted and then not be able to play in Lucious' senior year.

I don't think the doctors ever let me know how serious it was. I found out much later once I did some research on my own that it was something pretty serious, but once I got over that original discomfort, I never had any pain.

When I came back, I had missed the Baylor and USC games and I was in no condition to play football. They put me on a gradual conditioning program. I got into the Miami game for a few plays and gradually I got into shape. I started the Texas game, and that was a great way to get back into it because we played so well that day [a 52–13 OU win]. That was my first career start, and I played only three quarters because of the score.

We finished 10–0–1 but couldn't go to a bowl because of the NCAA probation. We would have liked to play in a bowl, but we accepted the fact that it wouldn't happen before the season began.

The Kansas game in 1975 I have tried to forget about. I just remember [Kansas quarterback] Nolan Cromwell, who was a great guy by the way, running over people that day. We just couldn't stop them. They did something that no other team did when we were there, which was beat us in Norman.

That was one of only two losses, with the other being the Colorado game of our freshman season, during our entire career.

One thing about those OU teams—it didn't matter if we were playing Utah State or Oregon or Nebraska, we approached them all the same and we were ready to play. We played hard and expected to win.

When we went to the Orange Bowl to play Michigan, we were not headed to Miami to horse around and to lie on the beach. We made sure we were focused and there to win the game. It was the same way the seniors approached the Sugar Bowl when I was a freshman. It was about business.

Once we found out that Ohio State lost [in the Rose Bowl], there was an opportunity to win the national championship. It was a great, hard-fought, low-scoring game—a fun game to play in and a fun game to win [14–6].

When you look at it from a cumulative standpoint, it is quite remarkable to think that we lost only two games and tied another in our four years there. We never lost to Texas, Nebraska, and Oklahoma State, so I consider us pretty fortunate to have done that. You count your blessings with that type of record, but you have a sense of humility about it.

It really shows the caliber of players and caliber of coaches we had. They were all great people, too.

When I look back on it, the appreciation for our record gets greater and greater for me. When you are there playing, you are young and you do not fully appreciate the experience at the time. You are just playing one game at a time and doing your best to win.

We were playing for each other and for the coaching staff. It was a bond that was truly remarkable.

Barry Switzer means an awful lot to me, not just as a football coach, but as a person. The way he cared for his players, the way he managed us, and in making the experience fun. He wanted us to be successful. He was unique. I had no other coach like him in my whole career and I hold him in such high esteem.

In 1994 I was inducted into the GTE Academic Hall of Fame and I sent out invitations to people who were important to me. I sent one to Barry, but the ceremony was in Washington, D.C., just a few weeks after he had been named head coach of the Dallas Cowboys. I never expected him to be there, but there he was, along with Larry Lacewell. I couldn't believe it. He had to be busy with his new job, but he took the time to fly up there for me. That's the Barry Switzer I know.

I am very proud that I am an OU alumnus. The things I learned there, academically as well as athletically, continue to help me in my life today. It is a great school and it is filled with great people. We entered a program that already was one of the best and we carried the banner for our four years and did the best that we could. I am very proud and very grateful for the experience.

Lee Roy Selmon is considered one of the greatest players in college football history. He was an All-American in 1974 and 1975. He won the Lombardi Award and the Outland Trophy in 1975. He finished his career with 325 tackles, including 40 for loss. He also was an Academic All-American. Selmon is a member of the GTE Academic Hall of Fame and the College Football Hall of Fame. He was taken with the first pick of the 1976 NFL draft by the Tampa Bay Buccaneers, with whom he played 10 seasons. He was inducted into the Pro Football Hall of Fame in 1995. He was President of the University of South Florida's Foundation Partnership for Athletics.

Jimbo Elrod | Defensive end | 1973–1975

To give you an idea of how much I loved football when I was young, Dick Butkus was my big hero when I was growing up in Tulsa. I remember when Frito-Lay put out a 45-record of his greatest hits. I would put on the headphones and listen to Dick hit people for hours. That was music to my ears. [I have a sports bar now and I have a poster of Dick Butkus right there on the wall.]

My first sport was baseball, and then I started wrestling in the fourth grade. I started Pop Warner football in the fifth grade. My first position with the Southeast Bears was guard, and once they saw that I moved pretty well they moved me to linebacker. I was just average size, a little soft, but I knew the game pretty well because I watched football—the Dallas Cowboys and the Sooners—all the time.

Yes, I was an Oklahoma fan from the start.

My father Bill was a doctor and a gigantic sports fan. He never really played any sports, but he loved football and boxing. My oldest brother, LeRoy, got a scholarship to play football at Oklahoma State, and my middle brother, Billy, was a good baseball and football player, but he had a birth defect in his neck that prevented from playing later.

I really loved wrestling, too, and I won the 132-pound city championship when I was a freshman. When I got to high school, I had a choice of schools. I could go to Tulsa Hale, where my first two brothers went, or I could go to East Central, the new school in town that had air-conditioning. I picked East Central, of course. And it had a really good football coach, a guy named Rod Goodsell, who had played some in the NFL.

I played center and inside linebacker and I learned to read defenses under coach Goodsell. I also learned that it was fun to block linebackers. We had really good coaching, which is paramount for any young player to develop. Coach Goodsell was an avid weightlifter, too, and he had a weight room in his garage. During the summers, the guys who wanted it badly enough were over there at his place hitting the weights.

When I was a junior, we were the only team to beat Booker T. Washington. We used to get 17,000 or 20,000 fans to watch the games when we played Booker T. During my senior year, we stopped them on a goal line stand and the game ended up in a tie.

We tied for the conference championship in my senior year, but lost 7–6 to Memorial during the season, so they got the opportunity to play Booker T. in the playoffs. We were the only team that could handle Washington, and they easily beat Memorial and went on to win the state title that year.

In wrestling, I won the state championship at 178 pounds and I knew I had a future in wrestling if I wanted it. Most people who know me know that my aspiration was to wrestle in the Olympics. I loved Oklahoma State wrestling and I loved Oklahoma wrestling, so I had a tough choice ahead of me.

However, Oklahoma State recruited me hard in wrestling, and Oklahoma recruited me hard in both sports.

I remember when Oklahoma State's football coaches made one final trip to my home. They said something like they weren't sure I could play football in the Big Eight, and from that comment on, my dad took over the process.

He told them, "We've heard what you've had to offer, now this meeting is over."

When [Oklahoma State wrestling coach] Tommy Chesbro heard what those football coaches had told me, he was very upset.

At the same time Leon Cross was recruiting me for the Sooners and he said I could wrestle all I wanted at Oklahoma.

"We would love to have you," he told me. So I signed with the Sooners.

When I checked in—they had all the freshmen check into a Howard Johnson's in Oklahoma City—I noticed how much bigger the other guys were than me.

I thought, "Wow! How is this going to turn out?"

You really question yourself at a time like that. We had other bigger linebackers coming in, guys like Marty Brecht, who was about 6'3" and 235. I might have been 6'2" and 195 at the time. It makes you wonder what Leon saw in me.

In wrestling, you don't have to worry about beating somebody out in practice. You just go wrestle, and whoever wins moves on.

At the time I thought, "Well, if football doesn't work out for me, I will just wrestle, go watch football games on Saturdays, and get a good education."

I never had any doubts about my wrestling abilities. I knew that I could always [drop] weight and go down to a lower weight class if I wanted. And my wrestling skills were pretty good.

My first memories of the practice field are when they took the freshmen down to the varsity's inside drill. There were guys like Lucious Selmon, Derland Moore, and Rod Shoate really getting after it. Rod Shoate was just killing people, knocking people out left and right, and [defensive line coach] Jimmy Johnson was yelling at everybody. That first inside drill really woke me up to the intensity of big-time college football.

That year, 1972, was the first year freshmen were eligible [under new NCAA rules], and they took Tinker Owens, Dewey Selmon, and Glenn Comeaux, another linebacker, up to the varsity for a while. When they sent Glenn back down after two weeks, I whacked him pretty good in practice one day and it was then that I figured I could play with these guys, too.

In wrestling, I had to wrestle heavyweight because of an injury to our heavyweight, and in my first match I was out there wrestling the previous year's national champion at Oklahoma State. I thought I would just try a quick move and get a fall and I caught him with it and put him on his back, but he was so big there was no way I could hold it. He pinned me. That was my first match, and I weighed about 195 pounds. I later went down to 190 and ended the season with a winning record. But before the Big Eight championships, I dislocated my ankle in practice.

When it was announced coach Fairbanks was leaving, I really don't remember much about it because I was off somewhere with the wrestling team. I had no interaction with coach Switzer at that point, and my first memories of him are when he brought us together at the 50-yard line in the spring and told us about getting the job.

I'll never forget what he told us: "I guarantee you that I am a fighter, I am a winner, and I am a competitor—and you guys will be, too!"

That's the first thing I heard Barry Switzer say.

Dad always taught me that the coach was the coach. Whoever it is, you do what they say.

The next season in football, I was fine with being redshirted. I was behind Rod Shoate. He was an idol of mine, and I watched everything he did, listened to everything he said, and went everywhere he went.

One day in practice, after I was set to redshirt, Lee Roy [was sick] and Dewey got hurt, so they moved some people around on the line because they needed a defensive end.

Larry Lacewell grabbed me by the shoulder and pulled me off to the side, telling me, "Go get at it at end."

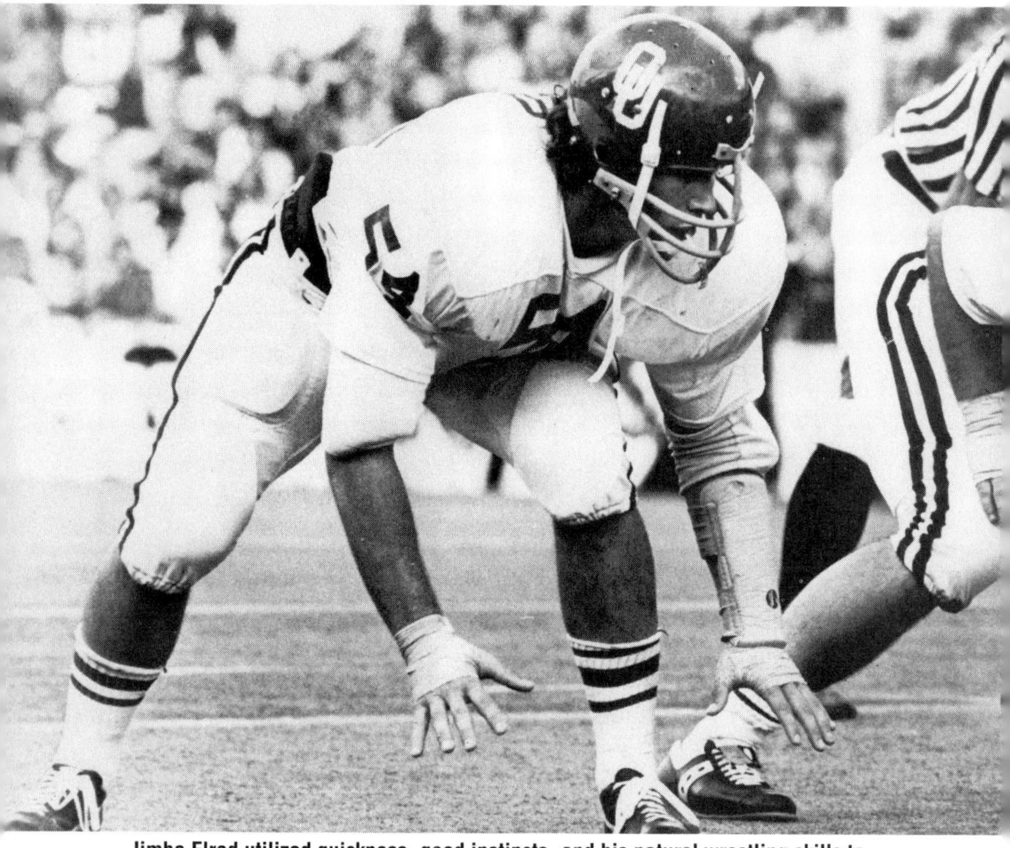

Jimbo Elrod utilized quickness, good instincts, and his natural wrestling skills to become an All-American at the standup defensive end position. He recorded 44 tackles for loss in his career.

I liked Larry Lacewell, but you wanted to be on his good side. He was tough. Would he get on me? You bet. I knew how tough he was.

While we were practicing, if the other players who were standing around made any noise at all, Larry would turn around, send them over to the stadium, and say, "Give me 20"—as in 20 times up and down the stadium steps. If he turned around, he shot panic in you, so you had better be paying attention.

Anyway, that's how it all started for me at defensive end. I played in the Baylor game, and Baylor had a fullback they called "Short Daddy." He was really good. I met him in the hole on a hard stunt and it was lights out for me. I nailed him and then I saw stars. I knew I was in the big leagues at that point, but that hit knocked all the scared out of me.

The next week, we were coming down the ramp at USC, and they had that stupid Tommy Trojan, about 200 players on the sidelines, and all their fans going against us country boys. But we were so ready for that game.

We had practiced on flowing into zone on pass coverage, and one time I got into my zone when Pat Haden threw it right at me. I could have run it in about 20 yards for a touchdown, but it looked like I had never touched a football before. It hit me in the hands and I dropped it.

Then I remember Rod Shoate hitting Anthony Davis so hard that he literally came out of his cleats. Anthony Davis started wincing and crying, and we didn't see him in the game for a long time. Hands down, we should have won that game, but we tied 7–7. I think we missed four field goals that day.

Adjusting to defensive end wasn't an adjustment at all. It put me closer to a body across the line of scrimmage. Switzer and Lacewell had an eye for positions and talent, and they knew I could handle tight ends. Getting leverage, like in wrestling, was a breeze for me. I could get my hands on the tight end and read the play. My best asset was my quickness.

We blitzed a lot out of that 5–2 defense. Well, they called it a 5–2, but it was really a 3–4 because the ends stood up like linebackers.

My position was the position Lawrence Taylor made famous in the NFL, and Larry Lacewell still believes we started it at Oklahoma and he's probably right.

Football had gone well for me that year, and when I moved on to my sophomore season of wrestling, I had a pretty good season. I would have been seeded second heading into the Big Eight championships, but I cracked three ribs in practice while preparing for it. If you have ever tried to do anything with a cracked rib, you know how painful it is. I tried everything I could do to wrestle, but I had to give it up.

After wrestling season, my left shoulder would fall out every once in a while—a rotator cuff problem—and I had to get that fixed.

Heading into the 1974 football season, coach Switzer told us we could still win the Big Eight even though we were on [NCAA] probation. That was always our first objective of any season, anyway, so nothing was different.

I look back on it now and I realize how dominant our defense was that season. We had Lee Roy, Dewey, Rod Shoate, Randy Hughes, All-Americans about everywhere you looked. I knew not many teams would be scoring on us, and most of them went three-and-out.

The coaches were incredible, too, and I was just in awe of how good we were. Everything was very precise. We also watched a lot of film. I would watch Lee Roy reach out with one arm and tackle a 245-pound fullback. I saw Randy Hughes make some incredible interceptions. And watching little Joe [Washington] from the sideline, how much fun was that? I will say another thing: [quarterback] Steve Davis needs to be given more credit after all these years. A lot of people don't realize how good he was at running that wishbone. He was great at reading the defense and knowing what to do to make the wishbone go.

These are the ingredients making up a dynasty.

In the Texas game, they were driving near the end of the game and we were tied [13–13], so we needed to make something happen. Larry [Lacewell] was upstairs and he made the call for a stunt. I don't think [Texas quarterback] Marty Akins read it right because he left the ball in Earl Campbell's hands.

I knew that when you took on Earl you had to hit him in the mouth and not in the legs because his legs were too big and too strong. You would never win the battle with him if you went low. So I hit Earl right in the mouth, and the ball just came out. It was a head-on shot and it was a big turnover. That was at about our 30-yard line.

Then we won the game [16–13], which was the most gratifying win because it was against Texas.

That 1974 team never lost, and we would have played any team anywhere because nobody was going to beat us that year. People compared us to some of the best college teams ever, and I think we stack up well. We knew we were national champions and we deserved it.

We lost a few people going into the 1975 season and had to play some younger guys. We had to replace Rod Shoate—and you can't replace a Rod Shoate.

That Kansas game [23–3 loss] was a big fluke because we dropped the ball on the ground about 11 times and we lost seven or eight of them, four or five of them in our red zone. If any other team had done that, they would have been beaten by 60 points. That really shows how good we were. It was a very weird day.

I really think some of our players didn't take things as seriously as they should have, and that's how that loss happened. I was one of those guys who took it all very seriously. I always did. But once the streak was over, we took 24 hours to get over it and we knew the national championship was still a possibility. We got ready for Missouri, and they were much more talented than Kansas.

We were behind at the end of that game, and I think Galen Hall upstairs in the booth spotted their cornerback, Ken Downing, leaving the game with an injury. So he called Joe Washington's number on a pitch to the right and he was gone. Then we had to go for two to win the game, and I was on my hands and knees praying. Fortunately, Joe snuck in there, and we won 28–27.

I just wanted to get out of there with a win and get to Nebraska at home for our final game.

We can say that we never lost to Texas and never lost to Nebraska, and I am pretty proud of that.

Right before the Orange Bowl, we found out in the locker room that [No. 1] Ohio State had been beaten [by UCLA in the Rose Bowl], so it was possible we could win another national title by beating Michigan.

We had practiced really hard leading up to the Orange Bowl, which I always liked. I loved hard practices and conditioning, so when the coaches made us run extra, I just laughed. It was always fine with me.

I remember one time when some of us missed curfew one night, and Barry had about 22 of us running extra. It was about 6:00 a.m., and we kept running and running. I came by once and said, "How many more times, Coach?"

There were about two or three guys behind me and George Davis, who later died of ALS. He and I were lapping people. I asked Barry, "If we let those guys pass us, can we quit?"

He said, "Elrod, you sumbitch!"

He was trying to run us into the ground, but George and I ran about 10 miles every morning, so we thought it was sort of fun.

The Orange Bowl was a real slug-fest. We completely shut down their running game of Gordon Bell and Rob Lytle, and that left them with a freshman quarterback [Rick Leach]. We flushed him out once, and Jerry Anderson and I hit him near the sideline and knocked him out. Later, Lee Roy sacked him and broke his finger. We really gave him a beating that night.

I look at Oklahoma football now like a long chain-link that has never been broken, at least I never broke my link. You keep it all together until the next class arrives. Everybody has ups and downs in life, and when you are down, you can always count on one of your teammates to bring you back up.

The people who came before me, the people I played with, and the people since are what's truly great about Oklahoma. It's not really a cliché, it is a family.

How do I sum it up? That school in Norman is magical to me. Those four years I spent there are branded on me. It had a big impact on my life. To be a Sooner, that experience, is a continuing process. I was a Sooner and I am still a Sooner.

Jimbo Elrod was an All-American in 1975 when he made 20 tackles for loss and 108 total tackles. He finished his career as the school's all-time leader in tackles for loss (44). In his career, he made 225 tackles and had seven fumble recoveries. He played four seasons in the NFL, including three with the Kansas City Chiefs.

Thomas Lott | Quarterback | 1975–1978

Growing up, I earned more baseball trophies than football trophies, but I soon got bored with baseball. The summers are so hot in Texas, and the game is slower than football, so I lost interest. Now as I look back, if I had any sense I would have kept up with it. I was a pretty good pitcher and shortstop.

Then again, I never would have become an Oklahoma Sooner if I had stuck with baseball.

In my neighborhood in the inner-city of San Antonio, I grew up mostly with Hispanics and blacks and there were gangs and trouble to get into. I was hanging with a group of friends that would have led me there, but I was one of the lucky guys. I did some things I had no business doing, but nothing serious. My mother said she would kill me if I got into trouble, and I believed her. Playing sports kept me out of trouble, too. While a bunch of my friends were headed to jail or prison, the thought of not getting to play sports scared me straight.

My mother, who worked as a nurse and raised me and two sisters, moved us to the suburbs during my sixth-grade year. I didn't want to leave our neighborhood, and it was a tough year on me, but I was in a better school and a better environment even though it was serious culture shock for me at first—there were only five blacks in the whole school.

The thing about athletics is that no matter who you are, you get an opportunity to meet people and make friends. That's the real beauty of sports. People always look at it as just a game, but it is so much more. All the friends I made and all the cultures I have been exposed to were through sports.

And I don't think I would have gone to college if not for football.

I made the San Antonio Jay varsity as a sophomore. I was a running back and a cornerback, but in my junior year our quarterback tore up his knee against MacArthur. We were running the wishbone, and my coach came to me during the game and asked me to play quarterback. They had to send the plays in and tell me exactly what to do on each play, but we ended up winning that game.

After the game, my coach came to me and said, "You did a pretty good job, so I would like to keep you at quarterback. I don't have time to get anybody else ready."

I really didn't like playing quarterback, although I would do anything to help my team. I did it with the thought of going back to running back after the season. I ended up rushing for more than 1,000 yards that year, and we finished 9–1, but I felt I was a running back playing quarterback.

At the end of the season, my coach asked me into the office and told me, "I've got some bad news and some good news."

I asked, "What's the good news?"

"I found me a quarterback—and the bad news is that it's you."

I protested a little bit and told him how I wanted to return to running back.

He said, "You don't understand. You rushed for 1,000 yards as a quarterback. If you have another season like that, you can go anywhere you want to go."

What made me mad was that I couldn't play cornerback or return punts or kickoffs any more. I hated coming off the field. If things happened on the field I didn't care for, I could go to cornerback and make somebody pay for it. I had to give all of that up.

But once I knew I had to stay at quarterback, I made my mind up to be the best in the state of Texas. That was my goal.

I rushed for 1,000 yards again as a senior but it was much harder. I didn't have much help since our star running back, Billy Taylor, went off to Texas Tech. I read in the newspaper that "if you stop Lott, you stop Jay."

We might have thrown the ball a few times each game, but in some games we never threw it. We finished 4–6 in my senior season. I hated losing . . . just hated it.

I remember a year earlier that Jerry Pettibone, Oklahoma's recruiting coordinator, came to the school to recruit a senior, and one of the coaches pointed to me and told him, "Come back next year and you need to get this guy right here."

Coach Pettibone said, "We'll just do that. I'll come back next year for him."

During my senior year, there was a black guy sitting in our stands one day during practice. In my neighborhood, everybody knew everybody else, but nobody knew this guy. Right after practice he walked up to me and introduced himself. It was Wendell Mosley, an OU assistant.

"Thomas," he told me, "I like what I see in you. I am telling you right now: OU will offer you a scholarship."

I visited Texas A&M, Arkansas, OU, Texas, and Texas A&I, and recruiting got to be heavy on me. At that time, the NCAA didn't govern it as much, and I would come home and have three or four recruiters sitting in front of my house. They would call me out of class to visit with them. It also interfered with basketball, so I ended up walking away from basketball because of it. I see now why the NCAA put more rules into recruiting.

I also knew that I had to live with this decision for the rest of my life. I had made up my mind not to go to school too far away like to the West Coast, but not too close, either. I knew I wanted to go to a school running the wishbone, too. Notre Dame wanted me as a running back, so they were out.

People always wondered where my hatred for Texas came from. When I visited there, I could tell things weren't a good fit for me in Austin. One night on my visit, two carloads of us were headed to a party and at the stoplight, everybody got out of the car in front of us and danced in the street. When the light turned green, they got back in the car and drove off.

I said, "What the hell is going on?"

Then I got to this party and I was talking to a young lady when Raymond Clayborn told me that we were headed to another party. The girl wanted to go with us, but she turned out to be another player's girlfriend. He got all upset and wanted to fight me. Like I said, things didn't go well.

The next day I was sitting across from Darrell Royal at his desk and he asked me how I liked my visit. I lied and said it was great, which it wasn't. Then he wanted to know what other schools I was considering.

"I told Notre Dame that I wasn't coming up there," I said. "And I have a visit to Oklahoma scheduled . . . "

When I said that, his mood changed. He nodded at his assistant to close the door. Then he stood up and said, "Oklahoma! What are you going to Oklahoma for?"

Now I had to defend my decision to visit Oklahoma, which was the No. 1 team in the country that year.

He went on and on about how much the state of Texas had done for me. How in the world could I consider leaving Texas?

I still held a grudge at the state of Texas because I was second-team all-state. I felt I should have been first-team and I thought it was because I was black.

When I visited Arkansas, the Arkansas players told me point-blank, "Don't come here because this school won't play a black quarterback."

On my recruiting visit to Oklahoma, I was all business. I didn't go to parties. Elvis Peacock showed me around, but I didn't do much but watch film. I told the coaches, "I want film on every quarterback you having coming back."

I stayed in the hotel and watched film on everyone of them, and Kerry Jackson was the only one who impressed me. I just knew I could play in this offense if they gave me a chance.

I ended up writing down 10 things I wanted from a university: things like national exposure, the opportunity to win, the opportunity to play, the coaches, location, etc. I knew that no school could give me all of them, but the one that gave me the most of those 10, that's where I would go. In the end, it was obvious that Oklahoma could give me more of those 10 than any other school.

During recruiting, I got to know George Cumby, Kenny King, and Billy Sims. I knew that Sims had rushed for 3,000 and some yards and King 2,000 and some, and I was wondering how they had put up numbers like that. It took everything I had to rush for 1,000, but I realized that their schools were playing in smaller classes in Texas. We got to know each other and talked about maybe going to the same place.

Then coach Switzer told me, "Billy's coming, King's coming."

I thought, "Shoot, I'd better go to OU, too."

Thomas Lott, shown here scrambling against Iowa State, is considered by many as the finest option quarterback in OU history. He rushed for 2,145 yards and 30 touchdowns in his career. *Photo courtesy of OU Athletics Media Relations.*

It turns out he was telling Billy the same thing. We all signed to go to Oklahoma, and one day we got to talking and we realized he had did the same thing to all of us. But I would have gone there anyway.

One thing about coach Switzer that I really liked was we had barbeque once and he sat right in the middle of the floor and ate barbeque with us like he had been there many times before. I felt so comfortable around him.

When I first got to Norman, I almost thought I had made a wrong turn and ended up at Grambling in Louisiana. There were so many black players and we had so much talent. It seemed like we had 150 players on scholarship.

I was eighth on the depth chart when I got there and there were even guys behind me! Everybody there was either All-American, all-state, all-city, all- district, or all-something. The speed of our practices was something incredible.

Our freshman team beat everybody by a margin of about 30 points, and I could tell our class was something special. It may have been one of the best classes ever in college football.

I almost left Norman during my freshman season, however. I kept hearing that I would never start in the future because I was black. I really didn't know the history of Oklahoma football, that all of the quarterbacks had been white. I just knew that Kerry Jackson was by far the best quarterback I saw in the school and he wasn't starting, but I didn't know why. I also realized from my move to the suburbs that everything wasn't about black and white.

When we ran the wishbone in my freshman season, we didn't read the defense on the option—it was predetermined in the huddle. We changed it to a true triple-option before my sophomore season. Defenses could stop two of the three options, but the third one you cannot stop.

Our defense was always in the top-five in the country, and I knew after playing against them during the spring that we wouldn't run up against anybody better than them in the fall. That next spring, I jumped ahead of about four or five people and was moving up the depth chart. I studied the option and watched a lot of film to understand it completely.

Steve Davis and a bunch of other seniors had graduated, and I was behind Joe McReynolds and Dean Blevins. I knew that none of them ahead of me could run like I could and all I wanted was an opportunity to win the starting position.

I told myself that I would be starting by the end of the fourth game of my sophomore season. By then, I figured Dean would have an opportunity to prove what he could do.

In that first game against Vanderbilt, we really struggled. In the second game, the same thing. I played a little, but not enough. At Iowa State in the fourth game, Horace Ivory made a long run to win the game, and I didn't play a down. I was very upset. Emotionally and mentally, I was quitting. I was mad at the world.

I had made up my mind that I was leaving Oklahoma. All through that Saturday night, that's what I was going to do. I tossed and turned all night, but when I woke up that Sunday morning, I was a little calmer. I had told myself that I would be playing after the fourth game, so that meant another week, I rationalized.

So for some reason, I decided to stay another week. I really can't explain my change of heart. I just felt different once I woke up. I like to tell people that the Lord spoke to me that night in a dream. I decided I would go through practice that week and see how things panned out.

Then coach Switzer and [offensive coordinator] Galen Hall pulled me into the office and said, "We're not happy with what Dean's doing. We want to work both of you with the No. 1 offense. We'll start Dean and if he doesn't move the ball, we'll put you in. If you don't move the ball, we'll put him back in. We're going to do this until one of you moves the ball."

It wasn't an ideal situation, but it was better than what I had. On Wednesday when I was coming out of class, someone said, "Coach Switzer and coach Hall need to see you immediately."

I was thinking something really bad had happened at home. I was thinking the worst. I walked into the office and both had serious looks on their faces. I thought, "Oh no."

Then one of them said, "Dean is sick and in the hospital and he will not be able to play against Texas. You are starting. Thomas, what do you think?"

"That's why I came here," I said. "If you ask me, it's two weeks late."

I had been named the starter at the brink of my self-imposed deadline.

All of us Texans who played for Oklahoma had a grudge against Texas for one reason or another. Nine of us from Texas were starting at Oklahoma at the time. I know Darrell Royal didn't like Switzer because he was young, brash, cocky to a point, and he had one hell of a football team. We didn't like them too much and they probably didn't like us.

Switzer told me that week they were going to scale the game plan down for me. And we did. We didn't run the option much, and Texas had kicked two field goals to go ahead 6–0. I thought the coaches gave Texas way too much respect. I think they thought since Texas ran the wishbone for so long that they could stop ours. We went against what we did best and didn't run the option that day.

Finally, we ran it on the final drive and went down and tied them, but then we muffed the extra-point attempt. A 6-6 tie . . . such a weird feeling, not winning and not losing.

I wish we wouldn't have been so conservative, but I understood why they were. It was my first game, so I couldn't tell them what to do. I can name you two games in my whole life when I was so pissed off. That was one of them. I'll get to the other later.

The Kansas game the next week was my breakout game. I showed the coaches that this was my position and nobody was getting it back. But it was a good thing I wasn't battling for a receiver position because I blew my first chance at a big play.

We had a play where I would pitch to Elvis [Peacock] to the right on a sweep and I would sneak out of the backfield to the left to catch a throwback pass from him. He threw the ball right on my hip. I reached back and started to turn before I closed on the ball and it rolled right out of my hands. There was nobody in front of me. It would have been my first college touchdown. I can still picture that play.

I rushed for over 100 yards and scored two touchdowns, and we won 28–10, so I felt a little better.

I never gave the quarterback job back.

We lost two in a row, to Oklahoma State and to Colorado, because we had lost two or three secondary players to injury, and those teams were passing on us. I got on the bus after the Colorado game and said, "I don't give a —— if we have to score 100 points each week, we are not losing another game this season!"

We didn't. We beat Nebraska 20–17 and beat Wyoming easily, 41–7, in the Fiesta Bowl.

That next spring was a lot different for me. I was coming off an MVP game at the Fiesta Bowl and I was not competing with anybody for the job. I had all the confidence in the world, too, now that I had shown what I could do.

In our last scrimmage before the season started that fall, I had gotten tackled and was lying on the ground when one of our guys was getting up, and he lost his balance and fell back on my right knee. It was one of those freak deals. The doctors were treating it as a bruised muscle but it wasn't getting any better. [Running backs coach] Donnie Duncan knew this chiropractor, and he diagnosed it as a bruised nerve. He started some treatment, and I felt a difference the very next day.

I don't know if Barry knew about it because I never told anybody, and I don't think Donnie did either. Chiropractors were known as quacks back then, so we didn't let anybody know. But what he did worked.

We won our first two games without me and all the talk was whether I would be able to play at Ohio State. I started the game and I was trying to protect my knee. I was running to the left and my good knee gave out. I had put so much emphasis on the other knee that I ended up hurting it and they took me out of the game. We got up 20–0 and then they came back to take the lead. At the end, I knew Uwe [von Schamann] had kicked two long field goals the year before, so when it came down to him at the end and when he led the "Block that kick" chant with the fans, I knew he was going to make it.

Before the kick, Switzer was on his hands and knees.

I looked down at him and said, "Get up off the ground! You are embarrassing us!"

Uwe made it, and we won 29–28, and I always believed we would have won by more if I didn't get hurt that day. But a win is a win, right?

As we prepared for Texas a few weeks later, I told the coaches, "We need to run the option."

"OK, Thomas, OK," they said.

So what happens? We get into the game and didn't run the option.

At halftime, I asked coach Hall, "Why aren't we running the option?"

"We will run it in the second half," he said.

It was the same thing over and over again. We didn't. We got the ball back with a couple of minutes left, and we were behind 13–6. They finally let us run the option, and we drove right down the field. We got inside the 10-yard line and faced a fourth-and-1.

On this play, we ran the option and I got down the line. [Texas'] Brad Shearer wrapped up my legs. I leaned forward to get the yard, but Johnnie Johnson knocked me backward, and that was the ballgame.

I was so upset with our coaching staff. I think they really dropped the ball by giving Texas too much respect for the second straight year.

The Orange Bowl game against Arkansas that year taught me a lot about percentages. We had rebounded to win the rest of them and beat Nebraska 38–7. Arkansas had suspended those players, and all the odds were in our favor.

Then some weird things started happening to us. In the last practice before the game I pulled a hamstring. We didn't tell anybody about it, especially not the media, and I entered that game not knowing if I could play or not.

We always had our routine the night before a game where we would go to dinner and then go see a movie. Well, the buses were late to pick us up, we didn't get to dinner on time, the food was not ready, and then we didn't get to see a movie. On the way back to the hotel, a couple of guys started arguing, and they were ready to get into a fight right there on the bus. We had to pull them apart. The whole thing was so unusual because we were always so close as a team. The atmosphere wasn't good at all.

The one thing I hated about playing in the Orange Bowl was that it was always the last game of the day. So you would sit around your hotel room, go to a few meetings, go back to your room, and you're watching football all day.

We watched Notre Dame beat No. 1 Texas in the Cotton Bowl. Then we saw Washington beat No. 4 Michigan in the Rose Bowl. Going into our game ranked No. 2, I figured, "Well, I guess we'll be the only top-ranked team to win today."

All day long it was supposed to rain, but it never did. We went out and went through the pregame warm-ups and then headed back to the locker room. Somebody came in and said, "It's raining cats and dogs out there."

That Orange Bowl surface was all sand with a little bit of grass on top of it anyway. After that rain, it made it just slick enough to make it tough on us. If you ran dive plays on it, it would have been OK, but we couldn't plant and make cuts that night. On the first play, we fumbled and I had a strange feeling this wouldn't be our night. We made [Arkansas coach] Lou Holtz famous that night. After that [31–6 loss], I learned that at certain times in your life, things don't always go your way.

We were determined that next spring to do everything the right way and bounce back from it. We made sure we dotted all of our i's and crossed all of our t's. We worked very hard that spring, and there was some serious competition between the defense and offense. I can honestly say that we wanted that national championship in 1978 more than anything in the world.

The last two Texas games had been so frustrating for me that I vowed we wouldn't play them the way we had the past two years. Coach Hall had been very conservative in that game, and I liked taking chances. That day, I refused to let anything get in the way of winning that game. I even changed plays coach Hall sent in.

He would say, "Thomas, that's not the play I called."

"Oh, sorry, Coach," I would say.

I told the players on offense, "If something comes in that I don't like, I am not running it."

Nobody in the country knew that offense like I did. I was a student of the game and I studied a lot of film. I always wanted to throw it more than we did, and we did have conflicts about that, but we jumped up on people so quickly sometimes—that was one reason we didn't throw more.

But in the Texas game, I kept changing plays and they were working. After a while, he stopped asking about it. Coach Switzer's attitude was, "Just get it done."

And that's what I was doing. We beat Texas 31–10, but it was bittersweet because I hurt my ankle late in the game and had to miss the next game at Kansas. That pretty much knocked me out of any Heisman race, and we were featuring Billy [Sims], so he jumped right into it.

Kansas scored to make it 17–16 late in the game, and they were going crazy on their sideline. If they had sent their two-point play in right away, there is no doubt in my mind they would have scored to win the game. But the quarterback was going back and forth, back and forth, from the huddle to the sideline, and they finally got a delay of game. They couldn't decide what to call. Once the penalty was marked off, I thought for sure they would kick the extra point for the tie, but they didn't. They tried for two and we stopped it to escape with the win.

When we got out of that game, I knew I had to try to come back the next week against Iowa State. I couldn't really cut too well, but we beat them 34–6.

We got to the Nebraska game undefeated and on the road to what we all thought would be a national title. While Texas was always personal for me, Nebraska was always business.

This time I felt no different about Nebraska than I had in the last three years. They didn't have the talent of other schools. I even thought Missouri had better talent than Nebraska. I knew we were much better than them and, if we protected the ball, we wouldn't lose. But with high rewards in the wishbone comes high risk.

It was cold and ugly that day and we just couldn't hold onto the ball.

How else do you explain fumbling nine times [losing six]?

Everybody remembers Billy's last fumble at the 3-yard line when we were ready to score to win the game, but we were still in the game after all those previous fumbles. We stopped them after that, and I thought we were going to get the ball back.

I was saying, "We'll be all right. We're gonna get the ball back and go score."

Then we committed a personal foul on defense that gave them a first down.

I said, "We'll be all right. We're gonna get the ball back and score."

Greg Roberts looked at me and said, "Homeboy, it's over. Now they can run out the clock."

At that moment, my heart just froze. I never have recovered from that game [a 17–14 loss]. It still breaks my heart to think about it. We lost everything in that game. We lost the Big Eight championship, the national championship . . . everything we had worked for.

We went out with a bang by beating Oklahoma State 62–7 the next week, and it was very, very emotional. We realized it was the last time we would play together at home. We were rushed into the locker room after that game and we found out that Missouri had beaten Nebraska. All of a sudden, we got a share of the Big Eight title and then the Orange Bowl people asked us if we wanted to go and play Nebraska again.

The locker room went crazy. You talk about one of the happiest moments of my life. We would have played them in the parking lot of a grocery store. I knew if we played them 10 times again, we wouldn't lose one of them.

We ran over Nebraska in the Orange Bowl [31–24], as I expected we would. One poll gave [the national championship] to USC and one poll gave it to Alabama, and we would have beaten either one of them. I guess it wasn't meant to be. We never got that national championship ring.

A lot of things I learned at OU I attribute to coach Switzer. People say we didn't have discipline. Let me tell you, you don't win as many games [41–6–1 record, 1975–1978] as we did without discipline. Coach Switzer understood that the speed of the game was more important than the bulk and brawn.

Sometimes, I thought of coach Switzer as my dad. He meant that much to me.

Playing at Oklahoma was an experience that changed my life. It opened doors that never would have been opened for me. It gave me the tools I needed to be productive in life. It gave me the opportunity to meet people I will love for the rest of my life. I have so many strong, passionate feelings for the University of Oklahoma.

I got everything that college football had to offer and I got it all at Oklahoma. My heart will always be in Norman and it always be with the Sooners.

Thomas Lott was named All–Big Eight in 1977 and 1978. He also was a team captain in 1978. He accounted for 3,035 total yards in his career in which Oklahoma won 23 of Lott's 29 starts (with one tie). He had eight 100-yard rushing games, including a career-best 195 on 24 carries against Kansas State in 1976.

Uwe von Schamann | Kicker | 1976–1978

I was born in Berlin, Germany, April 23, 1956, and raised by my mother. Mom was a teenager when I was born and she was always trying to improve our life, changing jobs and moving. When I was six, we moved to Luxembourg, and it was pretty hectic, having to make new friends.

When I was younger, there was a problem with my legs not getting enough calcium. I had brittle bones, and Mom didn't allow me to play on any competitive teams because I was in danger of breaking my legs.

We had friends from Germany who had moved to Fort Worth, Texas, and they had always encouraged us to visit them. Finally, in 1971, when Mom had won a trip to Iceland, we decided to go ahead and take it and then go on to New York.

I was 15 at the time and spoke a little English, but Mom spoke none. When we got to New York, we had no idea how big this country was.

We had about $100 left, and Mom asked me what I wanted to do. We figured we could try to go see our friends in Fort Worth, so I went up to the Greyhound bus ticket counter and got two tickets for us. The tickets read, "Memphis." We had no idea where Memphis was, but we had enough change left to buy four apples. That's all we had to eat.

We thought, "We'll go to this Memphis place and worry about the rest of the trip once we get there."

Two days later, we arrived in Memphis and we were out of food and drink, so we started hitchhiking. The first guy who picked us up was drunk, but he dropped us off at a truck stop. There, we found a guy who took us to Little Rock, Arkansas. He took us to breakfast and then took us to his house where his wife made some sandwiches for us for the road. They had a seven-month-old daughter and they were just great to us.

It was an act of kindness that Mom and I always remembered. That man and his family in Little Rock impressed us so much that Mom and I agreed that it must have been an example of all the good things we had heard about this country.

After that, we met another guy on the road who took us the final leg of the trip to our friends' house in Fort Worth. We spent two weeks in Fort Worth, and I went to school with my friend during that time. On our way home back to Luxembourg, I talked Mom into moving here, so we came back in the summer of 1972 for good.

After my sophomore year at Eastern Hills in Forth Worth, Mom let me backpack and hitchhike all over Europe for a couple of months. I really think she had hoped I would get homesick and want to move back there, but I loved it in Fort Worth.

One day in P.E. class at school, I picked up a ball and kicked it. One of the coaches happened to see me and asked what my name was. I told him.

"What kind of name is that?" he asked.

Then he told me, "Let's see you kick it again."

After I kicked it again, he said, "You want to come out for football?"

I didn't know what football was, but I went out for it.

When I first saw football, I thought it was a silly, stupid game. It looked like a bunch of guys with crash helmets on. I just didn't see the attraction to it, didn't see the point. In practice I kicked and it was no big deal to me. The ball had an odd shape and it was really different than the soccer ball I was used to. After a couple of kicks, I had it down. But our coach, Cecil Newton, had to teach me punting: how to hold it, drop it, and the whole thing.

The first game in which I kicked, they just told me to kick it through the uprights and I did. Then everybody started jumping up and down, but it was no big deal to me.

After my junior year, coach Newton told me, "Next year, maybe you can get a scholarship."

I remember asking, "What's a scholarship?"

In the last game I played in high school, in the city playoffs against Arlington Heights, the opposing kicker was Tony Franklin, who ended up at Texas A&M and later played with the Philadelphia Eagles. I kicked a field goal 52 yards, which was then the state record, but in the last minute of the game, Tony kicked a 58-yarder to beat us—and my record.

When Jerry Pettibone, then the recruiting coordinator at Oklahoma, came to practice to look at one of our receivers, our coach asked him if he needed a kicker. He introduced me that day, and then coach Switzer started recruiting me after that. I had visited Rice and Baylor, but the only schools that really pursued me were Oklahoma and Oklahoma State.

I remember meeting coach Switzer at the Ramada Inn on the east side of Fort Worth. Mom and I expected him to buy us dinner, but all we had with coach Switzer was a Coke. I thought maybe he figured this German guy didn't know any better. He tried to persuade Mom that Oklahoma was better for me than Oklahoma State.

When I took my recruiting trip to Norman, I had never seen a beautiful college campus like that before. The facilities were impressive and the whole atmosphere was great. We went to a basketball game, and I felt comfortable there right from the beginning.

Once Mom had me in college, she had no worries as far as supporting me. I was just glad I didn't have to play my freshman year at Oklahoma because the college courses were challenging for me. My English at that point was OK and I was making good grades, but I had to work at it. I entered school as a psychology major but ended up in journalism.

When I was a sophomore in 1976, Tony DeRienzo had graduated, and it was my turn to kick. The first pressure kick I remember would have been the extra point at the end of the game against Texas. We were tied 6–6, but the snap went over the holder's head, and I never got to kick it.

Our snapper, Kevin Craig, just felt horrible. I remember that President Ford, who was at the game and had been a center at Michigan, sent Kevin a letter of encouragement that read, "We centers have to stick together."

In the final game of that season, I kicked a 50-yard field goal in the Fiesta Bowl. The thing I also remember about that game—a 41–7 win over Wyoming—was some seniors smoking cigarettes and eating hot dogs on the sideline late in the game. I guess you could say we were kind of a loose bunch.

Let me get to the game that made my career memorable to so many people. The game at Ohio State, September 24, 1977.

I remember coach Switzer telling us that this was the marquee game in the nation for the week. He said that if we won the game, we would be the No. 1–ranked team. It was two powerhouses and the first time they had ever played each other.

Ohio State had Woody Hayes, who was old school, and we had Barry, who was this young, brash coach.

The night before the game, I remember my roommate, Bud Hebert, told me he thought I would win the game the next day with a field goal.

After I kicked two field goals and we were ahead 20–0, it looked like we might win it big, but they scored 28 unanswered points to lead 28–20. Then Phil Tabor caused a fumble, and Reggie Kinlaw recovered it. We scored, but failed on the two-point conversion. On the onside kick, I just tried to hit it hard and at somebody and make the ball jump around. Sure enough, it hit the first guy in the chest and bounced out, and Mike Babb recovered it. I knew we had a chance at that point.

We hit a pass and then ran Kenny King up the middle to get to the 24, and I noticed there was a little wind behind me. We called timeout with six seconds left. I said my little prayer and mediation that I always went through before a kick and then I was prepared to go.

Then Woody Hayes called a timeout. I went into the huddle and I don't remember saying this, but Sam Claphan told me later that I said, "Don't worry about it. I got it. Don't worry about it."

As I was walking around on the field, I could hear the crowd chanting, "Block that kick! Block that kick!"

I really don't know why I did this then, but I just started to raise my hands to lead the chant. It was a great snap, a great hold, and I hit it really well. The next thing I know is that I was on the bottom of a large pile of players. If it wouldn't have been for one of our offensive linemen shielding me, I may have died under that pile.

That kick, a 41-yarder, to this day, changed my life.

I still enjoy the stories when people come up to me and tell me what they were doing or where they were when I made that kick. They'll say something like, "I remember it like I remember JFK getting shot."

The funny thing about it is that one of our assistant coaches, Bill Shimek, had told his girlfriend the week earlier that he would marry her if we beat Ohio State. Five years later, I saw him and he told me, "I wish you would have missed that SOBing kick."

I guess the marriage didn't work out.

When we got home that night, it was crazy. People were waiting at the airport for us. People were driving around campus, honking horns. The next week, the Oklahoma City newspaper took a picture of my bare foot and ran it really large on the front page—it was just nuts after that game.

If I hadn't had made that kick I wonder now if they would have wanted to send me back to Germany. I think occasionally how my life would have been different if I had missed it. Even the way people reacted to me changed.

When I was with the Miami Dolphins later, coach [Don] Shula told me that he started thinking about drafting me after he saw that game. Then the first time I met Dan Marino, he walked up to me waving his arms like I had done at Ohio State.

Coach Switzer never did pronounce my name right. Sometimes he would get my first name right and then mispronounce my last name, or vice-versa. I think he knows it now, but the first thing I noticed about coach Shula was that he got it right the first time.

As long as I did my job, I never had much dealings with coach Switzer. He did get on my ass once as I came off the field after missing a field goal against Kansas.

Mom never did understand football. She couldn't figure out the difference between an extra point and a field goal, but she enjoyed seeing me play.

Uwe von Schamann was the integral figure in one of the defining moments of Oklahoma football history, his 41-yard kick in 1977 that beat Ohio State. He went on to have a successful NFL career with the Miami Dolphins. *Photo courtesy of AP/Wide World Photos.*

Growing up in Germany, obviously, it wasn't my dream to play football at OU. But when I came to Oklahoma, I felt like I found a home. I also found a family. The relationships I developed at OU I still have to this day. One of my greatest accomplishments is that I went back in 1996 and finished my degree when I was 40 years old. I am more proud of that than I am of what I did on the football field.

All these years later, I recently found the name of the man who was so kind to us in Little Rock. I had his name on a piece of paper: Robert Carson. I tried to call him, but I reached a woman who told me, "That is my son." Then she told me that he had died in a motorcycle accident soon after he had helped us back in 1972.

After the holidays last year when I was driving to Florida to see my mother, I decided to stop and visit her in Arkansas. When I got there, all the kids, grandkids, aunts, and uncles of this family came out to greet me. Robert Carson's daughter, who was seven months old at the time when he helped us, wanted me to tell her all about what her dad had done.

His mother even told me, "You brought my son home for Christmas for me. Thank you."

Now we talk all the time. It's as if I have a new family. Robert Carson was one of those people you meet by circumstance, but I will never forget him. Meeting him helped change my life, bringing us to the United States and me to Oklahoma.

Uwe von Schamann finished his career with a streak of making 125 consecutive PATs, which was an NCAA record at the time. He made 149 of 150 PATs and 33 of 51 field goals in his career. He was named All–Big Eight in 1978. He played six seasons with the Miami Dolphins.

Billy Sims | Running Back | 1975, 1977–1979

I was raised in St. Louis, Missouri, and that made me a huge baseball fan. I loved my Cardinals . . . still do. I grew up idolizing Bob Gibson, Lou Brock, and Curt Flood. Those guys were big heroes to me.

In the eighth grade, I moved to live with my grandparents in Hooks, Texas. Miss Sadie, as she was called, and Clarence Sims, were special people. They raised me and loved me and cared for me while I was growing up. They were spiritual, hard-working people who wanted me to do my best at whatever I did.

When I got to Hooks, it was obvious to me that football was the game you had to play. I first had to learn how to play it because I really didn't know much about it. I knew one thing right away: the guy who had the ball was catching hell all the time and I wanted to deliver the hits, so I became a linebacker.

They switched me to running back in the ninth grade, and that position was my future.

Hooks had a population of about 2,500 people then, and Hooks High was a 2A Class school in Texas, which meant we would have about 22 or 25 guys on our entire team. So, yeah, you had to play both ways.

What was our offensive system?

"Billy left, Billy right, Billy punt, and Billy kick off."

That was fine, because I learned to do it all.

Seriously, we ran the I-formation in which I gained more than 7,000 yards in my career. I was the second-leading rusher in Texas history. Nobody will catch the guy who holds the record, Kenneth Hall, of Sugarland. He rushed for more than 11,000 yards, which still is the national record. I met him recently and I think he was about 6'3", 220 pounds and could really run. Could you imagine a guy like that in the fifties?

Back in those days, when it came to recruiting, you could visit a school about every weekend, and I think I did before I narrowed it down to about six schools: Baylor, the University of Texas, Oklahoma State, Arkansas, TCU, and Oklahoma.

My first inclination was to go to Baylor because they were graduating their running back and I saw an opportunity to play right away. But eventually, I saw the bigger picture.

People always ask me why I didn't go to Texas, but they had Earl Campbell down there. I knew of coach Royal, but let me say this, growing up I wasn't a big fan of football. I didn't have a favorite team and I didn't watch that much, so it wasn't like I was a kid who was a Longhorn fan. Like I said earlier, I watched baseball.

Bill Shimek recruited me for Oklahoma, and I think he spent about 77 days with me in Hooks. He was there so much that we made him an honorary citizen.

On my recruiting visit to Norman, there was Greg Roberts, George Cumby, Thomas Lott, Kenny King, and many other Texas players who got together and talked about where we came from, what we wanted out of a college, and our plans and dreams. We were all talented players and we knew that if we played hard and worked hard, we would win championships if we stayed together.

Coach Switzer sure knew how to sell the program, too. All of those guys I mentioned sat around one night and bragged about who got recruited the hardest. What we all found out was that Barry told us all we would win a Heisman Trophy if we came to Oklahoma. I told him once much later that one out of 10 ain't bad. We always laughed about that.

I knew one thing: Miss Sadie liked him from the start. One thing about Coach, he could relate on all levels. Once you started talking to him, you realized he was no fake. He was genuine.

I knew I wanted to play for somebody like that.

Once I got to OU, I also knew I wouldn't start because Joe Washington was there. That was OK with me because I didn't know the wishbone from a chicken bone. A lot of people thought I should go to a college where I would have been able to play right away, but I always figured I could compete on Oklahoma's level.

I learned a lot from Joe, like how to work out and about having a work ethic and those type of things. I played on special teams that first year, but then I fractured my shoulder that next year and had to redshirt.

I ran a lot of scout-team plays in those days, even when I was hurt. It was no big deal to me, really. It was a maturing year for me.

The next year, 1977, I was sharing time with David Overstreet at the left halfback, Elvis Peacock was at the right half, and Kenny King was at fullback. I had about 400 yards in the season, scored a touchdown in

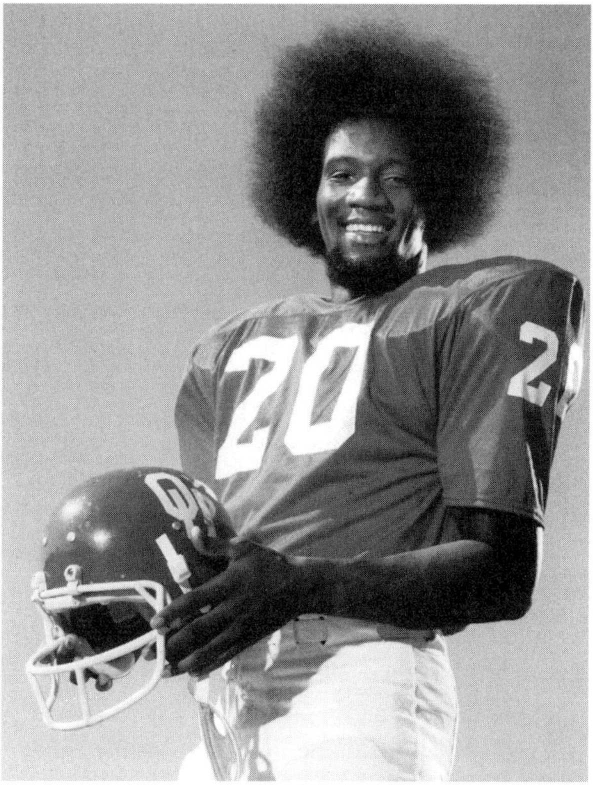

Legendary running back Billy Sims is remembered as one of the greatest players ever to suit up for the Sooners. He won the Heisman Trophy in his junior season, finished second his senior season, and was taken with the first pick in the 1980 NFL draft. *Photo courtesy of OU Athletics Media Relations.*

the first half of our big game at Ohio State, and then I hurt my Achilles tendon later in the first half.

I was so frustrated that I really wanted to quit football. The injuries really caught up with me. I thought I would just go to class, get my degree, and then go get a job. I was frustrated. It's tough being injured. I mean, coaches who used to talk to me were not talking to me all of a sudden. It was like I wasn't adding anything to the team, so I was forgotten.

You need to know that the game of football was never my life. I liked the game, but I didn't *love* the game. I was never consumed by it. At the same time, when I was out on the field, I always gave my all.

Coach Switzer talked me out of quitting. He knew I had been a great player in high school, but things just weren't working out for me. He understood all of that and told me to be patient and things would work out for me eventually.

I had good summer workouts in 1978 and I was finally healthy for a change. There was no publicity about me, no Heisman build-up or anything like that. I just got my chance and history happened. It was a fun season and everything just seemed to click for me. I just got into a zone and I had a great supporting cast, such as our great offensive line.

I am sure I would have gained much more than 2,000 yards if I had ever played more than three quarters of each game, but the other guys practiced hard and worked hard and they deserved to play, too. That was OK with me. [Sims rushed for more than 100 yards in every game except for the third game of the season, a 66–7 win over Rice. He finished with a school-record 1,896 rushing yards, a 7.41-yard average, and 22 touchdowns.]

People over the years have brought up that fumble at Nebraska. [Sims fumbled on Nebraska's 3-yard line in the final minutes of a 17–14 loss when the Sooners were 9–0 and ranked No. 1.] I tell them that if it weren't for the other eight fumbles that day, we would have won. We had nine fumbles that game and lost seven.

I was at the 5-yard line along the sideline and I was carrying the ball on my right side when the defensive back made a great play. He just punched it out. I later told my offensive linemen that if they hadn't been watching me run, they would have recovered it.

After that fumble, we still had a chance to pull it out, but we committed a personal foul on defense that was the killer. Not many people remembered that as the years go on, but they remember my fumble.

I know this: Nebraska people have thanked me a lot over the years, but they had a great team, too. We celebrated like we won the national championship after we found out we could play them again in the Orange Bowl. It was satisfying winning that rematch, and I have to add that we had no fumbles that day.

I had no idea of what to expect about the Heisman Trophy, but Steve Owens gave me a little insight on it. Until you experience the aura and history of it, you have no idea of how big it is. Now, more than 25 years later, 99 percent of the people I meet relate me to winning the Heisman rather than the NFL or the Detroit Lions or anything else.

It was the first time I ever bought a suit, and I borrowed some luggage for the trip to New York. Coming from Hooks, Texas, where all we had was trees and grass and countryside, I had never seen a place with so many buildings and concrete. It was quite an event and something I will never forget.

I had another season of eligibility left because of my injuries, but it never really entered my mind to win another Heisman. A lot of people thought I had a good chance to win it twice, but it really wasn't a big deal to me.

I could have left college after the 1978 season if I wanted, but I was having so much fun and enjoying the college atmosphere, I wanted to stay.

There were several games that season in which I played about a half and [USC's] Charles White was having a really good year. I never gave it a second thought because I ended up with a pretty good season [1,670 rushing yards, 23 touchdowns] and I was happy.

I did enough to become the first pick of the NFL draft, which is not necessarily a good thing because that means I was headed to the worst team. The San Francisco 49ers were picking second, and my career may have been different if I ended up out there winning Super Bowls with Joe Montana.

Anyway, I got married my senior year, and Barry helped me out greatly and I stayed to get my degree. That extra year really helped me in getting my degree, and that was something that had been so important to Miss Sadie. She had passed away during my freshman year and that was a very tough thing on me because she was my heart and soul.

The thing about Oklahoma, as I travel all over this country, is that when I say the words, "I played at Oklahoma," people take notice. It is a matter of pride. We have alumni all over the country and we are very proud people. I think we have 10,000 alumni here in Dallas and another 6,000 in Houston.

We call Oklahoma football "the monster." It was what Bud Wilkinson created and what Barry Switzer fed for a long time and what Bob Stoops feeds today. But it is a good monster. It represents a commitment, a love, and a sharing among the people who played football at OU. I owe a lot to coach Switzer and to the people who support Oklahoma.

I am awfully grateful that he talked me into staying and remaining a part of it.

Billy Sims won the Heisman Trophy in 1978, a season in which he gained 1,896 yards and scored 22 touchdowns. He finished his career as OU's all-time leading rusher with 4,118 yards on 593 carries (6.94-yard average). He totaled 20 100-yard games and seven 200-yard games, which is another OU record. Sims finished second in the 1979 Heisman Trophy balloting, won by USC's Charles White. Sims, the top pick in the 1980 NFL draft by the Detroit Lions, gained 5,106 yards and scored 42 touchdowns in his first five NFL seasons before a knee injury forced his retirement. He was inducted into the College Football Hall of Fame in 1995.

| chapter five |

The Eighties

J. C. Watts | Quarterback | 1978–1980

My hometown is Eufaula, Oklahoma. To find it on a map, look eastward from Oklahoma City and south-by-southeast from Tulsa. I like to call the ethos I grew up with "Oklahoma values," but you'd be just as accurate if you said "American values." Except for our lack of a seacoast, Oklahoma has a little bit of just about everything that is American.

I know exactly where I come from. Where I come from, I was taught that I didn't spend more than I took in. I was taught that education was important. I had to go to school and act civilized when I got there, respect my teachers as well as all adults, work hard, and exercise personal responsibility. I was taught that doing the right thing matters a lot.

My first and best teachers were Helen and Buddy Watts, with a backfield of grandparents and aunts and uncles and family friends who got me where I am today.

My father was named J.C., but his initials didn't stand for any proper name. Everybody called him Buddy. My father knew about the hard lessons in life, even though he lasted only two days into the seventh grade. He had to start working full-time because of the Depression.

He was never scared of hard work. At one point, he tried his hand at the food business and built a concrete-block barbeque stand.

In 1969, at the age of 46, he became Eufaula's first black policeman. It was speeders who got under his skin. Anyone willing to risk the lives of children to save themselves a few minutes could expect no mercy from Buddy Watts. One of his favorite jokes was about a cop who pulls a guy over for slowly cruising right through a stop sign. The driver gets out of his car and demands to know why.

"You didn't stop back there," the cop says.

"Yeah, but I slowed down," the driver tells him.

With that, the cop starts hitting him over the head with his nightstick.

"Ow! Stop!" the man pleads.

"Do you want me to stop—or should I just slow down?"

Buddy Watts loved that joke.

When I was born, they named me J.C., just like my father, but my initials stand for Julius Caesar. For the most part, everybody just called me "Junior."

During my elementary and junior-high years, the Selmon brothers played for the Eufaula High School's Ironheads and they became the closest thing to genuine heroes that I knew.

I dreamed of being a singer, but it was Lucious Selmon who opened my eyes to a whole new world of possibilities. I remember the moment as if it were yesterday. It was the Oklahoma-Nebraska game on Thanksgiving Day, 1971. Seeing Lucious on the TV screen, my adrenaline pumped like I was right there with him. That was nothing less than a life-changing event for a 13-year-old kid like me.

"Did you see Lucious on TV last Thursday?" was all you heard around town. I heard it over and over again.

Most of the kids I hung out with wanted to finish high school, get a job, get a car, and hopefully, get out on their own. I knew I wanted more than that, but I really didn't know how to go about doing it. A couple of friends in my neighborhood had fathers who were airmen, and they would come home and look good in their uniforms.

I had thought, "Twenty years in the Air Force and then you retire? That sounds pretty good to me."

But seeing Lucious on TV that day completely changed the direction of my life. I realized I could set my sights higher than just getting a job and my own car. I began to think maybe that can happen to me—to get an education and play big-time college football.

J. C. Watts persevered through many frustrations early in his career to become one of OU's all-time great quarterbacks. He later became a four-term U.S. Congressman. *Photo courtesy of OU Athletics Media Relations.*

Another Selmon opened my eyes even wider.

When I was a sophomore in high school, I had heard talk that Lee Roy Selmon might be a number-one draft choice.

My high school coach, Paul Bell, told me one day, "You could accomplish the same things the Selmons are accomplishing if you stay out of trouble and make good grades."

That's all I needed to hear.

At the time, Barry Switzer was "the King" in Oklahoma. Everybody loved the Sooners and everybody loved Barry. They threw a parade for Lucious Selmon down Main Street in Eufaula, and it seemed all 2,000 people of the town came out for it. Right behind Lucious on a red flatbed trailer was coach Switzer.

I will never, ever forget this: I was standing in front of the pool hall with all my friends. As the parade passed by, Lucious yelled to coach Switzer: "Hey, Coach, see that kid over there? That's going to be your quarterback some day."

Lucious had pointed to me. Coach Switzer asked him what my name was. Then he wanted to know what the J.C. stood for. The thing I remember is that we made eye contact that day and he had asked about me in front of all my friends. I am telling you, I don't know if life gets any better than that for a 15-year-old kid.

During my high school career, the Eufaula Ironheads compiled a 25–9 record. I had totaled more than 7,000 yards, was named a high school All-American, and perhaps most importantly, I was voted team captain.

When it came time to being recruited, signing with Oklahoma wasn't as easy as I thought it would be. My daddy was leaning to Oklahoma State. Notre Dame wanted me, too. But I could never get that picture of Lucious on television out of my head, and my heart had always been with OU.

My first months in Norman were pretty rough and I actually quit twice, as most people know. Like most freshmen, it is a time where the rubber meets the road. Most freshmen think they should be starting, but looking back, I know now that there was no way I was prepared to go lead that offense at that time.

As a freshman, you always buy into the hype of how good you are, but you don't understand how to practice. You don't understand there are people ahead of you who have already paid the price to be playing. You don't understand delayed gratification. Once you hit a little adversity, you say, "Well, this is not my cup of tea," and you do the easy thing—you quit.

The second time, I headed home and my father knew it was time to nip this thing in the bud. He told me, "You are a man now and you have to make your own decision, but let me tell you this: if it were easy, everybody would be doing it."

I was really ripe to hear something like that. It was exactly what I needed.

Then coach Switzer called me.

He said, "Come back and let's talk about it and, if you still want to leave after that, I will let you go."

When I got back to Norman, he told me, "I am going to redshirt you next year. You will be a backup the following year and then you will start for two years."

For some reason, I didn't think he was lying to me and I decided to stick around. The one thing about Barry Switzer—some people may not like him—but I've always known him to look me straight in the eye and shoot straight with me.

I learned some hard lessons that year, especially that some things in life are worth waiting for. I had to work harder each day without the recognition. I had to trust both people and the process.

In learning to run the wishbone offense, I really have to give Jack Mildren a lot of credit. When I was struggling with it all, I could go look at film of Thomas Lott, our starting quarterback. I watched his mechanics and learned from him. His mechanics were awesome, almost perfect. But Jack started the wishbone at Oklahoma and there was nobody for him to go watch on film.

I felt like I had the tools to run and throw and be a good option quarterback, but you have to learn all the small things that go into running the wishbone. It is taking that first step in the wishbone. You take that step, about a 45-degree step back toward the fullback, and you have to get the proper extension. In a two-hour practice, we worked on that one motion for probably about 40 minutes.

If you got good enough depth on that first step, then you focus on making all of your reads. In three seconds, you had two or three different reads to make and, if you made them the right way, the wishbone was fun to watch. But it had to become instinctive. I compare it to a kid struggling in math. Finally, he gets it and the light comes on and he goes from a C to an A.

I became the starter in 1979 when Thomas was gone, and now the job was mine. What coach Switzer had told me was exactly the way it worked out, but he didn't tell me there would be struggles once I became the starter.

Against Tulsa, I seemed to hit my stride and we played pretty well [49–13 win], but the Texas game was the worst game of my life. I fumbled four times and threw three interceptions. We lost [16–7].

Winning seven straight and winning the Big Eight title and then beating Florida State in the Orange Bowl was a highlight for me.

Going into my senior year, there was no rookie quarterback to break in, and we were convinced that we had a chance to win it all that year. But after four games, we were 2–2. We lost to Stanford and to Texas again. At Oklahoma, a 2–2 record is a travesty. It was a tough time for me. It is true that when you win, the head coach and the quarterback get more than their share of glory, and when you lose, they get more than their share of the boos.

But in the end, we won eight straight games and beat Florida State again in the Orange Bowl and all that adversity was forgotten.

Coach Switzer and I are friends to this day. He taught me a lot, like my father and my high school coach.

I will tell you that I cannot imagine anyone better than Barry Switzer at giving those pregame speeches. He would stand there and talk about having a patent on winning at the University of Oklahoma. He would recite statistics, data, circumstances, and analogies. He used everything to fire you up.

We expected to win at Oklahoma, and that was the bottom line. In the five years I was at OU, we never entered a game thinking we would lose. We lost some, but we never expected to. Once you created that feeling, Sooner Magic usually prevailed. That had a lot to do with Barry Switzer, that coaching staff, recruiting, the tradition, and the pride.

That's what I found from my time at the University of Oklahoma. The tradition was intact when I went there, and that air of expectancy followed me into politics and into business. I expected to succeed.

Another thing it taught me was this: because you lose doesn't make you a loser and because you fail doesn't make you a failure.

In the end, I will be forever linked to the University of Oklahoma and that tradition. But I never got caught up in the beating of my chest and patting myself on the back about it. I didn't need anybody else to do it for me, either. I have never worn my letter jacket from Oklahoma. When you do that, you say, "Hey, look at me, I am a jock at OU."

The big reward to me is to have done it. That's where the gratitude is: To have done it. To have lived it. That is something they can never take away from you.

I do have one regret from my time at Oklahoma. Port Robertson, the old hard-nosed wrestling coach, was the guy who kept us on the straight-and-narrow. Your mission in life at OU was not to get into the cross hairs of Port. Anyway, he literally begged me to major in business. I didn't: I majored in journalism. I would change that if I could, but not much else.

I don't know what's next for me. I cannot say that I wouldn't ever get involved in elective office again. My athletic background has taught me to "never to say never," but it's certainly not on my "top five things to do in life before I die" list. I am enjoying life away from office right now. I am enjoying my kids right now.

I know this: if my life ended tomorrow, I would not have much to groan about.

J. C. Watts led the Sooners to a 22–3 record as a starter. He completed 96 of 213 passes for 2,081 yards in his career. He passed for nine touchdowns and was intercepted 19 times. He had five 100-yard rushing games and finished with 1,520 rushing yards. He had 18 rushing touchdowns in 1980. He was named MVP of the 1980 and 1981 Orange Bowls. In the latter, he rallied the Sooners from a 17–10 deficit in the final minutes to win 18–17. He played in the Canadian Football League 1981–1986 and was named MVP of the Grey Cup. Watts served the state of Oklahoma 1994–2002 in the House of Representatives of the U.S. Congress.

Terry Crouch |Guard | 1979–1981

I never dreamed of being a football player. I was too big to play pee-wee football and when I finally got the chance to play in the sixth grade, I didn't know if I could play or not. But they put me at defensive tackle and I do know it was fun. I grew up in a predominately black neighborhood of Dallas, and when I transferred to middle school, I met a man named coach Smith. He was the meanest man I ever met. A retired Marine, he put us through holy hell.

"How bad do you want to be out here?" he would scream at us every day.

Not too bad, I thought. But he taught us how to win, and when I was in the ninth grade, we played for the city championship. By the time I was in 10th grade at Skyline High School, they wanted to put me on the varsity, but my mom said no.

"They are too big," she said. "You'll get hurt."

Mom was always worried about me. (By the way, I want to dedicate this chapter to my mother. Without her, I wouldn't have accomplished anything in life.) But when I did get to the varsity, I made all-city my junior year even though I was double- and triple-teamed a lot. I got beat up in one game—I hurt my knee, ankle, and back. I really took a beating at times.

I learned I had to surprise people by jumping the center on the way to the quarterback. I was very, very quick for my size. I remember in one game, Steve Rhodes played for Spruce and he was a senior when I was a junior. It was fourth-and-goal and they gave the ball to him and they ran it right at me.

Today, if you ask Steve to pull up his pants leg, you'll notice there is a big mark on his shin. That mark is from my helmet on that play. I stopped him cold.

Once he got to Oklahoma, coach [Jerry] Pettibone asked him if there were any good high school players down in Dallas.

He said, "Terry Crouch at Skyline."

So coach Pettibone recruited me the next year, but our coaches told him I had an attitude. Coach Pettibone said, "No, he doesn't. You just don't know how to coach him."

He was right. I never had a bad attitude. We just didn't get very good coaching in high school. I was sick of the recruiting process, but when coach Switzer, coach Pettibone, Lucious Selmon, and coach Duncan showed up at my house one day, coach Switzer said, "I came here to get you."

I thought, "This is one of the winningest football coaches right here in my house."

"Come visit Oklahoma," he told me. "You will like it and you will make All-American someday."

I said, "Coach, you been drinking?"

At a banquet I attended, Greg Pruitt was there and he told me, "You can go somewhere else and watch us win, or you can come win with us."

I came to find out later that people at Oklahoma were that good, not arrogant. When I visited, everybody was cool and calm and laughing and joking with each other. I could tell they all liked each other. It wasn't like that at all at the other schools. Houston, Baylor, and SMU wanted me, but when coach Pettibone asked me what I was going to do, I just said, "Coach, I am coming to OU."

They had no idea because I was always so quiet. The confidence is what sold me. Everyone at OU was so confident, and I could sense that. I also figured if I wanted to be the best I could be, I had to go to the best school I could. I thought OU was the best football program in the country and if I didn't make it there, I could always go somewhere else later.

I was 6'2" and about 250 pounds. When I first got to Oklahoma I played nose guard. Another freshman, Richard Turner, was at the position, too.

The first time I practiced against the wishbone, I blinked and they were gone. Elvis Peacock was nice to watch, but I only saw him from behind. I know I couldn't tackle him. Lucious Selmon came to me one day and said, "Richard has been coached more in high school and we have to move one of you to offense."

So guess who it was who got moved? I walked across the south end zone to join the offense.

Coach [Gene] Hochevar was coaching the offensive line, and he looked at me and said, "You are a smart little freshman, aren't you? Well, you are mine now!"

I had the furthest to go of anybody. I really did. I had switched positions. I had to learn a new stance. Everything was against me. I played a little offensive tackle in high school, but I could have cared less about it back then. And now I was a guard in college. As I learned the position, I just took the attitude that "I am going to beat you before you beat me." I figured I would get in the first punch.

My biggest adjustment was practicing on Sunday. I had never done that before. That first Sunday, I thought, "Man, this is crazy." The second Sunday, they must have noticed because coach Switzer said, "Go home and come back Tuesday morning."

That was the best thing he ever did for me.

I went home and I thought long and hard about it. I just thought, "This is part of the deal and I have to work my way through it." I came back to Norman and I was homesick for a month or so, but I was fine after that. When you look at the depth chart and you are number eight, that's a real blow to your ego. I knew there was always somebody better, and during my freshman year, I learned and accepted that.

When the bus pulls off with the varsity on Friday, you are sitting in your dorm room and you think about leaving. But the thing that kept me at Oklahoma was that I refused to be beat. I thought I could become a starter someday and I made that my primary goal.

Coach Hochevar was about 5'9" and 170 pounds soaking wet, but he was one of the meanest coaches. One day there was a fight between two guys who weighed about 300, and coach Hochevar jumped in there and grabbed a facemask and treated this guy like a rag doll.

After that, I said, "Whatever you say. I am cool."

That was my first look at real intensity. He demanded respect and you gave it to him, but what I learned from him was that the offensive line makes the team. He always said, "If you get your ass beat, I am going to beat your ass!" And I came to believe him.

When we practiced on offense, I called Thomas [Lott] "Hitler." He ran the practice. If the play didn't run right, he stopped it and ran it again. You ran the play until Thomas was happy with it.

On one play, I didn't run far enough and Kenny King came up to me and said, "Look, you run the play with us . . . even if it goes 40 yards." You had to be quick with Kenny behind you. He would run right up your back.

What impressed me most during this time was the other players actually cared about the freshmen. There was a legacy there about that. Coach Switzer would always say, "This is not my team. It's your team."

In a way, he was right.

One day in practice, I knew I had arrived when I hit David Hudgens. I knocked him up into the air and he said, "Freshman! You did good that play."

That was the beginning for me. Practicing against such great players on defense made you so much better. I bet you that out of three years

Terry Crouch, here preparing to block a North Carolina player in 1980, made the successful switch from defensive to offensive line, becoming an All-American guard.
Photo courtesy of OU Athletics Media Relations.

chasing George Cumby, I probably blocked him only twice. I remember blocking Daryl Hunt the first time. Wow, what a thrill. [Nose guard] Reggie Kinlaw was like a cobra. He would hit you and get off of you.

As far as blocking, I learned that the wishbone was all about angles. You knew where the ball was going, so you had to figure out the best angle to block it on every play. I learned the steps and the rhythm to it.

I had never really lifted weights the right way before Oklahoma. In high school, we had those Universal weights, and one day at OU I walked in and started using the Universal weights that other sports had used.

"What are you doing over there?" coach Switzer asked. "Get your butt over there with everybody else!"

I put about 135 pounds on the free weights and couldn't lift it. Guys were making fun of me. That was so embarrassing. That's why I became so strong later on, because I was embarrassed the first time I ever did free weights. While other guys were out on Friday nights, I was in the weight room. I knew I was quick and fast, but I needed to get stronger.

In the summers, I would be out picking up this 1969 Camaro at our house to stay in shape. I would put my little sister in the driver's seat and would tell her when to turn the wheel. I would push that car up and down the field. And I would beat on the side of the house with my fists to get my hands ready for the season.

One day, my dad said, "What are you doing?"

I said, "Getting ready for the season."

"Well, don't tell your mom you are doing this."

I didn't. Mom always worried about me getting hurt.

That second year, coach Duncan and coach Switzer got into an argument about whether to redshirt me. I really didn't have a problem with it. Coach Switzer just said, "You are redshirting." So I did.

During that year, Reggie Kinlaw and Daryl Hunt got tired of me hitting them in practice. Coach would say, "What's the problem, Reggie?"

And he would answer, "Goddamn it, I am tired of him blocking me."

So they took me off the scout team, but practice was boring for me. I watched and learned the wishbone, but it was tough to re-enact the intensity during practice.

In 1979, coach [Merv] Johnson came over from Notre Dame to coach our offensive line. He had those Notre Dame colors on and he was all "rah-rah," but we were just the opposite. We lolly-gagged through practice, but come game time, we were mean and ready to play.

The pressure was on me that year and I knew I had to produce. Early on, I kept jumping offside because I was so anxious. I was busting assignments. I would think, adjust, then play, and all those things I learned in practice had to be done at full-speed in the game. It took me about six games to adjust.

I remember in the Kansas game I kept jumping offside. Some of us had a problem with coach Johnson at that time because he had us thinking too much. In the wishbone, you have to react to what you see and not be out there thinking. You don't have time to think. I think [guard] Don Key talked to coach Switzer, who said, "If I tell him to back off of you, will you play better?"

We all agreed we would. He said, "If you don't get it done, I will go find two junior-college guards who will get it done."

Coach Johnson backed off of us, and life became fun by the end of the season. I remember Billy Sims having 255 yards against Missouri. Now that was fun.

The guy I became very close to was the left tackle beside me, Louis Oubre. We were roommates for two years and we had a special bond. That whole offensive line was like one big family. I have never found a cohesiveness anywhere else in life like what we had. Louis one day just looked at me and said, "Let's be roommates," so we did.

He was funny, boy, was he funny. And he hated to get up in the morning. I had to get him up for class. One day when he wouldn't get up, I called Port Robertson on him. Port was the guy who handled study hall and made sure we worked hard studying. Port got him on the phone and when Louis got off the phone, he said, "I want to hit you so bad."

We had as much fun on the field, too. At times we would get to the line of scrimmage during a game and Louis would look at the defensive lineman and say, "We are going to run the ball right here."

I would say, "What are you telling him the play for? Be quiet!"

Then the play would go to the other side and that lineman would be lost. Or Louis would come up to the line and I would ask him, "Louis, what are you going to do to him?"

He would answer, "I am going to take out his kneecap."

I would say, "OK."

Then neither one of us would touch him because I was pulling and Louis had to block somebody else and that lineman would be all confused. Other times we would get to the line of scrimmage and we would be arguing. We talked right up to the snap.

Louis would tell me, "Big T, if we are talking when we get to the line of scrimmage, those fools will be paying attention to us and thinking." He knew that thinking was not an option when you are playing against the wishbone. You have to react to it.

But I guess I was mean on the field. Louis would say, "Off the field you are the calmest, nicest guy. But on the field you are pure crazy."

I didn't think like an offensive lineman. I was in scraps on the field all the time. My objective was to intimidate you, scare you, or hurt you. I knew if the guards didn't do it well, the wishbone wouldn't go.

The 1980 season was the most fun I had. We lost two games that year, and the first was to John Elway and Stanford in Norman. I never saw a guy like John Elway before. He would run one way and throw it across the field 50 yards for a touchdown. And he was laughing as he did it. And we lost to Texas [20–13].

We played North Carolina later that year, and they had the great Lawrence Taylor. Early in the game, he would be on the backside of a sweep and come around and make the tackle behind the line of scrimmage. We figured it out, though. Coach Johnson said, "Just turn out to block him." So we started doing that, and Lawrence soon got really pissed off. We won 41–7.

At Nebraska we were behind with about two minutes left, and I made a block on the cornerback with Buster Rhymes behind me as we won the game. After the game, Buster said, "How fast are you? I run a 4.2 [40] and I had to run to keep up with you."

My senior year wasn't much fun because there was a lot of stress. I was a captain, but we had two quarterbacks, Kelly Phelps and Darrell Shepard, playing, and it wasn't working. We always had to calm Darrell down while Kelly was more laid back. The offense was struggling, too. I had been running "31 lead" for four years and I had never run into the quarterback before, and now I was running into Kelly Phelps. Each game, I was worried about running into our quarterback on what is supposed to be one of our bread-and-butter plays. I ran into him during the Southern Cal game [a 28–24 loss] and he fumbled.

The timing on the wishbone was way off and we were divided because of that. When Thomas [Lott] was there, everything was fast and quick. When J. C. [Watts] was there, it was fast and quick. Now we were slow.

Barry called me into the office one day and asked, "What's the problem?"

In my opinion, we just had too many different mentalities on that team. We had guys who didn't follow orders and new guys who wanted to change things.

One day, Kansas State had us down 21–0, and coach Switzer said, "We are going to run behind you the rest of the day."

We did and we won 28–21.

Never beating Texas is my biggest regret. It's an empty feeling. After that final loss to them [34–14], the Texas defensive line coach ran me down on the field and told me, "I just want to shake your hand. I've never seen an offensive lineman beat up my defensive linemen like that."

We finished 7–4–1, and it was tough on all of us. We lost games we should have won, but that's the way it goes sometimes. After the season coach Switzer called me in and asked, "How do you feel about the Hula Bowl?"

I said, "I don't know."

He pulled out a letter saying that I was to head to the game. Then he said, "Remember when I recruited you and I told you that you would make All-American someday? Well, I want to read something to you . . ."

It was the Kodak All-American team, and my name was on the list.

"Now do you believe me?" coach Switzer asked. "Now do you have faith in me?"

I was an All-American!

I thought back to my freshman year when Darrol Ray told us that "the guy you least expect in your class will make All-American." I was the one in my class to make it. My buddy Louis had made it the year before, so now we both did it.

My time at OU was so much fun. Pro football was no fun. When I entered college, I didn't have that much confidence because I didn't have good coaching in high school. Sometimes even today I wonder, "How the hell did I do that?"

I have to smile at the whole experience. I still get goose bumps when I think about my days at OU. It was very special . . . it really was.

Tradition—that's the magic word. OU won because the players understood what it meant to be a Sooner. We had the best athletes and the best coaches. And we had the nicest people you would ever meet in your life. And it's not just about football. I met people such as my good friend Jeri Hente whom I met in English class. Jeri taught me how to study, and we just became good friends.

Norman was such a small town, too, that you got to know a lot of people. One time I was driving down one street and the cops yelled out over their loudspeaker on a police car, "Terry! Slow down!"

Can you imagine that? The cops recognized me and reminded me I was going too fast in a small town. That would never happen in a big city like Dallas.

I attended an autograph session recently, and this Sooners fan pulled a magazine out of a plastic bag and he had all of the offensive players' signatures of our team but mine. He saved that all these years to get my autograph.

After I signed it, he said, "Now I can preserve it."

It was 25 years ago, but it all remains very special to me. I was just an offensive lineman, but I played for OU. That is something they never can take away. It always tickled me to meet guys who played before me. I may not have known them, but I would say, "I am proud of what you created."

And I knew I now was a part of it.

I remember one day seeing Bud Wilkinson, who came out to watch practice, and coach Switzer talking together. I think about that now and wish I had a picture of it. Better yet, I wish I had a picture with me standing with them.

There is nothing better than being a Sooner!

Terry Crouch was named an All-American in 1980 by The Sporting News and a consensus All-American in 1981. He also was a team captain in 1981. He was named All–Big Eight in 1980 and 1981. He was drafted in the fifth round by the Baltimore Colts.

Jackie Shipp | Linebacker | 1980–1983

I lived a rock's throw from Oklahoma State's stadium while growing up in Stillwater, Oklahoma, and I went to most of OSU's games from the time I was nine years old through my high school days. Dad taught class at OSU and he was a really good baseball player in his day. He also coached some high school football, so he knew the ins and outs of recruiting when it came time for me to decide on a college.

Growing up, I was not one of those guys who had a favorite team. I was a fan of whoever won the Super Bowl that year, while all my friends were Dallas Cowboys fans. I couldn't tell you I was a big Oklahoma State fan, either, but I could tell you all of those players' names. I knew all the Big Eight players at that time and I remember seeing Joe Washington do some outstanding things during one OU-OSU game in Stillwater. But I never saw an OU game in Norman until I was a senior in high school.

I was a skinny kid, probably only about 5'10" and 155 pounds in the ninth grade. But by the time I was a sophomore, I started to grow some and I played a lot for the Stillwater High Pioneers. I was a safety, and then they moved me to linebacker. We were state runners-up that year. As a junior, I also played some as running back, and then as a senior I played some tight end. I always knew that my position for the future was linebacker.

The first letter I ever got from a college was a questionnaire from Tulsa. Right then, I said, "Wow, I am going to Tulsa!"

When I was a sophomore, [OU assistant] Larry Lacewell came to one of our practices to watch some seniors and he asked about me, thinking I was a senior. It was then I knew that I may have a future in college football.

When it came time to be recruited, I started to think that I wanted to play on the West Coast, and my choices came down to UCLA and Oklahoma even though I also visited Nebraska, USC, and of course, Oklahoma State. I ruled out OSU though because I didn't want to stay right at home.

When coaches came to recruit me, I didn't say much. I remember sitting on a bean bag in the den while my mother and father did all the talking. If they asked a question, I would answer it, but other than that, all I did was listen.

What I remember is that coach Switzer was the most-relaxed coach ever to visit my house. He had a different aura about him. Recruiting wasn't a business trip to him, it was like visiting family. Some coaches sat in my den with a suit and tie. Coach Switzer took off his shoes and moved around the house like he had been there a thousand times. You couldn't help but like his personality.

When he left, I told Mom and Dad, "I didn't know you already knew coach Switzer."

They didn't, but it just seemed that way.

And I was a country boy at heart, so I was not ready to live in L.A. at that time. Coach Switzer made me see that Oklahoma was a great fit for me, and my parents would get to see me play every Saturday, so the choice was easy in the end.

Once I made my decision, a lot of people in Stillwater were upset with me and my family. I signed that morning at home and when I went to school, I had to go to the lady to get a pass because I was late. She made a nasty remark about me not going to Oklahoma State. Then when I took my mother's laundry to the cleaners, the lady there made a remark to me. I heard it all, especially, "You will never play at Oklahoma."

When I got to Norman and got out on the football field, I realized there were 100 Jackie Shipps out there. Those big dreams you dream? Sometimes they come with a big price, and I realized it was time to work a lot harder than I worked at Stillwater High. So much is expected of you and expected of this program, it naturally makes you more competitive.

I'll never forget our first inside drill during practice. You know on those ESPN shows when they have players miked and you hear all that grunting and groaning? I always thought that was fake.

When we ran that drill in practice, we ran it downhill off the crown of our field. I never realized how fast the game was until our offense was coming at me that day. Then I heard all that moaning and groaning and the pads clacking together.

I thought, "Damn, this is what it's like!"

Coach [Warren] Harper looked at me and another linebacker that came in with me, Thomas Benson, and said, "Are you all ready?"

I think Thomas and I both made some plays in that drill, purely from adrenaline, but the offense was coming downhill at us and it was so much faster than anything I was used to. It opened our eyes about college football in a big way.

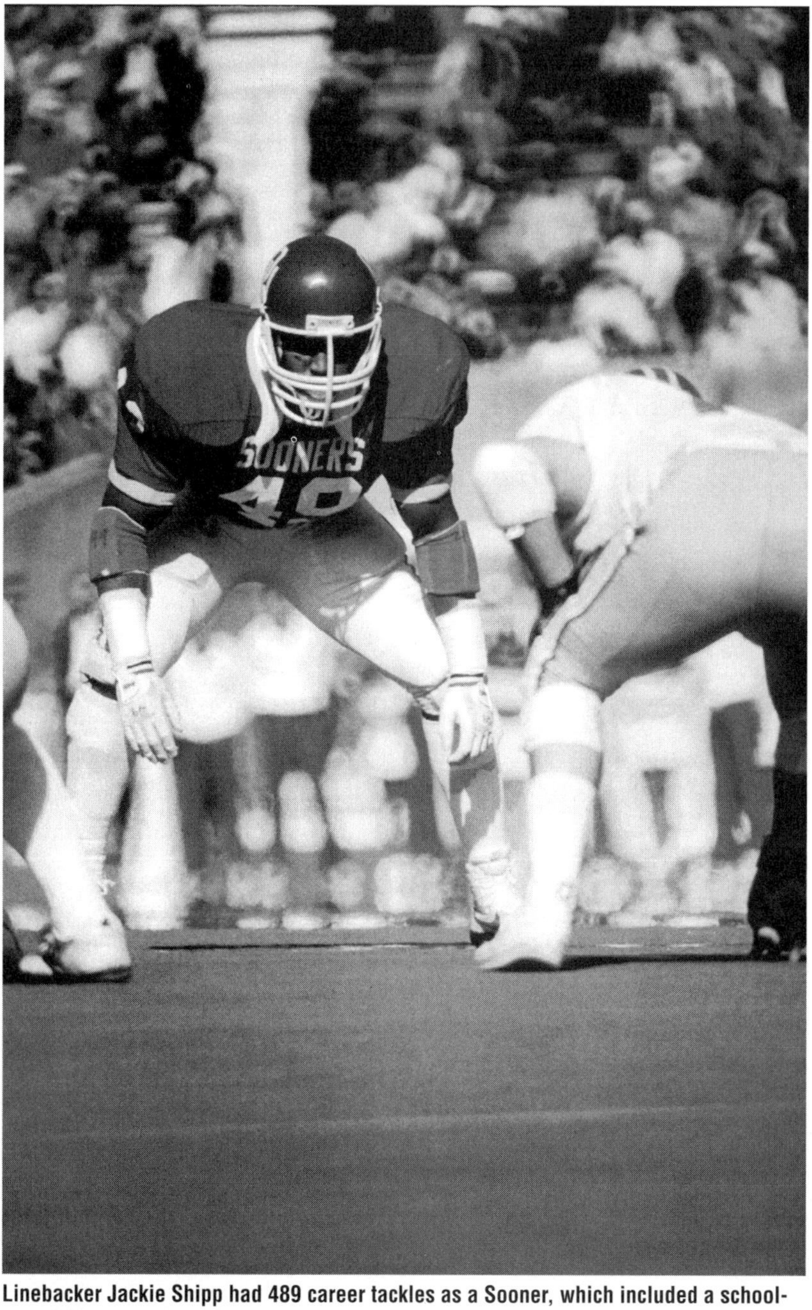

Linebacker Jackie Shipp had 489 career tackles as a Sooner, which included a school-record 23 tackles in a single game. *Photo courtesy of John Williamson.*

I played that year on special teams and when the games got out of hand. I remember playing against North Carolina and putting a hit on "Famous" Amos Lawrence that knocked him out of the game. That was a cocky team. I remember them coming to Norman and talking smack to us before the game. I can still hear [OU tackle] Louis Oubre in that high-pitched voice, saying, "Can you believe this shit? They are talking smack to us?"

We won easily [41–7] that day.

Later that season at Nebraska, I showed what being a freshman is like. Nebraska had the ball near midfield, and the coach sent the defensive call in with me. As I ran in from the sideline, I looked up and saw that big side of the Nebraska stadium. I was just looking at it in awe and when I got to the huddle I forgot the call.

Somebody in the huddle muttered, "Damn freshman."

The next season I broke my hand in camp, so I couldn't start the Wyoming game to open the season. After the game, I had played well enough to be nominated for Big Eight Defensive Player of the Week. Then we lost to USC and tied Iowa State.

I had always asked Terry Crouch about this feeling you are supposed to get when you walk down the ramp before a Texas game. I had heard so much about it. I asked, "Terry, what is this shit about the feeling you get when you walk down that ramp? That's all I have been hearing about."

Terry giggled at me and just said, "You'll see. You'll see."

So we walked down the ramp, I saw all of those fans in the Cotton Bowl and we ran the length of the field to go down and stretch before the game. I bent down to touch my toes and I started throwing up right there. I had puke all over my facemask, and Terry looked over at me and asked, "Now you understand?"

We lost to Texas that day and we were 1–2–1, and it was a funny feeling. It wasn't like Oklahoma.

I set the [single-game] school record for tackles [23] against Missouri that year, and after the game, I was walking in a hallway and I remember coach Switzer shaking my hand. "You are a heck of a football player," he told me.

That is one thing I'll never forget.

The funny thing was, we had a team doctor, Dr. O' Donahue, and all the older guys had a superstition they passed on about him. They would say, "Whatever you do, don't let him touch you before a game. Every guy he has touched before a game has blown out a knee."

So before that Missouri game, I was sitting there when Dr. O'Donahue walked by and touched my knee and said, "Have a good game."

And that is the day I set the tackle record.

As a junior, the coaches moved me from weakside linebacker to strongside. People always ask me why my tackle production dropped off from year to year, but that is one reason—and we started to play more passing teams.

We had some tough losses in my years. USC beat us 12–0 and we hadn't been shut out in [16] years. Then we got shut out again by Missouri during my junior year. We had made the switch to the I-formation for Marcus Dupree and it wasn't working as well. We probably weren't as close as a lot of Oklahoma teams in the past were. But that happens when you are not winning championships.

It wasn't that we didn't have talent, but it just never came together for us in those years enough to win championships.

And we did have a lot of fun.

One time I am walking back to the dorm one night and it was very dark. All of a sudden, a guy in a trench coat and a mask jumps out from nowhere and yells, "Jackie Shipp! You've been messing with my girlfriend and now you are going to die!"

I throw my hands up in the air and say, "Oh Jesus!"

I thought that was it for me and then all of a sudden the guy throws his mask off and it's Spencer Tillman. We still laugh about that one.

You want to know about coach Switzer and his ability to motivate? The week before we played Oklahoma State in 1982, they had a running back who was leading the nation in rushing, Earnest Anderson. That's all coach Switzer talked about with the media.

"Oh, I wish we had him on our team," he would say. "He is such a great back. I wish we had him. I don't know how we're going to stop him."

We heard this every day that week and it was starting to irritate everybody. Before the game, everybody started to leave the locker room when coach Switzer called us back in.

He said, "Now you remember that bullshit I have been saying about Anderson? To hell with that! I didn't even recruit the little SOB. Now go out and stop him!"

On the first play of the game, he caught a screen pass, and out of 11 of our guys on defense, nine of us ended up on top of Anderson.

That's how well coach Switzer could motivate you.

As you may know, I now coach at Oklahoma on Bob Stoops' staff and I am in position to sell this university to recruits. Oklahoma coaches such as coach Harper were honest with me when I was being recruited, and that's how I approach it. I just tell a recruit how this university can help him obtain a degree, grow into a man, and help him once he has finished his career and has that degree.

As you get older, you realize how important this university is to us who have played here. You are talking about years of great tradition. I don't know what it is, but there is something special about this place. It isn't so much the games and the plays, it is the people and the players. For example, after we played Washington State in the Rose Bowl a few years ago, coach Switzer was in our hotel lobby and he just sat down to visit with our players. From about 11:00 that night until 2:00 the next morning, he sat there and talked to them, and I could tell how much he missed it. I realized how much players had meant to him.

Being at Oklahoma is just like having another family.

Would I do it all over again? No doubt about it—I love Oklahoma.

Jackie Shipp is second in OU history in total tackles with 489 (Daryl Hunt is number one with 530). Shipp holds single-game (23 tackles) and single-season (189 tackles in 1981) school records for tackles. He was named All–Big Eight in 1982 and 1983. Shipp was a first-round choice of the Miami Dolphins and played eight seasons in the NFL.

Rick Bryan | Defensive Lineman | 1980–1983

As a young boy, I always wondered what it would be like to play football for the Oklahoma Sooners.

Growing up with two brothers, sports was always a big part of our lives. We grew up in Coweta, Oklahoma, a farming community of about

5,000 people about 25 miles southeast of Tulsa. Our farm wasn't that big, about 200 acres which was large enough for 30 head of cattle.

When we—Mitch was one year older, Steve two years younger than me—weren't working, we would be in the yard playing football or down at the barn playing basketball. No matter what we played, it always ended the same way—in a fight. None of us liked to lose.

My dad, Jack Bryan, was a workaholic. In addition to farming, he drove a truck for Hale Halsell, a food company based in Tulsa. Many days I would watch him farm all day and then drive a truck all night just to make sure we had what we needed as a family. He expected us to pull our weight and help take care of the farm. Some days, I remember driving a tractor from dawn to dusk. Dad taught us how to work hard and how never to quit until the job was done. Later in life, I realized how important his teachings were.

Playing sports in school came easily for me. I started playing football in the fourth grade and loved it. I was way ahead of the other kids in my class because of all the experience I had playing with my brothers. Heading into seventh grade, I hit a growth spurt and grew about six inches, but then I injured my back. For the next two and a half years, I couldn't play, but I did a lot of watching and realized how much the game of football meant to me.

During that time, Barry Switzer became head coach of Oklahoma and they had changed their offense to the wishbone. I remember on Saturdays that my eyes were locked onto the TV watching the Sooners play. I was a huge fan, watching names like Billy Sims, Daryl Hunt, and George Cumby.

When they would win a big game against Nebraska or Texas, everything seemed great in my world. But when they lost, I would have tears in my eyes. No doubt about it, the Sooners were my team, and their players were my idols.

In my sophomore year in high school, my parents decided to let me go out for football since my back had finally healed. I was almost 6'5" and I weighed about 190 pounds, but I was a raw-boned kid. And I was scared to death. I hadn't played in three years and now I was playing against guys two or three years older than me.

The one thing that gave me confidence was that my brother Mitch was a junior and he was starting at tight end and defensive end. I worked hard in practice and became a starter at offensive tackle and defensive end, but I guess it wasn't that hard when you had only 28 players on your entire football team. Mitch and I were bookend defensive ends. Teams didn't do too much running outside on us that season. I grew up a lot that year and gained so much confidence in myself. But we went 4–6 because we couldn't score many points.

We got a new coach the next season. Coach Tom Beller's system called for a two-tight end set on offense and I moved from offensive tackle to tight end, but Mitch and I were still bookends on our 5–2 defense. And now we were both tight ends, too. By that time, we were both about 210 pounds. Mitch was 6'3".

I loved playing tight end. I still blocked a lot, but now I got to catch the football. And we had a good quarterback and we were throwing the ball a lot. Colleges were noticing Mitch, and I was being seen as well, although I was a year younger. I have to say that football was very fun during that time. Playing with my brother was like playing in the backyard again. He caught more passes than I did that season, but I had more tackles. We finished 6–4 and missed the state playoffs on a coin flip.

Oklahoma State, coached by Jim Stanley at the time, pretty much told Mitch they would offer him a scholarship. During his recruiting process, I was always in the background, listening and learning. I thought if Mitch went to Oklahoma State, I would be there the following year, too.

OU never really entered into my thinking because I figured I would never be good enough to play for the great Oklahoma Sooners. I knew only the elite got to play at OU and I knew I wasn't in that category.

The 1978 Oklahoma team was the greatest OU team I ever saw, but Billy Sims' fumble near the goal line resulted in a loss at Nebraska that year.

But just like Billy's fumble, things happen. Stanley got fired at Oklahoma State and Jimmy Johnson was hired. For some reason, Mitch's scholarship never materialized. I entered my senior season with bad feelings toward Oklahoma State because of what they had done to

Defensive lineman Rick Bryan, a two-time All-American, chases down Oklahoma State's quarterback in 1983. *Photo courtesy of OU Athletics Media Relations.*

Mitch, but I also felt that they were still my best chance to play Division I football.

Heading into that year, I was receiving letters from a lot of colleges. I was up to 235 pounds. That year, coach Beller hired a defensive coordinator, Ben Wasson, who moved me to middle linebacker. That way, he figured offenses couldn't run away from me. By now, my brother Steve was a sophomore and once again, Bryan brothers were at tight end and at linebacker, too.

I loved playing linebacker. I tried to make every tackle, and I played sideline-to-sideline. We went 8–2 that season, but again missed the state playoffs. I ended up making all-state at tight end.

As soon as my senior season finished, the recruiting battles heated up. Nebraska's Tom Osborne was the first head coach I met. I was so impressed with that man. His gentle sincerity really won me over. But Nebraska, just like OU, intimidated me, and Nebraska was farther from home.

Merv Johnson was the first coach from Oklahoma whom I met. Like coach Osborne, he had a sincere and gentle way about him. I could tell that he was a very classy man. He told me that they wanted me at tight end and that I would be backing up Forrest Valora, a tight end who would be named All–Big Eight in 1980.

Suddenly, my dreams were coming true: OU wanted me! Any normal kid would have signed right then and there, but not me. I still never thought I would be good enough to play for OU. I figured Oklahoma State was where I belonged. They weren't as good, and if I could play Division I football, it would be for them.

But then I met coach Switzer. He came out by my home near Tater Hill, a name which coach Switzer fell in love with. Later on, I would become known as "Ricky Bryan from Tater Hill."

I don't know how many times I've been asked where Tater Hill is.

The night coach Switzer and Merv Johnson came to my home was very cold, and Mom and Dad grilled steaks. I didn't eat much that night because I was too nervous. It was one thing to have Barry Switzer in your home, but my dad was a frank-talking man and he always said what was on his mind. I knew it was a matter of time before he said something that would embarrass me.

When we moved to the living room after dinner, Dad had the fireplace blazing and coach Switzer sat down in the recliner next to the fireplace. Nobody could sit in that chair for very long without burning up.

As we talked about football, coach Switzer and coach Johnson knew I was leaning toward Oklahoma State. Coach Switzer asked why I would pick OSU over OU and I ducked my head because I couldn't answer. I mean, how do you tell Barry Switzer that you don't think you're good enough to play for him?

So I just sat there.

So my dad answered for me. He said, "Coach, we have always heard that you have to be black to play for OU."

I don't know whose face got more red, coach Switzer's or mine. Pretty soon sweat balls were running off of his head, as he sat next to that fireplace. Then he jumped up and headed toward the door.

"Coach, I didn't mean to offend you," my dad said.

"No, Jack, you didn't," Coach said, "but this damn fire is about to kill me!"

I still laugh when I think of that. Before they left that night, coach Switzer challenged me. He told me, "Ricky, you can go to OSU and be a great player, but you will never know if you are the best unless you come to OU."

They didn't realize it, but that night they became part of our family. In a couple of months, I signed with OU and became a part of theirs.

When I left home in August of 1980, I felt lost. I was leaving home for the first time and didn't know what was ahead of me. I wasn't even five miles from my house when I became homesick. I didn't want to leave. As I drove toward Norman, I started talking to God and I know He listened to me the entire way there.

When I arrived in Norman, I realized I had reported two days early. I almost got back into my car and headed home. But I knew that if I did, I wouldn't come back. For the next two days, I left my dorm room only to eat. The freshmen dorms were very small, with bunk beds against one wall, a desk against the other, and a closet. That was it. No TV. No telephone. Nothing.

I laid in that bed for the next two days and cried, talked to God, and cried some more. I was scared, I was homesick, and I was lost. After those two days, I think the Lord got tired of listening to me. He finally told me, in my mind, to go out and do the best I could every time I walked onto the field and that He would give me the strength to survive.

So that is what I did.

Brent Burks, an offensive lineman, was my roommate and he showed up the night before two-a-days began. We were as different as peas and carrots. He was big, 6'7" and 275 pounds, and he was kind of prissy. When I say prissy, I mean he was neat, clean, and very organized. I was just the opposite. I was a slob. Worst of all, I dipped Copenhagen.

The worst argument we had that year was when he caught me spitting the juice in his plants. But by the end of the year, I became more like him in the clean-and-neat department and he was dipping Copenhagen and spitting in his own plants. We became very close friends over the next four years.

Freshmen practices were split up with the offense practicing in the morning and the defense in the afternoon. In the afternoon, I tried to go with the linebackers, and they told me I was too slow to be a linebacker, so they sent me to be with the defensive linemen. I wasn't too happy about it, but it turned out to be the best thing that could have happened to me.

Rex Norris was our defensive line coach and our defensive coordinator. He wasn't a big man, but his demeanor was very large. After practice one day, he called me over for a talk. He told me he thought I would make a great defensive end. He said if I switched positions, he would make me a two-time All-American. I thought he was full of crap, but I told him I would do whatever they wanted.

The week before the Colorado game, the third game of the season, defensive end Keith Gary had been injured. Coach Switzer called me to his office. He said they needed more depth on the defensive line and he wanted me to switch to defensive end. I had been sharing time as the second-team tight end and I figured I would be the starter the next season, but I made the switch the next day. I didn't care much for tight end anymore anyway because all the tight end did was block. They didn't do much receiving.

Lucious Selmon, who helped coach Norris coach the defensive line, always had been one of my idols. So whatever Lucious told me, I did.

By halftime of the Colorado game, we were leading 42–0, and coach Norris said I was going to play in the second half. It was the longest half of football I ever played. Colorado scored 42 points on the subs in the second half that day, but we won 82–42. From that game on, I was a defensive lineman and I loved the change.

I backed up Richard Turner for the remainder of the season. He was a senior that season and he ended up All–Big Eight. To a degree, he took me under his wing and taught me a lot about playing the position. Richard also liked to hunt quail and he called me his "pup."

By my sophomore year, Richard was gone and I had earned the starting spot, but I was still a pup and I knew it. Pleasing coach Norris meant more to me than anything else. I never wanted to lose the confidence he showed in me.

When we entered the week of the USC game we were ranked No. 2 and USC was No. 1. That was a beautiful Saturday in the L.A. Coliseum, and the game was on national television. It was the first big game I had ever played in and I was terrified. I was afraid of letting down those who believed in me and my family. Once again, I was asking God to get me through it. USC scored with six seconds left in the game, and we lost 28–24. Even though we lost, I played a great game: it was the first time I received the Big Eight Defensive Player of the Week.

I had a lot of big games that year, but we finished 7–4–1. We also lost to Texas, Missouri, and Nebraska, but went to the Sun Bowl and beat Houston, and I was named Defensive Player of the Game.

My junior year started off very rocky. I had gotten married during the summer to my high school sweetheart and we moved all of our things into an apartment in Norman a couple of weeks before I had to report to camp. When we arrived back to Norman the day before camp started, everything was gone. The thieves even stole the telephone off the wall!

My wife was devastated. Coach Switzer was very sympathetic and he helped us out every way he could legally. I will always appreciate him for all the support he gave us. During those times, I really found out how big that man's heart is. He still intimidated me, but I knew he cared about me not only as a football player but as a person. He became like a member of the family to us.

Marcus Dupree came to Norman that year. We had a solid defense, and now with Marcus' help, our offense would be potent again. Marcus was an incredible athlete. He could do it all. The only thing was that Marcus really didn't want to be there. He was using OU as a stepping-stone to pro football and that was it.

No matter what coach Switzer said to him, he would never push himself hard enough in practice to get in great physical shape. He had a great year, but he still cost us some games because he would get caught from behind during big runs in the second half. Or his hamstrings would tighten up and he would have to come out of the game. The next year he left OU and went to the USFL. I think if he would have stayed and done what the coaches asked of him, he would have had been one of the greatest Sooners in history.

When USC came to Norman that fall, we were both ranked high, and it was supposed to be an offensive showdown. Once again, it would be on national television. Our defense played great that day, but USC scored on a reverse and added a couple of field goals and that was it.

Our offense never got on track. USC won 12–0 and it was the only time we were ever shut out [it was OU's first shutout loss in 16 years]. I wanted to win that game probably more than any other game I ever played in. That's how big that game was to me.

After the game, I remember sitting in the training room totally exhausted when coach Norris came in looking for me. When he told me I played a hell of a game, I just ducked my head. He put his arm around me and said, "Today you showed everybody who the best defensive lineman in the country is."

He knew how much I hated to lose, but I felt good inside just because he was proud of me. He will never know how much that meant to me.

We went on to beat Texas 28–22 that year, but we came up short against Nebraska 28–24, and the Cornhuskers won the Big Eight championship.

When I was voted the Big Eight Defensive Player of the Year, I examined the coaches' ballot and the only name I looked for was Tom Osborne. If he voted for me, the award meant something. He did. I respected him tremendously.

My senior year seemed like a dream. I fell asleep and when I awakened, it was all over. It seemed like nothing went right that season.

Marcus left in the middle of the season, and our offense was struggling to score. Our defense wasn't playing as good as we should have been playing. We lost to Texas 28–16 and on top of all that, I had pulled something in my foot and I could hardly run.

They held me out of the Kansas game and it was the only game I ever missed. We lost to Missouri the next week because we just couldn't score. I struggled with my injured foot the rest of the season, but managed to have a decent year. We ended up losing to Nebraska 28–21 and finished 8–4. It was a very poor year by OU standards.

The three years I started turned out to be the worst years in OU football since coach Switzer became head coach. He was catching a lot of heat and I felt bad for him, but I knew he would turn it around, and he did.

A couple of years later in 1985, the Sooners would win the national championship again, and my brother Steve was a part of it. [Mitch also became a Sooner, lettering in 1982–1983.]

Anyway, OU was back on top where it belonged.

Looking back to my childhood, I always wondered what it would be like to play for OU. In the end, I got my chance and it was so much more than what a little boy from Coweta, Oklahoma, could ever imagine. Playing football with the great teammates I played with was magical, and playing in front of 75,000 people almost every week was unbelievable.

The relationships I had with coaches, players, and fans will be with me the rest of my life. The lessons I learned at OU helped me through 10 years of pro football. More importantly, it helped me with how I deal with my life now.

You always hear about "Sooner Magic." To me, that magic was the relationships I had with coach Norris, coach Johnson, coach North, and coach Switzer. And the most important relationship of all was the one with God. He carried me when I couldn't walk and gave me the courage when I was too afraid to try. Without Him, I never would have made it.

My dad passed away a couple of years ago, and coach Switzer and coach Johnson both called my mom's home that day. After I got off the telephone with them, I went down to the barn and cried. They both will never know how much they meant to my family. I want to thank them for allowing me and my brothers to realize our dreams.

I want to thank them all for letting us be Oklahoma Sooners.

Rick Bryan was an All-American in 1982 and 1983 and was named the Big Eight Defensive Player of the Year in 1982. He was All–Big Eight in 1981, 1982, and 1983, and Academic All–Big Eight in 1981, 1982, and 1983. He finished his career with 365 tackles. He was selected with the ninth pick of the 1984 NFL draft by the Atlanta Falcons, with whom he played 10 seasons.

Spencer Tillman | Running Back | 1983–1986

My memories of first playing ball came in Grace Carry's lot adjacent to our house in Tulsa. She really didn't want all the kids playing in her lot, but one day Mom walked down to her house and asked if the wayward kids of the neighborhood could use her lot to play, and she agreed. Mom was a stately woman, about 6'1", so you didn't say no to her too often.

It was in that lot where I started playing football.

One day when I was nine or 10, I shook a guy named Bobby Pendleton, and that's when it hit me that I could play. When I grew up, I attended Thomas Edison High which was a predominately white school. I felt like a fly in buttermilk, but everybody wanted me on their team and I made friends pretty easily.

I made all-city and all-state and all that stuff, but I want to say right here that numbers, honors, and stats never mattered to me. Never. I remember the relationships, the people. That's how I always measured my experiences. And that's how I will always measure my experience as an Oklahoma Sooner.

When it came time to pick a college, I went to Alabama, Nebraska, UCLA, SMU, Oklahoma, and Texas. I watched football a lot on TV and tradition was very important to me.

I was really close to going to Nebraska because I could tell that academics was the real deal there. But I wanted to major in petroleum land management, and a counselor at Nebraska told me they didn't have that major. It's a fact that I probably would have wound up at Nebraska if they did.

On my visit there, they put on a show one night and there was a problem with the piano being where it was supposed to be. On cue, three of their linemen—one of them was Dave Rimington—picked up that piano and put it on stage. It was probably staged, but they said something like, "See, if you come to Nebraska, that's how'll strong you'll be."

But Oklahoma wanted me, too. Merv Johnson recruited me directly, and then Rex Norris and coach Switzer came later. Barry did his number on me once I got to visit Norman, but he never came to my house. I thought about him what most people in Oklahoma thought about him: that he was bigger than life.

And I signed to play for the Sooners.

Norman was intimidating to me at first like it was for a lot of freshmen. I remember times were tough. Some nights, my roommate, Roy Owens, and I would be looking for loose change in the couch to be able to buy a pizza.

I know I felt I could play at this level, and I signed before Marcus Dupree had signed. People always said I was crazy if I went there while he was going there, too. I looked at it rationally—"Sure, they are going to play this guy, but it's the wishbone," I thought.

I figured everybody in that backfield will get some opportunities.

As a freshman, I decided to redshirt because I was looking at the big picture and I thought it was the right thing to do.

During that season, 1982, the better Marcus did [Dupree rushed for 1,144 yards and 12 touchdowns that season], the more difficulty I had with my decision. I had relinquished that position by choice. I didn't have regrets, but I was faced with discouragement.

But the next season Marcus got hooked up with the wrong people and didn't stay focused. I replaced him in the third game against Tulsa and then had a big game against Kansas State [131 yards on 21 carries]. That season I was chomping at the bit to get more carries because I think I could have had 1,800 yards in the I-formation. But it was a good year [1,047 rushing yards, nine touchdowns].

A lot of fun things happened that season.

I became close with Barry Switzer and his kids, Doug, Greg, and Kathy, and baby-sat them some. Barry knew I was a relationship-type of person, and right as we were ready to take the field against Nebraska he walked up to me. He wrapped that arm around my shoulder and jutted out that jaw as he always did and said, "Spencer, I just want to tell you that I love you."

Now that was right as we came out of the tunnel there and ready to take the field! I knew he meant it, too, and it meant so much to me. And I had a great game, too [134 rushing yards on 16 carries in a 28–21 loss].

Barry always told us one thing, "Nobody remembers what you did. They remember that you were part of something special."

And he was right.

The next game, at Hawaii, I got all those carries [178 yards on 37 carries] but it was a frustrating game for me. They were a better team that we thought they were. They very physical and quick. I remember that whole day I didn't get beyond that second level of the line of scrimmage, but they kept giving me the football.

Hey, we were Oklahoma: we didn't pass much.

Then my frustrations started the following year, 1984. I pulled a hamstring and missed a lot of time, and Lydell [Carr] had a great year [688 yards]. I realized then that there are crucibles in life and that's what happens to us sometimes. It shapes us. It forces us to get stronger and to persevere.

As we opened the 1985 season at Minnesota, I had about 94 yards in the first quarter and then I blew out a hamstring. My injuries and frustrations actually helped me, though. I changed the way I approached life. I changed my major to journalism, and when I got hurt, I started thinking about where my passions lie. I got hired my sophomore year by KTVY, the NBC affiliate in Oklahoma City. I was an intern in every position they had during the summers.

After my hamstring injuries, I came back to play but I didn't do well numbers-wise. I contributed some, but we shared the wealth in those days when it came to carries. It was still tough on me, because I knew what I could do if I were healthy.

Having the type of injury I had, the doctors said it was OK, but I knew I was injured. It turned out the fibers in my muscle were torn. It's not like a broken bone where everybody knows the injury and everybody is cool with it. It's frustrating not to know exactly why it's bothering you, but you know you are injured.

The disappointment was evident in the minds of other people. I could almost tell what people were thinking: "Here's this kid who can hit the home run, but he's always hurt."

It was a burden to have, but like I said, those things shape us for the future.

At that time, I met Rich Leitka, who was a systems analyst for Farmer's Insurance. Rich knew a lot about nutrition and keeping your body healthy. He was great at teaching you how to keep your muscles

Spencer Tillman, shown here diving for a touchdown against SMU in 1985, rushed for 1,047 yards as a redshirt freshman before battling injuries throughout the remainder of his career. *Photo courtesy of Lisa Hall.*

flexible. Rich taught me about nutrition, hydration, resistance training, and rest and recovery. He said if you take only one of those away and don't do it, you would receive a C grade. You take two away and you are flunking.

After that, I never had hamstring problems again.

And I finished strong with a good Orange Bowl [109 yards on seven carries in the 42–8 win over Arkansas], and that helped a great deal toward my NFL future. I later had great performances in the Senior Bowl and Hula Bowl, which didn't hurt, either.

Let me say that I love coach Switzer. He was the most loyal individual in terms of player relations. If you want to go to war with somebody, you want to be in his corner. People don't know him like I know him. I've seen him cry. I've seen him care. I've seen many aspects of his life.

I was working with NBC when Barry lost his job. I went to Norman and interviewed him, and many players spoke publicly to support him: J. C. Watts, Steve Owens, myself, and many others, all trying to prevent what happened.

In the end, he just got a bad deal.

Barry would always throw out little nuggets of information, trying to teach you things. He always tried to make everybody a team player, and those are the type of things that help you in life. That's why I don't remember the statistics really well. They don't matter, do they?

I remember the people, the teammates, and the funny moments.

Guys like Tony Rayburn, a defensive back. He was very talented. After we won the national championship [in 1985], we were having a big celebration at one of the hotels downtown and Lorne Greene of *Bonanza* fame was asked to be there.

I remember going into the bathroom with Tony and, as we waited, Lorne came out of a stall. Tony just stood there and pointed, saying, "Look, Pa . . . Pa . . . Pa's taking a shit."

In that deep *Bonanza*-like voice, Lorne Greene just said, "Pardon me, excuse me . . . " and went over to wash his hands.

Or seeing Raider, Brian Bosworth's dog, sitting up in the stands watching the game. He would be sitting in a seat just like a paying customer. Brian was about Brian. He created the monster and the system fed it. He was painting his hair before we ever heard of Dennis Rodman. But what people don't know about Brian is that he was a sharp guy and a very good student.

We had a Sooners' legends' reunion once, and Brian wept like a baby and apologized to all the great players there. He apologized for all the selfish things he did during his career.

Tony Casillas and I became good friends. He was a big Hispanic kid, fun-loving and strong as a bull. What a great player. He was a two-time All-American and he won the Lombardi Award. Another fun guy to be around was Jeff Tupper. I have so many great memories of my teammates and all the people at Oklahoma.

I remember the moments, too. Over the years, I have tried to dissect reasons of what allowed teams to win championships like we did in 1985. Sometimes, it's an error by someone else. Sometimes, it's your own excellence. I remember the bus ride back to the hotel after beating Penn State in the Orange Bowl. I remember the parade in downtown Oklahoma City and all the confetti in the air.

Would I do it all over again? Absolutely.

I wouldn't want it any other way than the way I had it. I had blips here and there, and the injuries, but I had a decent career. People who have the ultimate success in the strictest sense are the people who never get the depth out of life. You have to struggle. You have to have failure at times. The people I know who have the greatest success have some scars. They have had some failures. That's what makes us deep and strong people in the end.

I still do a great deal for my university. All athletes make the university what it is. All students and graduates make the university what it is. But I know you are not defined by your university's football success. When the Sooners had a resurgence in 2000, my importance as a broadcaster did not increase.

The tradition is what we use as a bridge to get from one point to another. None of it would have happened without the Oklahoma tradition. And that tradition as well as my memories resulting from it will always remain very important to me.

Spencer Tillman led Oklahoma in rushing as a freshman in 1983 and finished his career with eight 100-yard rushing games. He finished his career with 2,425 yards on 456 carries and scored 22 touchdowns. He was a fifth-round draft choice of the Houston Oilers and played nine seasons in the NFL. He currently works as a football analyst for CBS.

Brian Bosworth | Linebacker | 1984–1986

I grew up in Irving, Texas, but I spent a lot of time being shipped off to Oklahoma where my grandparents lived. Mom and Dad worked full-time and they wanted to come home in the summer to a house in one piece, so I spent a lot of time at my grandparents' place. It was a good situation for me. I would help my granddad out on the farm, getting up early and doing farm stuff. I would help with the cows and chase chickens. Let me tell you, their cows produced the best milk you could ever imagine.

Those were happy times. I had a lot of fun with my grandpa. He was a man who did what he wanted. He would drink his beer and smoke his Camels and he lived his life on his terms. He had a handicap. I think one leg was a foot and a half shorter than the other. It was like having a Frankenstein foot, but I never heard that man complain. Every day was a blessing to him. He never had much money, but we would go down to the bar and he would get a beer and he always made sure I had a Coke.

The real thing I learned from him was this: don't let others dictate who you are—just be yourself or whatever you want to be.

My dad, Austin Bosworth, was always tough on me. He was, and still is at times, a headstrong man. He didn't have much flexibility. I thought there had to be something wrong with him. Why was he so tough on me?

Dad had played football in the service as a linebacker and fullback. He was about 220 pounds in his prime and mean as a drill sergeant. He worked me so hard when I was young because I think he wanted me to achieve. That's a big reason I always worked so hard, so I wouldn't disappoint him. We have earned each other's respect over the years and we know where our boundaries are.

He started me playing football in the Pop Warner League, and I loved it from the beginning. I played basketball and soccer, too, but I loved football.

My weekends as a kid were made by whether Oklahoma won or lost on Saturday and what the Cowboys did on Sunday. If they both won, it was a good weekend.

When I first got to MacArthur High, I played quarterback and defensive end as a freshman. Our defensive end position was really a standup outside linebacker. They picked me to go over to the varsity during spring ball following my freshman year. That is a key time in a player's life. I was standing there with the other freshmen and the coaches are saying, "I want you and you and you."

When they picked me, it was like getting picked for an Oscar. I'll never forget that moment.

It was a good memory, but when I got over to the varsity, I thought, "Holy crap, these guys are huge. I've got my work cut out for me."

At first, I was tip-toeing around, trying not to make a mistake. I was taking on blockers, but not making any real plays. During two-a-days that fall, we were practicing long and hard. In those days, there were no rules about practice limits. You practiced as long as the coaches wanted you to, in those old Riddell shoes with no support, with no water breaks, and you couldn't take your helmet off.

We were doing a load-blocking drill one day when you had to take on the fullback and try to stay alive to make the tackle. All of a sudden, the guy in front of me got his foot caught in the dirt and blew a knee out, and I went from second team to first team just like that.

I felt bad for the guy, but I was excited and scared at the same time. The juniors and seniors were relying on this young sophomore who was 5'10" and probably 150 pounds dripping wet. After that guy in front of me got hurt, however, something turned around inside of me. I didn't want to be a liability for the upperclassmen and I didn't want people to think I was given the job.

All of a sudden, I was like a wild animal who hadn't been fed. I threw caution to the wind. I thought, "By God, if I am going to be out there, at least I will make an impact. They will know that No. 89 is out on the field."

I just turned it loose and played footloose and fancy free. I wasn't big, like I said, so I would play a punch-and-move game like a lightweight boxer. Suddenly, I was making plays, and the coaches liked it.

When we played Highland Park, they had these two massive tackles. I walked out there and looked across the line of scrimmage, and this guy was like a mountain. We may have got our butts kicked 26–3 in that game, but they didn't do anything on my side of the field.

When we played Trinity, somebody on our team blocked a field goal at the end of the game and the ball was bouncing right in front of me. I grabbed it and started to run down the sidelines as fast as I could. All of a sudden, I could see a flash on the side of me and I could hear one of my teammates yelling, "Boz, Boz, Boz!"

As I was about to be tackled, I slipped the ball out to him and he scored. That play won the game for us and that was when all the other guys accepted me. You have to do something that you don't think you are capable of and that was the first time for me.

We finished 6–3–1 during my junior year, but we were better than that. The coach ran off some of the black players and I never understood why. For my senior year, they moved me to middle linebacker, and we had a good defensive coordinator, Russell Weisner, who was a Longhorn, but he was like my daddy. I never wanted to make him feel like I didn't give my all for him. He had that way about him. As a team, we had an abysmal year, finishing something like 2–8.

When it came time for recruiting, I committed to SMU right off the bat. I had a self-esteem problem and didn't think I would measure up anywhere else. They were coming off some pretty good years with Eric Dickerson and Craig James and the Pony Express, but I was 18 years old and didn't know how to say no to anybody yet.

Then I started to get some calls asking what size shoes I wore and what kind of car I drove. I wondered, "If they are offering me this stuff, what are they doing for the real blue-chip players?"

I just knew that school was going to get into NCAA trouble, and they did. I visited LSU and had a really good time, but I ate some crawdad heads and got sick. I drank a case of Pepto-Bismol just to get over that recruiting trip. I didn't have a feeling I would fit in there anyway.

Mom and Dad made me visit Baylor, but that felt like a small school to me. I visited Texas A&M and it was a very impressive campus. I respected coach [Jackie] Sherrill, who was the head coach, and I loved it there. The stadium was huge and it felt like home. So then I committed to A&M.

The very next Monday, I was sitting in the cafeteria telling my buddies, "I am going to A&M," and I look up and see this huge mink coat standing at the entrance to the cafeteria. Nobody in Texas wears a mink coat.

Brian Bosworth was one of the more celebrated players in the Sooners' long history, earning All-America honors in 1985 and 1986 and being the first player selected in the 1987 NFL supplemental draft. *Photo courtesy of OU Athletics Media Relations.*

Then I heard this booming voice coming from the mink coat, "Where's Bosworth? Where's Bosworth?"

Somebody at our table said, "That's Barry Switzer!"

The guy in the mink coat raised his hands and he was wearing a huge national championship ring. Then he said, "I know he wants one of these. Where is he?"

"He's over here, Coach."

I was hiding under a chair. That's when you really feel like a fish in the bowl. You are in front of all your peers and here's this guy in a mink coat screaming your name.

I had yet to visit Oklahoma and he wanted me to move up my recruiting trip. I said, "Sure, I'll be there."

So I went to Norman and walked into that stadium and got that haunting feeling like someone does when they realize they had married the wrong person. I suddenly had that feeling about A&M. It was a pretty weekend and as I walked around I just knew, "This is where I am supposed to be."

When I talked to Switzer that weekend, I told him, "I don't understand why you are recruiting me so hard. I don't know if I am Oklahoma material."

He stared and me and said, "Don't you ever think that about yourself. I want you to be a part of this family and make this family better than it is. Don't you ever question yourself!"

I thought, "Well, this guy knows football talent better than anybody."

"OK, Coach," I said. "If you insist. I will come to Oklahoma."

It was a big load off of my shoulders, like finding the perfect girl who you want to walk with forever.

Those first couple of days when I arrived as a freshman seem surreal. You really have to learn how to practice all over again. We were doing a seven-on-seven drill and coach [Gary] Gibbs, the defensive coordinator, called "man coverage." It was my first time in a 5–2 defense, and all of a sudden Coach was screaming at me, "What the f*** are you doing?"

That was so embarrassing, but that was the last time he ever screamed at me.

I knew coming in that I wouldn't be part of the team during my first year. They were going to redshirt the freshman class. I went to watch most of the games [in 1983] and I remember walking out of the Ohio State game [a 24–14 OU loss] in the third quarter. There was no excitement on the field that day. That team just looked mentally dead. I just didn't feel connected to that team at all. Jackie Shipp and Thomas Benson were on that team, and I never liked their attitudes.

I don't think Switzer did, either. He told them, "There will be no bowl game this season. Hawaii is our bowl game."

We all went over there to Hawaii, including the freshmen, and at the training table one day, coach Switzer came over to me and said, "Boz, next year, I need you to be my senior. I redshirted you so you wouldn't be part of this squad. I didn't want you to be poisoned by this team's attitude."

That team [which finished 8–4] had no camaraderie. There was friction between the offense and the defense about who was better. It was like, "Let's not get hurt, let's just play the game and get inside."

Switzer had a great sense of things like that. I mean, nobody on that team hung out together. He was very strong in voicing his opinion of what he expected of me and he was counting on me to be a leader. I know he wanted everybody on the same page because he was feeling a little heat at the time after three straight four-loss seasons.

I entered the next season backing up Evan Gatewood, who had backed up Jackie Shipp the year before. Evan and I were an awful lot alike as far as our mental approach to the game. His footwork and angle of pursuit was so good. Everything was technically perfect with him, so I knew I had my work cut out to beat him out. I knew I had to separate myself from him somehow.

What I separated was my shoulder. One day in the spring, Jerome Ledbetter came through the middle and hit me, catching me flat-footed. As soon as I stood up, I couldn't pick up my shoulder. There were three or four days there, even the day when we took the team pictures, when I couldn't even comb my hair. I think that's why that picture from that season turned out so bad.

I remember watching practice from the sidelines, and coach Gibbs would be saying, "Great job, Evan. Good job, Evan. Way to go, Evan!"

Finally, I had enough of that and I told the trainer, "Just tape it up. If I don't play now, I will be second-string next year."

During one scrimmage, it was like I had a flashback to that day back in high school when I decided I couldn't just be out there. Spencer Tillman got the handoff and I jumped over a blocker and just destroyed Spencer for about a 7-yard loss. I got up screaming like a banshee. Switzer went crazy. He came running over screaming, "That's exactly what we need on this team! I want everybody to do that!"

That's when I realized you had to play with emotion on a level above everybody else. I decided right then, "That's what I have to do."

I was contemplating leaving Norman for the summer when a few of us got to talking about working out together. We would train in the morning and eat lunch together and we started to become a tight group. Marcus [Dupree] was gone, and we had Troy [Aikman] coming in as the quarterback. He could really throw it. I thought, "Holy shit, we are going to be really good."

The week before the opener against Stanford, my girlfriend (who I ended up marrying) decided we were breaking up. That screwed up my whole week. It was enough that Stanford was a complicated offense—and then I had to deal with that.

Good thing for Kevin Murphy, who was the only guy on that defense who had a sense of calm about him. We got out there and Stanford went right down the field to score on the first series. We got over to the sideline and Kevin said, "Look guys, just relax. We need to forget about the past and forget about that drive and make your marks right now."

We started to play one play at a time and not worry about the whole series. It was one-two-three and get the hell off the field. (I got the only interception of my career that day.) We started to do that and everything took care of itself [OU won 19–7].

In the next game, we went to Pittsburgh in what would be our first physical test. On the first series, Kevin, who was playing over [Pittsburgh All-American tackle] Bill Fralic, went down with a broken foot.

There was about a five-minute break to get Kevin off the field, and I got in the huddle and said, "Well, the last senior guy on this team is gone. It is up to us to step up right here, right now. Let's make our mark!"

We started to beat the shit out of them. No matter what they ran, we just stopped them cold. We won 42–10 and now we knew we could physically match up with anybody.

When the Texas game came around, they were ranked No. 1 and we were No. 2. One day that week, the girl who just broke up with me asked me for some tickets to the game.

"Why do you need them?"

"Because the guy I am dating is going to Texas," she told me.

Can you imagine how I felt? That was the same day that I walked into the locker room and some writer asked me why I didn't go to Texas. I just went off.

"I f***ing hate them. I hate their colors. I hate the city of Austin. I don't like Fred Akers. That's why I didn't go to Texas! I am so mad, I can't wait to play them Saturday!"

That's when the Boz was born. I wasn't even thinking at the time, but that quote was going from my mouth to this guy's pen to a newspaper to the bulletin board at Texas.

Coach Switzer called me in and asked, "What are you, 'Bulletin Board Bosworth?'"

I said, "Sorry, Coach. I do hate them. I will play my hardest Saturday, I promise you that."

Before that Texas game, it was raining and I was so nervous and hyped up that I was vomiting in the locker room. I walked down the tunnel, and all those Texas players started yelling at me.

I wondered, "What the hell did I do?" But once you back a dog into a corner, he's going to fight.

Neither offense did much that day in the first half. I think we held them to about 10 total yards. So we walked up that tunnel at halftime still yelling at each other. It got to be late in the game and we were leading 15–10. Then they got a safety and got the ball back at about midfield. They ran that dump screen and the guy caught it, fumbled it, and we recovered. That should have been the game, but the officials called an incomplete pass. They got down to about the 30 and threw it up in the air and Keith Stanberry intercepted it, secured it on his knees, but they called him out of bounds—that the catch was no good. They ended up getting down to the 20 and kicking a third-down field goal to tie the game 15–15.

The officials took that one from us.

Playing Texas was extremely personal to me. I never lost to them or Nebraska or Oklahoma State. A loss to Texas really would have haunted me all these years.

What changed the course of our team and really stayed with me was what happened when we got home from Dallas. We were so down that we were all going to meet at this certain bar, but it was raining hard. All of a sudden we heard sirens and we ran outside. Keith Stanberry's red 300ZX was upside down against a telephone pole. As soon as I saw it, I started crying.

Keith had a broken back and pelvis. Andre Johnson had broken both of his knees. We knew their football careers were over, and that changed the way all of us looked at things. We started to take care of each other off the field.

The next few games were surreal. Danny Bradley got hurt in the Iowa State game and we barely won [12–10], and then Kansas played out of their minds [OU lost 28–11]. Troy came in and was trying to run the wishbone. He couldn't run the wishbone. I think that is the game he realized he didn't belong at Oklahoma or in that offense.

We went to Nebraska with one loss and one tie and saw that Sea of Red and we knew it would be a war. Coach Gibbs came into the defensive huddle and he showed us that national championship ring and told us, "If you guys ever want to win one of these, you have to win a game like this."

We were very prepared for that game. As we played Nebraska over the years, we learned their cadences and their checkoffs no matter who the quarterback was. We knew they were running that power-I right at us, it was just a matter of seeing if we could stop it. We needed a goal-line stand at the end of the game and we stopped them. It was like we told Nebraska to get off the [Big Eight] throne, we are sitting on it from now on. [OU won 17–7.]

We played Oklahoma State the next week, and thank God it was at home because that was a good Oklahoma State team. They had Thurman Thomas and Leslie O'Neal. We were on such a high after winning at Nebraska, we weren't going to ruin it by losing to them.

After we won [24–14] to clinch the Big Eight—it was the first time I had ever won anything in my life—I'll never forget us crying and hugging each other in the locker room. We won it as a family. When you get a chance to share something like that with your teammates, whom you've gone to battle with, side-by-side, shoulder-to-shoulder, it is such an honor.

Our whole goal was to win the Big Eight championship and get to the Orange Bowl, not to *win* the Orange Bowl.

We had accomplished it, so then we went down to Miami and had a really good time. We went to all of the functions and partied too much. Washington did a phenomenal job, I give them credit. They trapped us all night. You would think you were going to get to the ball and you would get hit in the ear. We had too much tequila and didn't study the game plan enough. Still, the turning point in the game was that Schooner thing [when the Sooner Schooner was penalized for being on the field during play]. It just wasn't our day [28–17 loss]. Lesson learned.

Every day you play at Oklahoma you are reminded of the national championships by that big scoreboard there. I know I always wanted to be on a team that would be a part of one.

We all stayed around that next summer and worked out as a team. We had two sessions of weight training, two sessions of running. Everybody was doing it. If somebody didn't do it, he got razzed.

We still had an identity crisis on offense of whether it was an I-formation team or a wishbone team early that season [1985]. The offense just didn't have any rhythm. It took a goal-line stand just to beat Minnesota [13–7]. We beat Kansas State and then completely shut down Texas: I mean Texas cried to get off the field that day [a 14–7 OU win]. When Miami came to Norman, we had already blown our emotional load against Texas.

What I couldn't believe was how Miami acted when they got to our stadium. They were like a bunch of hoods. I am just a redneck from Oklahoma, but they all had mouths on them. That was the first real pro team we had faced with a pro offense and a pro defense. They could run and be physical, and Vinny [Testaverde] was hot that day.

Troy started that way, too, but then all of a sudden Jerome Brown came up the middle and broke his leg. Nobody at the time realized the impact of what that play would be in the long run. Jamelle Holieway was young and raw. We didn't rally in that game because we were in shock over losing our quarterback, but we recovered quickly after that loss [27–14].

We won the rest of them, beating Nebraska 27–7 and Oklahoma State 13–0 in the Ice Bowl. Those first four games of that season didn't feel like Oklahoma. I signed up to play at an Oklahoma that had redneck defense and the wishbone offense. Finally, when Jamelle came in and got better and better, that's what we had.

In some respects, I am glad that injury happened to Troy. He went on to have a fabulous career at UCLA, and we got back to Oklahoma football. The Midwest is a place to bow your neck back, have a square dance, and get nasty on the football field. That's the way it should be.

When we got back to the Orange Bowl, before the game, I heard somebody say, "Hey man, Miami just got beat in the Sugar Bowl."

That meant we could win a national championship by beating Penn State. That was pretty easy [OU won 25–10], because they weren't very good.

More than 20 years later, that team and that national championship means a great deal to me. It was the way in which we won it. I always believed that defense wins championships, and that was a great defense. We dominated and we intimidated.

After seeing the 2004 team in the Orange Bowl, I think OU could take a lesson from that. It seemed the coaches weren't spending the quality time on defense the way they do on offense.

My junior year was tough in a lot of ways. We lost to Miami again and then the T-shirt thing [after Bosworth tested positive for steroids and was suspended for the Orange Bowl against Arkansas] happened.

I have always regretted wearing that T-shirt [that read: "The NCAA: National Communists Against Athletes"], which everyone saw on national TV. I never regretted the message, but it was the way I put that message out there that was wrong. I made a statement on a stage in which my team was the main cast member and I shouldn't have done it. And I certainly shouldn't have done it with that T-shirt.

I made a poor choice in Miami and, after that, it kind of forced Switzer's hand that it was time for the Boz to move on. So leaving after my junior season was the right thing to do, according to the people around me. In my heart, it really wasn't.

I wanted to be a student at OU until the day I died, but I was advised that it was time to get out and go to the NFL because of the fear of being hurt. It is a rough contact sport and it was a money issue.

Looking back, given that risk, I would have been satisfied to stay for my senior year to get another championship.

I have to thank coach Switzer, though. He is one of those people in my life who really helped define who I am. He gave me confidence. Like my father, he was one of those guys who I never wanted to disappoint. I wanted to satisfy that man with my play on the field. He was so instrumental in giving me my identity.

To a certain degree, I felt somewhat responsible when he was forced to resign. The things I talked about in my book, the shooting on campus and those type of things, might have had something to do with it all. I don't know. I didn't specifically target my school or intend to, but I felt responsible even though he assured me that wasn't the case.

I felt they took a piece of history away from his legend. I just thought it really was contradictory the way he took care of his players all those years and yet the school turned its back on him and used him as a scapegoat.

Reality is that when you recruit somebody, you hope they become a great person or a great citizen, but you don't always bat 1.000. If one or two of them make a wrong turn, that's life. That's reality. He would always guide us back to the right path, but some guys he probably couldn't do that to.

In recent years, he has been a very good friend to me. He told me when he recruited me that I would be part of that family and you never turn your back on your family. A lot of people turned their backs on me, but he wasn't one of them. He believed in Brian. I wasn't the Boz to him.

That was my creation, but I don't regret that. You've got to be who you are. Being the Boz allowed me to be free and it allowed my game to be taken to another level.

I made mistakes, but I learned from them. I am married and have three kids now and time does go by pretty quickly, but that program and school still are important to me. I still watch their games and it is important to me that Oklahoma does well. It hurts me when they lose.

The funny thing is, I still dream about my time there. I dream a few times every month about being in the locker room, hearing one of Switzer's speeches, or I dream something like being stuck in traffic while the game is starting without me.

I guess playing for Oklahoma was a dream to me. It was a dream come true.

Brian Bosworth was an All-American in 1985–1986. He won the Butkus Award as the nation's best linebacker in both of those seasons, becoming the only two-time winner of the award. He also was All–Big Eight in 1984, 1985, and 1986. He finished his career with 413 tackles. He finished with 39 tackles for loss. He also was an Academic All-American in 1986. Bosworth was the first pick of the 1987 NFL supplemental draft by the Seattle Seahawks. He currently is an actor who lives in Malibu, California.

Mark Hutson | Guard | 1984–1987

Growing up in Fort Smith, Arkansas, it was natural to be a Razorback fan, and I was. But Fort Smith is only 13 miles from the Oklahoma state line, so I received plenty of exposure to Oklahoma Sooners football. Both of my parents were born in the state of Oklahoma, and my earliest memory of OU football was listening to the games on the radio with my grandfather Bill Hutson in the midseventies.

When I started playing football at the age of six, I played in the backfield. When I got to the sixth grade, my coach, Doug Lowrey, pulled me aside one day and told me he was moving me to the offensive line. My world was shattered. After practice that afternoon, I sat down under a tree and cried.

To me, that was the worst position anyone could play.

But coach Lowrey, who had been an offensive lineman in pro football, convinced me that it wasn't the end of the world. He told me that if I wanted to keep playing the game, that would be the position for me.

Coach Lowrey was the first of several good coaches who helped me develop. My junior high coach, Billy Joe Releford, had the enthusiasm and ability to relate one-on-one with all of his players, which sparked my decision much later to get into coaching once my career was finished. Once I got to high school, I was fortunate to have a coach who had coached the offensive line in college: coach Joe Fred Young prepared me mentally and fundamentally so I would be prepared to play college football.

I have to thank them all for preparing me, but what coach Young couldn't prepare me for was the recruiting process. At the age of 17, I was not ready for the phone calls and all the letters that I was inundated by. When the recruiters started to come around the house, looking back on it, I guess I was too honest with most of them. I either checked "not interested" on their forms or simply said "no."

Coaches such as Larry Coker and Ken Hatfield entertained my family in our living room. And of course, so did Barry Switzer. He was the one whom my family and I felt most comfortable with.

Maybe it was his appearance—he showed up in blue jeans and cowboy boots. But I think the thing that really won me over was the way he got along with my younger brother, Mike, who was mentally and physically handicapped. Barry took the time to visit with Mike and talk to him, unlike some of the other recruiters.

During the fall of my senior year, I attended all of the Razorbacks' home games and took my official visit to the Fayetteville campus. My first airplane trip was to Athens, Georgia, to visit Vince Dooley and the Georgia Bulldogs.

I really thought Georgia was a great place with great people, but it was too far from home, so I committed to Arkansas and canceled trips to Oklahoma, Oklahoma State, and Baylor. I asked all of the other recruiters not to call me. Charley North, OU's tight ends coach, who had done a tremendous job recruiting me, wished me luck and told me he may check back with me in a couple of weeks.

Two weeks later, I received a call from coach North on a Friday afternoon. He told me he was in Little Rock picking up a tight end named Keith Jackson and he wanted to know if he could stop by Fort Smith to pick me up for a recruiting visit to Norman.

I told him I was interested, but I didn't know if I had any clean clothes. This embarrassed my mother, but coach North laughed and told me to put some clothes in a bag and that we would do the laundry once we got to Norman.

As it turned out, I found some clean clothes at the house prior to coach North and Keith arriving in Fort Smith.

Once we got to Norman, I thought the people and the facilities at OU were outstanding and I was very impressed with the offensive line coach, Merv Johnson. He was up-front, honest, and sincere and I could tell he was someone I could play for in college.

When I returned home, I told my parents how great it was and that I was interested in attending the University of Oklahoma. I asked if they wanted to go back with me the next weekend for an unofficial visit. They did.

They came away with the same feeling I had, that Oklahoma was a great place for me.

We all agreed that I faced a tough decision between Arkansas and Oklahoma.

The next week was the national signing day. I had not heard from any of the Arkansas coaches for several weeks after I had committed to them, but once they found out that I had visited OU, their coaches started calling me again. I told them I had changed my mind and that I would be signing with Oklahoma.

Coach Hatfield called and told me I was making the biggest mistake of my life. He told me that Oklahoma had too many good players and that I would get "lost in the shuffle" and that my parents wouldn't get to see any of my away games since OU played in the Big Eight. (My parents ended up missing only two of my games through my career.) He also said that I would never be able to work in the state of Arkansas for the rest of my life. In the end, he was unable to wish me well with my decision.

"I am sorry you feel that way," I told him, "but my decision is final."

Arkansas did make one last effort, however. My parents and I went to pick up a pizza one night and when we returned home, my brother told us that Governor Clinton had called and that he would call back later.

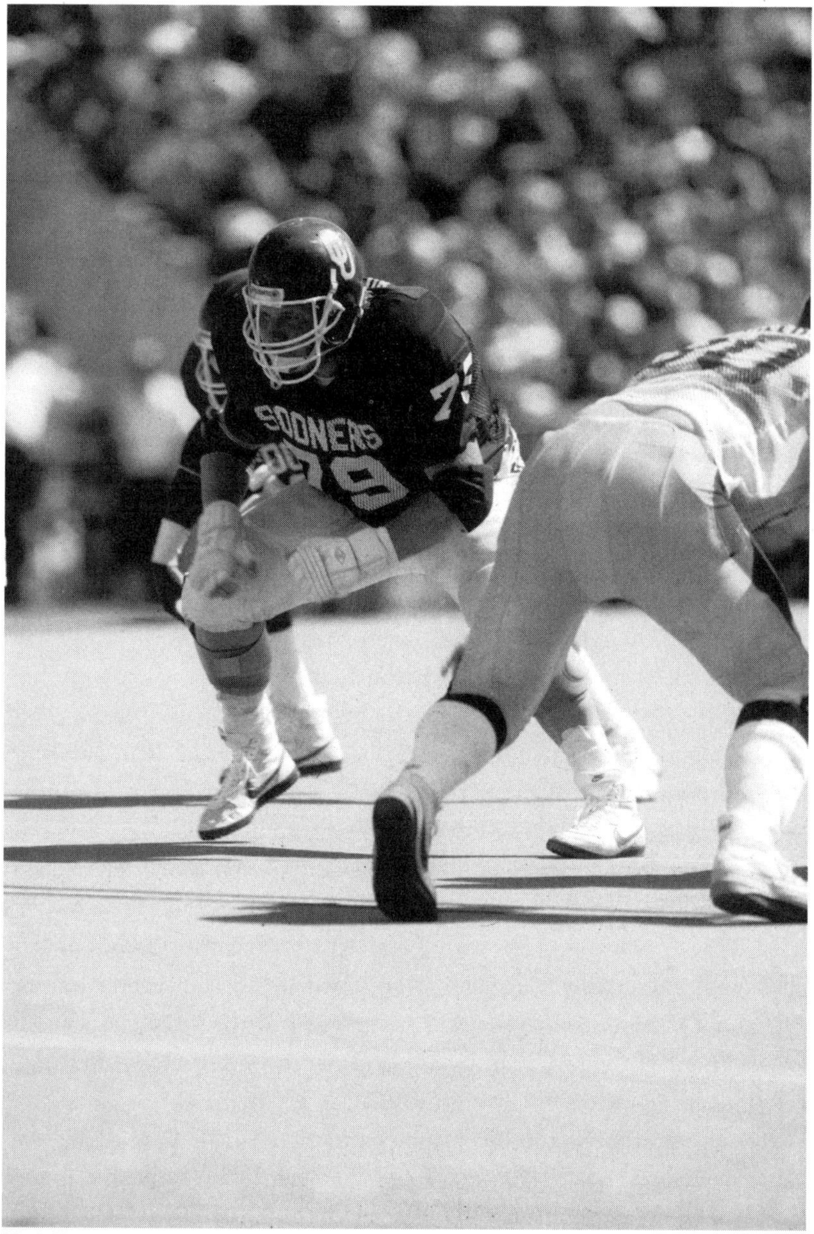

Mark Hutson, an Arkansas native, was so bent on becoming a Sooner that two phone calls from then–Arkansas governor Bill Clinton could not sway him to reconsider the Razorbacks' scholarship offer. He became a two-time All-American at OU. *Photo courtesy of John Williamson.*

Of course, my brother had been known to stretch the truth a little in the past, so we had a big laugh about it and didn't think anything about it.

About two hours later, Mom summoned me to the telephone. It was Governor Clinton. He told me that Arkansas was a great school and that if he had a son, he would want him to be a "Fighting Razorback." I listened to him, thanked him, and told him that both of my parents were graduates of the University of Arkansas, but that I would be attending the University of Oklahoma. Unlike coach Hatfield, he wished me well and I did the same for him.

Little did I know, I had just rejected a request from the future President of the United States.

The next morning was signing day, and by 9:00 a.m., I became a proud Sooner.

The first time I stepped foot into Memorial Stadium on a fall Saturday was in the 1984 opener against Stanford. I remember standing on the 45-yard line on the kickoff return team, staring up at the crowd of almost 80,000. That crowd was larger than my hometown! I vaguely remember the sound of the ball being kicked off and then someone knocked me down to the turf, officially beginning my OU career.

I played second-team offensive tackle and on special teams during that freshman season. We tied Texas 15–15, beat Nebraska, and won the Big Eight championship, but lost to Washington in the Orange Bowl. It was a good learning experience, but it made me even more determined to win a starting job that next spring.

In 1985, my sophomore year, I started the first four games at left tackle. I became dehydrated and I cramped up in the second half at Minnesota in the season-opener. I spent most of the second half with our starting right guard, Anthony Phillips, with IV's stuck in our arms, watching the game on TV from the training room.

After we lost to Miami 27–14 in a game in which [Miami defensive tackle] Jerome Brown had 18 tackles and Troy Aikman broke his ankle, coach Johnson made several changes on the offensive line. He moved me to left guard and Jamelle Holieway took over for Troy, becoming our starting quarterback.

I have to say that playing against other defenses on Saturdays was a relief because our defense, led by Tony Casillas, Brian Bosworth, and Kevin Murphy, was simply great that year. They made it very difficult for us during the week of practice.

We beat Texas 14–7, and the meaning of the Red River Shootout really sunk in for me that game.

The Big Eight championship came down to us and Nebraska, like it usually did in those days. In coach Switzer's pregame speech, he told us that we were the two best teams in the country and that this game was for the national championship.

The same Keith Jackson who had made that recruiting visit with me two years earlier broke the game open on a tight end-reverse, and we won 27–7, as oranges flew onto the field at Memorial Stadium at the end of the game.

The coldest game I ever played in was the next week at Oklahoma State. During the second half, it had literally rained ice and the field was frozen solid, but we won what became known as "the Ice Bowl" 13–0.

That Orange Bowl game against Penn State was as tough and as physical as any game that I had ever played in, but we broke it open with big plays by Keith and Lydell Carr to win 25–10, making OU national champions.

Walking off that field that night, knowing we were the best team in the nation, it was the best feeling I ever had in any form of athletics.

In my junior year, a tough loss to Miami prevented us from repeating as national champions, but we did repeat as Big Eight champions. We trailed at halftime at Nebraska, but coach Switzer gave us a speech about tapping into some Sooner Magic. Sure enough, Jamelle hit Derrick Shepard late in the game to pull us to within 17–16. I can still remember Nebraska fans booing us as we kicked the extra point to tie the game.

The booing stopped with 18 seconds remaining when Jamelle passed to Keith to set up Tim Lashar's game-winning field goal. The ending to that game was filled with Sooner Magic!

We were headed to the Orange Bowl for a third time.

This Orange Bowl had special meaning for me and for coach Switzer because it was against Ken Hatfield and Arkansas, which had upset

Oklahoma in the 1978 Orange Bowl, costing coach Switzer another national championship, so he wanted to beat them as much as I did.

And as you know, I had my own reasons for wanting to beat the Hogs.

We did, 42–8.

At the beginning of my senior year, I was voted team captain by my peers, and that is the one individual honor that I am most proud of.

We started No. 1 and rolled through the regular season. On a down note, Jamelle hurt his knee and a freshman, Charles Thompson, replaced him. The saddest day of my career was that final home game against Missouri. Walking off the field after the game, I realized I would never play on that field again.

Charles Thompson led us over Nebraska 17–7 the next week, setting up another game with Miami in the Orange Bowl.

We lost 20–14, but the game did provide one of the most exciting plays of my career. Coach [Jim] Donnan, our offensive coordinator, had put the "fumblerooski" in our game plan. We worked on it in practice, but I thought he did it just for conditioning at the end of each practice. I never dreamed he would call it during the Orange Bowl.

When the play came in, my gloves were all wet and slippery and I tried to take them off, but I thought it might give the play away. Our center, Bob Latham, snapped the ball and held it between his legs. The quarterback ran an option [without the ball] to the left. The ball was stuck briefly between Bob's legs before I could get hold of it. This allowed more time for the defense to converge on the quarterback. Then I ran around right end 29 yards for a touchdown—it was the only carry of my college career.

Still, that was the most disappointing loss of my college career.

What does it mean to be a Sooner?

It is being part of a family—a family rich with winning tradition. Coach Switzer said it best once during a pregame speech: "As a player, being on the inside, you take for granted the awe and respect people have for Oklahoma football."

But I see that now.

Looking back, I realize that I was very fortunate to have played for one of the greatest programs in college football history. I know it was the best decision I could have made.

Mark Hutson was an All-American in 1986 and 1987. He also was All–Big Eight in 1985, 1986, and 1987. He was a team captain in 1987. Hutson was drafted in the third round of the 1988 NFL draft by the Dallas Cowboys.

Anthony Phillips | Guard | 1985–1988

I guess you could say it wasn't a foregone conclusion that I would become an Oklahoma Sooner. Being a blue-chip player from the state of Oklahoma in my day, it was almost automatic that you would go to OU, not to mention the fact my brother Jon was already there, as well as several others from my high school.

However, I was born in Dallas and lived many years in Tennessee and had grown up a Texas and Tennessee fan.

I would later become an OU fan while living in Jenks, Oklahoma, a suburb of Tulsa. Jenks is a football powerhouse, having won about seven of the past nine state championships.

When I was a senior, I was blessed to have the option to go about anywhere in the country and visited many schools: Texas, USC, Notre Dame, Tennessee, and of course, OU.

As I said, I had followed the Volunteers and Longhorns, but neither of their head coaches at the time got me too excited. When I sat in front of Johnny Majors, it appeared to me he was close to retirement. He didn't have that fire I expected. Neither did Fred Akers of Texas.

A guy named Barry Switzer was the hands-down winner when it came to head coaches. My brother Jon was already at OU, but I still tried to be objective about my decision and not let that influence me.

After making the rounds during recruiting, I liked coach Switzer and I felt Oklahoma was the place to be to compete for a national championship.

Coach Switzer told me it would happen, that the ingredients would be in place if I and several of the other top players in the state would come to OU. I believed him, too. Fortunately, so did all the top players in the state that year: Troy Aikman, Lydell Carr, Patrick Collins, Bob Latham, Scott Garl, and myself. All of us would go on to make meaningful contributions for the Sooners.

I was recruited to OU as a defensive lineman and would eventually become an offensive guard. It was common for the Oklahoma staff to recruit defensive linemen and convert some of them to offense because they wanted athletes to run the option-oriented offense. We had to be able to run, run fast, and run often.

I quickly realized that would be my best chance to get on the field, but I broke my foot during my freshman year and ended up redshirting. This gave me a chance to spend more time in the weight room to get bigger and stronger, and then have a real chance to compete for a starting position in the spring.

Fortunately, this worked out as I planned and I ended up starting for four years.

Nineteen eighty-five turned out to be an interesting year, to say the least. Troy Aikman was our starting quarterback and we went to the Metrodome in Minneapolis to face a mediocre Minnesota team. If you looked at the film of this uninspiring 13–7 win, no sane person would believe this would be a team that would be good enough to go on to win a national title that year.

It was an auspicious start to what would turn out to be a wild season, culminating with a win over Penn State in the Orange Bowl for the national title. Of course, along the way we would lose Aikman to a broken leg in the game against Miami when Jerome Brown knifed in unabated to sack him. We would lose that game, however, but gain the services of Jamelle Holieway at quarterback. It was a moment which made us begin running the wishbone again.

This would take most of our remaining opponents by surprise as we romped through the rest of the season with victory after victory. The Nebraska and Oklahoma State games stick out as the memorable games that year.

We soundly beat Nebraska at home 27–7, ending in a downpour of oranges at Owen Field, highlighted by Keith Jackson's 88-yard end-around that went down as one of the greatest plays in OU history and vaulted him into super stardom.

"The Ice Bowl" at Lewis Field in Stillwater to end the regular season is a game I'll never forget. We clinched the Big Eight title during that game while being pelted with about two inches of ice along the way. We looked like beasts of the high plains pawing at the ice on the field in order to get any traction on the line of scrimmage. That 13–0 win and another over SMU at the end of the season vaulted us to No. 2 in the polls by the time we were to meet undefeated Penn Sate in the Orange Bowl.

Miami was No. 1 and a heavy favorite who was about to play Tennessee in the Sugar Bowl. It was pretty much a foregone conclusion that the same Hurricanes who broke Troy's legs would beat Tennessee and win the title. I think we were as shocked as anyone to see the Vols whipping Miami as we watched the game in the locker room of the Orange Bowl before our game kicked off.

All of sudden, we were all looking at each other and thinking, "This is it, we are now playing for all the marbles."

We knew if we beat Penn State the title would be ours. It was a surreal feeling, to say the least, and we went out and soundly beat Penn State 25–10 that night.

Looking back on it, I truly think we were better off preparing for that game without the added significance of the presumably out-of-reach title. Instead, we played in the moment. We were loose and we left it all out on the field that night.

After all the celebration of the 1985 national championship, and, believe me, we did celebrate, we turned our attention to the next season. It was almost scary to think we should be even better, and the pollsters believed it, too, as we came into the preseason ranked No. 1. But we had to play Miami again in the regular season, this time in Miami which always proved to be a hostile environment and a tough place to win.

We thoroughly drubbed UCLA 38–3 in the opener in Norman and geared up for Miami, a No. 1 versus No. 2 showdown. Once again, they were our chief nemesis, beating us 28–16 in the miserable Miami heat.

I have to say that Miami's fans were the worst in the country. I can't imagine anyone nastier to an opposing team. They would throw stuff at us coming out of the locker room, spit on us, and shout every expletive ever known to man. In fact, one time the referee had to stop the game in order to remove a large Army knife that someone had thrown onto the field during the game.

Still, Miami was the only team in the country that had the same caliber of athletes as we did, and coupled with their balanced offensive attack, they proved to be the only team that could regularly defeat us.

After that loss, we stormed through the 1986 season with the hopes that Miami might eventually stumble and gain us another shot at the title. The Nebraska game in Lincoln was memorable to me. I guess all Cornhusker games were. We were down 17–7 with only a few minutes remaining and had no apparent chance of pulling off a miracle.

Low and behold, the miracle unfolded with a bit of Sooner Magic. A quick touchdown, a field goal, and then a miracle catch by Keith Jackson placed us in field-goal position again. After we won 20–17, the Nebraska fans were in complete shock and dismay. They sat in the stands for what seemed like hours wondering what they had just witnessed as my brother Jon ran around Nebraska's home stadium, claiming this was "our house."

The Nebraska fans are truly great fans, however. They respect good football and they respect their worthy opponents. Lincoln was always a great place to play college football.

Miami never lost in the regular season, and for that matter, neither did Penn State. Those two teams were to meet in the Fiesta Bowl, eliminating us from any national title consideration. We settled for an underwhelming Arkansas team in the Orange Bowl.

However, this did provide us the opportunity to avenge, for coach Switzer anyway, an earlier loss to Arkansas in the 1978 Orange Bowl. We thoroughly whipped Arkansas 42–8 in what turned out to be a mismatch as we settled for the No. 3 final ranking.

Anthony Phillips was recruited as a defensive lineman and moved over to the offensive line, where he was a two-time All-American at guard.

We were fired up again for the 1987 season, coming in as the preseason No. 1. This time, Miami was not part of our regular season, so they weren't on our minds. At least not yet.

We pretty much rolled through the season and over all of our opponents until the showdown with Nebraska. My favorite pregame speech occurred during this run. We were in Manhattan, Kansas, to play Kansas State and, apparently, Switzer had a little too much fun the night before the game. He was pacing through the locker room, back and forth, in his typical pregame manner. We were all patiently waiting for his choice words of motivation. He stopped, lifted up his glasses to show his bloodshot eyes, and stated, "Men, don't play like I feel today!"

We went out and rolled over Kansas State 59–10. Of course, this wasn't the K-State of today. The Wildcats weren't that good back in the eighties.

Flying into Manhattan was always especially exciting. We had to fly on a 737 because it was the only large jet that could stop fast enough on the airport's short runway, which appeared to be in the middle of a cattle pasture. It was typically windy that day, and the airplane would inevitably be bucking around like a wild bronco. Many of the players were not accustomed to flying all that much, especially some of the younger guys. It would sound like a Sunday morning revival on that airplane with all the people praying out loud. Once the airplane hit the ground, you always wondered if it would be able to stop in time before we ran out of runway.

In the next game, Colorado gave us a spirited game in Norman. Mark Hutson, the opposite-side guard, and I collided on two separate occasions while pulling, and we nearly got into a fight right on the field. He was sure he had the play right and that I was in the wrong.

Of course, I was right. We blew past Kansas in Lawrence the next week in a real track meet, 71–10. The Kansas press didn't take kindly to many of us eating hot dogs on the sidelines with our pads off late in the game. We moved by Oklahoma State the next week 29–10, but we lost Holieway to a knee injury that would turn out to be a season-ending injury for him.

The speedster from Lawton, Charles Thompson, would come in and start the next game against Missouri in a lackluster 17–13 win. This was a great setup going into the Nebraska game in Lincoln. The media was so unimpressed with our win, they moved Nebraska ahead of us in the polls to No. 1, bumping us to No. 2.

This set up Game of the Century II.

We were headed into a hostile environment, we had lost our starting quarterback, we had dropped in the polls, and Nebraska was talking trash. We kept our mouths shut. I knew that we were going to find out what we were really made of in this one. How would we respond?

We beat Nebraska from the word "go" that day. We thoroughly dominated the line of scrimmage on both sides of the ball and we were facing some pretty big names: Neil Smith and Danny Noonan, to name a few. The score [17–7] doesn't look so dominating, but consider that Nebraska's offense crossed midfield only three times and we fumbled the ball four times and threw one interception. We basically ran up and down the field at will and had three players with over 100 yards that day, including Thompson.

This was one of the most memorable wins of my career.

I'll challenge anyone to show me better offensive line blocking than we had executed that day against what was a great Nebraska defense. We really whipped their asses. Suddenly, we were back in the No. 1 spot and headed to the Orange Bowl to face Miami for another shot at the national title.

We weren't going to let this one get past us. Miami had already cost us one title, and we weren't about to let them make it two. We went to Miami two weeks before the game in order to focus and have extra preparation time. We actually had two-a-days for the first week and literally knocked the hell out of each other, in addition to quite a bit of conditioning.

In retrospect, we probably over-prepared and over-conditioned. We weren't as loose as we should have been, and we were probably a bit leg-weary to boot. It was a good game, finishing with a score of 20–14, but it was a loss nonetheless.

With many of our starters graduating, I knew it would be tough to be in the running for a national championship during my senior season.

What most teams would celebrate as a great season at 9–3, I could only characterize as mediocre, at least by Oklahoma standards. This would pretty much define my last year as a Sooner on the field. No doubt, much of the talent had graduated the previous year, but we could have won every game on our schedule that year.

We had lost at USC 23–7 in the third game of the season and then lost close games to Nebraska in the final game of the regular season and to Clemson in the Citrus Bowl. Still, it was nice to go somewhere other than Miami for a bowl game, although not playing for any type of title made it bittersweet for us.

Several milestones were achieved that last year, accomplishments that I am very proud of today. We defeated Texas for a fourth year in a row, the first time since the seventies that OU had a four-year run in that rivalry. We also beat Oklahoma State for the fourth straight year, and they had the great Barry Sanders. Both teams forgot how to play defense that day, and it was basically a Mike Gaddis-versus-Sanders track meet. We won it 31–28.

As everyone in Oklahoma knows, coach Switzer's final year was 1988, which happened to be my final season. The shooting on campus and Charles Thompson getting busted happened after the season and, suddenly, it was somewhat like the perfect storm. All of these events happened in a short time, and it was a tough to end a career that way. You watched your fellow teammates suffer. You watched your coaches suffer.

I can say this about it: when you get 100 kids together like that from all different backgrounds across the country, there will be issues. Switzer had the philosophy of being hands-off and letting kids be themselves. When you have the right people, that works really well. When you have some bad people, it doesn't. I know you probably couldn't run a program like that today.

The sad thing was that the media back then labeled us all bad people. We had 90 guys with great stories, but you never heard those stories. I always made a point back then to tell the media how proud I was of the program and the people in it.

I can't say enough about the experience I had as an Oklahoma Sooner. The great players I played with, the great players I played against, the exceptional coaches, and other people associated with the program, as well as the fine academic schooling I received while obtaining a business degree. The value of an OU degree increases with value over time as President Boren has taken the school to new heights.

I still believe the offensive line I played on was arguably the best in Sooner history: Greg Johnson, Bob Latham, Mark Hutson, and my brother Jon.

There are several coaches I hold in high regard to this day. Coach Switzer was always a players coach, which is a subjective term. My definition of it is someone who cares about you above and beyond your contributions on the football field, and he fit that definition. The players played and worked hard for the man.

Merv Johnson was a coach of high integrity and he instilled a great sense of pride, character, and work ethic in his players. He treated us like men and expected us to act like men, and we did. Jim Donnan, our offensive coordinator, was a coach also filled with pride and integrity. He called it like it was, and I still use one of his favorite phrases to this day, "Men, you can't make chicken salad out of chicken shit." He would say that, referring to our opponents. Our weight coach, Pete Martinelli, was a fiery Italian about 5'5" and all muscle. He would call you every name you ever heard and some you never heard of. He would run us until we puked and then run us some more, but we loved him like a brother.

I stay in contact with these folks to this day.

With a record of 42–6 over four years, three Big Eight titles, and one national title, there wasn't a better program to be involved with 1985–1988. You can take all the success, all the awards and titles, and the things you keep, but what lasts a lifetime are the bonds and relationships that you forge with your teammates, coaches, and others associated with that success. Being an Oklahoma Sooner will always be a part of me, inextricably intertwined into the fiber of my being.

And one more thing made it special for me—playing for the Sooners became a family affair for us. Jon played with me, and our oldest brother, Greg, took pictures of our games for *Sooners Illustrated*.

For all of those things, I count myself a lucky man.

You take on the responsibility and the tradition of all the great players and coaches who came before you, those with you, and those who will follow you. This is something you carry with you for the rest of your life. It is a part of you. With time and with reflection, you begin to appreciate it all so much more. I always proudly wear my OU letterman's ring.

Tradition, pride, excellence, winning, national titles, All-Americans: these are all the words that come to my mind when I think about being a Sooner.

Anthony Phillips was named an All-American in 1986 and 1988. He is one of only three Oklahoma players to be named all-conference in four seasons, joining Wade Walker (1946–1949) and Darrell Reed (1984–1987). He also was named Academic All–Big Eight four times and was named Academic All-American in 1987.

| chapter six |

The Nineties and the New Millennium

Rocky Calmus | Linebacker | 1998–2001

I've asked my parents a few times how they named me "Rocky Ayers," but I have never been given a straight answer from them. I do know that I weighed a ton when I was born—about 11 pounds, 11 ounces—so maybe that had something to do with it.

Basketball and T-ball were my first sports while I was growing up in Jenks, Oklahoma, a suburb of Tulsa. I played flag football in the second grade but got bored with it. We didn't have tackle football when I was kid as they do now.

I wasn't a big sports fan growing up. I was more of an outdoors kid, playing around the town with my buddy. We would play around the creek, catch some frogs and bugs and stuff like that.

Dad was a pretty big baseball fan and had played in the minor leagues. My uncle also played pro baseball. My oldest brother played baseball and got drafted out of high school, but he went to Oral Roberts University on a baseball scholarship.

When I did start to play the game of football, I was always a running back and linebacker as far back as I can remember. I was a little taller than the other kids, but not really big. It seemed that everybody was skinny back then.

I became a starter during my sophomore year at Jenks when a starting linebacker got hurt and I went in for him. We lost in the state semifinals that year to Midwest City. Then during my junior year, we went 13–1, but lost to Broken Arrow. In my senior year, though, we blew everybody away, finishing 14–0. It was like men playing against boys that season.

Kansas State, Oklahoma State, and Oklahoma were the main schools recruiting me. Kansas State was the powerhouse of those three at the time, but I was an Oklahoma boy and I wanted to stay in the state.

At the time, Oklahoma was at rock bottom. But there was something about my visit that made me want to go there. I will tell you that John Blake knew how to recruit—how to talk to the players and the right things to say.

He is an Oklahoma guy—he'd been with the Dallas Cowboys and won some Super Bowls with them, so he had a great track record. As far as I was concerned, there were still plenty of reasons to choose the Sooners.

I went to Norman early that next summer to work out, and Merv Johnson found me a job. I didn't want anything easy, like watching the grass grow, but my job was really tough. I spent the summer roofing houses and then trying to lift weights after work. It was awful. And it was hot. That has to be one of the worst jobs in the world.

I really didn't want to play in the all-state all-star game that summer because I was worried about getting hurt. But the guy running the game begged me to play, so I gave in and agreed to do it. Early in the third quarter, I pulled my hamstring. So I spent my first weeks of two-a-days at Oklahoma rehabbing my hamstring.

Some people wonder how I got jersey No. 20 as a linebacker, but I had worn that number in sports since little league. My brother had it and Spencer Tillman had it, and I loved the number. I never talked to Billy Sims about it, but I figured that would be one of the first numbers OU would retire, if they retired numbers at all.

We had a very good defense my freshman year, but I can't say much about our offense. The defense would be out there on the field the whole game, and we would wear down over time, but we kept playing hard.

A lot of us were just glad to be on a Division I team, but I was a little depressed. I had never lost that many games in my whole high school career, and here we had lost five in a row at one point.

It was tough to do anything when the offense went three-and-out on every series. After a while, there was some real finger-pointing going on between the offense and the defense within the program.

We were fighting ourselves instead of the opponent.

My first career start was against Missouri, and I think I played pretty well over those last five or six games. I was holding my own and trying not to screw up too much.

But the losing was tougher than anything I went through individually. I will never forget sitting on the bench late in the game at Texas A&M [a 29–0 loss]. We were getting killed that day. It was cold and raining and they were blowing those cannons off every time they scored. I was almost in tears.

I just sat there in the rain, thinking, "Man, this stinks."

We just kept losing. You would lose a game, pick yourself up, and get ready for the next week, and then lose another game. It brought back memories of when I was being recruited and had told people I was going to OU. There were even some teachers in my own school trashing me for that decision. Maybe they were joking, but I don't think they were.

After the [5–6] season, we supported coach Blake, getting together and having a meeting when he was fired. We were really upset about it, and some guys wanted to leave, but as you get older, you realize that some coaches just don't pan out as head coaches. In the end, everybody realized we were Sooners and we had to stay.

Personally, I never thought about leaving.

We had a long, long break between coaches. I think we played our final game November 21, and all through December, we pretty much had time off.

They started the job search and this guy named Bob Stoops kept coming up. What did I know about him?—just that he was the defensive coordinator at Florida and they had won the national championship there in his first year [1996]. I figured they would bring in an offensive guy, since our defense wasn't the problem.

One of the toughest players in OU history, Rocky Calmus had a nose for the football, winning the Butkus Award and leading the Sooners in tackles for three consecutive seasons. *Photo courtesy of Lisa Hall.*

You are suspect of somebody who has never had a head-coaching job, because this is *Oklahoma* we are talking about, but now we all know that [athletic director] Joe Castiglione knew what he was doing.

When coach Stoops arrived on campus and met with us, I remember some of the guys were staring at his wife because she is very pretty.

Coach Stoops joked, "Y'all don't stare too long!"

That really broke the ice between him and us.

His first message that day was that he was not there to rebuild and regroup; he was there to win with the people in that room.

Remember I mentioned all that time off we had between coaches? Well, coach Stoops brought this little stocky guy named Jerry Schmidt with him from Florida [as the new strength coach]. We didn't know what to expect, but it didn't take long to find out.

We were out there in January at 5:30 a.m. for that first workout and after about an hour, I thought our workout was finished. That was just our warm-up and already, guys were throwing up. I was dead-dog tired. We knew things were changing in a hurry at that point. You would go through that intense workout and then you wanted to go home and sleep, but you would have to go to about four or five classes and then go lift weights after that.

That is what is tough about being a student-athlete.

I knew we had the talent, we had good players—the name players from the state of Oklahoma. We weren't getting them all at the time, but we had been getting a lot of them.

That first year under the new coaching staff, all of the finger-pointing stopped.

We had to push each other and lean on each other just to get through those workouts, and I think that brought us together even more. That was the first step. We were building some rapport and everything was happening so fast. I never missed a workout that summer, and a lot of other guys were there every day, too. The next year, nobody missed workouts.

We were in great shape heading into the [1999] season. We were so close to being so good, but we were just a play or two away. We had Notre Dame down by 17 points but let that game slip away. Then we went to Dallas and lost to Texas after we were winning that game.

Now if that had happened the year before, we would have been pointing fingers at each other again, but this time we were positive.

I had battled a wrist injury for more than a year. I had hurt it during my freshman year and it never healed properly. So the summer before my junior year, I was still rehabbing it. I usually played and practiced with a soft cast on it, but it was still difficult to get that punch on offensive linemen when they came out after you.

Then I had broken my lower leg against Texas Tech as a sophomore. In fact, I have broken a bone every year I have played football since my junior season in high school. That's hard-nosed playing for you! Seriously, I don't think I have ever been completely healthy.

As I look back now, the 2000 season is sort of a blur. It felt like we were underdogs the whole season. We would win and everybody said the next game would be the "big test" for us. Once we won that game, they would say the next game would be the "bigger test," then the "biggest test."

In a game that really got people's attention, against Texas, I had a big interception against [Chris] Simms, and Quentin Griffin really went off that day [scoring six touchdowns]. That was the worst beating [63–14] for them in that series, and by halftime, the stadium was half-empty.

Then we had to play No. 2 Kansas State. We beat them, even though that was the loudest I had ever heard any stadium. And then we had to play No. 1 Nebraska in the big showdown.

We got behind 14–0 very quickly, and I said, "Crap, what is happening?"

I never, not even for one minute, thought we were going to lose that game. We came back and blew them out, too [31–14], and that is when people started to finally believe in us—although some thought we would have a letdown after that game.

We then got behind A&M, but we stayed positive. We beat Oklahoma State in a real tight game and then people said, "Well, it's tough to beat someone like K-State twice."

That [Big 12 championship] game went back and forth, and it was just freezing that night. No matter what the score was or what happened during the game, we knew we would come back and win. We were very confident, but not cocky. Coach Stoops would never let us get cocky.

I can honestly say we were very hungry to win every game that season. We believed in ourselves and we always had something to prove to somebody.

The day we were to leave for the Orange Bowl, the airport was shut down because of bad weather, so we had to drive almost two hours from Jenks. It was freezing and the roads were bad. I rode to the airport with Matt McCoy and his father that day, and I think our flight to Miami was the only one they let go that day.

We got off the plane and walked out into that Miami weather, but then we had to go work out. I don't think any of us realized that we had to go run that day until we got off the plane, but that team never shied away from hard work.

Florida State didn't give us the respect we deserved. They said that we hadn't faced a team like them, an offense like theirs. They were scoring 40 points per game and had the Heisman Trophy winner, but we knew you had to respect your opponent as you prepared for them. I don't think that they knew that.

Once the game started, that high-powered offense of theirs was doing nothing to us. It was a strange game, because the momentum went back and forth, but nobody was scoring any points. We threw an interception and then Torrance [Marshall] made an interception for us. We were playing with them and realized their offense wasn't that explosive. The only big play I made was stripping [Florida State quarterback Chris] Weinke.

What really would have been the perfect ending would have been to shut them out 13–0 to go with our 13–0 record. That would have been the perfect script, but we had that safety at the end of the game.

Hey, we'll still take it.

We totally dominated them on defense. Our defense was made for linebackers and safeties.

We mixed it up pretty well, too, and confused people. We would bring two linebackers one time and then a linebacker and a safety the next time.

Oklahoma has a great coaching staff. Once we got to be around them, we could tell they knew what it took to be a great program. They made it exciting and fun because of their enthusiasm for the game. Mike Stoops had a little too much enthusiasm at times, but I grew very close to coach "V" [Venables]. I still stay in touch with him. They both are great coaches.

People bring up all the time that I passed on the *Playboy* photo shoot for the All-America team before the 2001 season. Let me start by saying that I have tremendous parents who brought me up in a Christian home. I had a great foundation, so when that opportunity came up, I realized that it was an All-America honor and you want to be named an All-American any time you can, but when people think of *Playboy*, they think of one thing—and it is not football. And that is not what I am about. The decision wasn't hard for me.

What was hard were those two losses during my senior season.

We went up to Nebraska and played in a great atmosphere against a great team and all of their tradition. They really have great fans, nice fans. We lost Jason White early with an injury that day, but we were stopping them on defense. Then they ran that trick play, that throwback pass to [Eric] Crouch, and I think the defensive end didn't contain on the play. You aren't going to catch Crouch once he's running free.

We saw Colorado kick Nebraska real good at the end of the season and knew we still had a shot, but we gave it away by losing to Oklahoma State [16–13]. Their kicker made two 50-yard field goals that day—how often does that happen?—and they completed that one pass in the corner of the end zone when Roy Williams got beat. That didn't happen very often to him.

It was Senior Day and the last game I ever played at home. That was by far the worst loss of my career.

We played as well as a defense can play in the Cotton Bowl because we wanted to go out on top. We held Arkansas to 55 yards, and that is unheard of. One of my last plays as a Sooner was making the fumble recovery on their final possession.

It goes by so quickly that it is tough to recapture every big moment, but I hope I did a good job of it.

I was one of the Oklahoma boys who wanted to help rebuild the tradition, to be a part of it. What happened our freshman year and then with coach Stoops coming in and laying that new foundation, that makes me proud.

We brought the magic back to Oklahoma football. That was one of the main reasons I decided to go there in the first place. The program is strong again, to match the tradition, and it will continue to be that way.

Rocky Calmus was an All-American in 2000 and 2001. He won the Butkus Award as the nation's top linebacker in 2001. He led OU in tackles in 1999, 2000, and 2001, totaling 431 for his career. His 59 tackles for loss is a school record. He also was a two-time team captain. Calmus was selected in the third round of the 2002 NFL draft by the Tennessee Titans.

Josh Heupel | Quarterback | 1999–2000

My earliest childhood memories involve playing with a ball of some kind. I didn't get a lot of toys, because sports was my toy. Everything I did growing up in Aberdeen, South Dakota, revolved around athletics. You name the sport and I played it. I loved hockey and basketball, and I also wrestled.

My father was a coach in high school and ultimately became head coach at the college in town, Northern State University, a Division II school. As soon as I could walk, I spent my time with my dad. It wasn't so much about the game of football at that point, as it was an opportunity to spend time with my father. But naturally, whether I wanted to or not, I soaked up his knowledge of football.

Before he was a head coach, Dad worked on the defensive side of the ball, so that is what I learned first. I never even experienced an offensive practice until I became a player myself. I would get dropped off at Dad's practices after school every day, or I would go with him into the office at 5:30 a.m.

I was in a lot of football meetings and watched a lot of film when I was a kid. What I noticed was how the good athletes became great players and what it took for them to get there.

Dad had worked hard, growing up on a farm, so the one thing he wanted to instill in me and in my sister was a hard-work ethic. He didn't want me sitting on my butt watching TV or playing video games. He encouraged me to do a lot of different sports and to compete hard in each one of them.

Still, when I started to play football, he never forced the game on me. But then again, he didn't have to.

For some reason, I loved the control that the quarterback had on the game. That is what drew me to the position. I played quarterback in the eighth grade and loved it, and then started every game from the second game of my sophomore season at Aberdeen Central High.

We had a coach who had been a graduate assistant at the University of Houston under John Jenkins when they ran the run-and-shoot, so our offense was wide open. I remember having an autographed poster on my wall of Andre Ware, who played at Houston, because I loved their style of play.

We weren't very successful in my first two years, but we had a very good team in my senior year. We got beat in the second round of the playoffs, but we were as good as anybody in the state.

I had scheduled a recruiting visit to Houston, but a quarterback who had committed somewhere else changed his mind, and all of a sudden, there wasn't a scholarship available for me. A couple of Division I-AA schools, Montana and Weber State, wanted me, so I took the best opportunity I had at the time to play for four years—that was Weber State. Weber State was like all the Big Sky schools back then—they threw the ball around quite a lot. Mike Price had coached there before taking the Washington State job, and they always produced some good players and had some tradition.

When I got there, I decided to redshirt and then compete for the starting job the following season, but I tore my ACL [knee] in the spring game after my freshman season. I came back that fall and competed for the job during two-a-days, but it was only three and a half months later, and it was too soon after the injury. I started a few games at the end of that [1997] season, but I had to rest the knee to get it completely healthy.

My head coach took a job at Utah State after that season, and I was left in limbo. I decided to stay long enough to get familiar with the new coach's offense to see if it would fit me, but it was a pound-it-down-your-throat and play-action-pass offense. I knew that wasn't the best thing for me, so I transferred to Snow Junior College in Ephraim, Utah, in March 1998.

My dad had some players who played there. I knew they threw the football around a bunch and always had good quarterbacks. I also knew that if I transferred to a major school from Weber State, I would lose a year of eligibility. I needed to play, so I thought that was the best thing for me.

I had a good year at Snow, passing for a lot of yards and making Junior College All-American. That season led to me being recruited by Utah State, New Mexico, and Minnesota.

I was visiting Utah State when my dad called and said he'd got a call from a guy named Mike Leach, who was leaving Kentucky to become offensive coordinator at Oklahoma. When I got back to my hotel room, I made a quick call to coach Leach. But there is no such thing as a quick conversation with him.

Being a football fan, I knew what Kentucky had done with their offense, and I wanted to make sure that was what they were going to do at Oklahoma. I never figured in my wildest dreams that a school like Oklahoma would be throwing it around like he was planning.

About 10 days later, right after New Year's, I visited Norman, and coach Leach picked me up at the airport. He had to have Merv Johnson, who had coached at the university a long time, ride along with him so he could find his way back from the airport. Remember that he and coach

A coach's son, Josh Heupel was exactly the leader new coach Bob Stoops was looking for to run Oklahoma's wide-open offense. Heupel passed for more than 7,400 yards and 53 touchdowns in only two seasons as a Sooner. *Photo courtesy of Lisa Hall.*

Stoops and the staff were new to Oklahoma, too, so they were as lost as I was. I really had no idea of where I was.

On the way from the airport to campus, I noticed that the highest building around was the stadium. Then I saw the Barry Switzer Center and all the portraits of the great players in the past. I knew that it wasn't a 5- or 10- or even a 15-year stretch of greatness. It was decades and decades of greatness, dating back to Bud Wilkinson, and the school had won six national championships.

If the offense fit, which I still didn't know, then it would be the place for me.

That day, we had lunch with coach Stoops, and he asked if I had any questions.

"Just two," I said. "Can we compete for a conference championship and can we compete for a national championship?"

He said yes to both.

I could tell he was genuine. He has that ability to make people buy into his system, even though I knew turnarounds like that don't happen very often.

Every other minute of that trip was spent in the film room with coach Leach. I think he wanted to get a good feel of what I saw defensively in certain situations and make sure that I was the right guy for him to run his offense.

While watching film, he would ask me things like, "What would you do here?"

And I wanted to get a feel for him and his offense.

I would ask, "Now, what do you want your quarterback to do here in this situation?"

When we realized it would be a good fit for both coach Leach and myself, I left there knowing that's where I wanted to be. I got home and talked to my parents about it. I then called coach Stoops and told him, "I am coming."

I was home for two days before I came back to Norman for good. When they had showed me around campus on that earlier visit, the guy who had taken me to the indoor facility acted like his key wouldn't fit. It was pitch dark and late at night, and I couldn't see inside the place, but this was Oklahoma, so I took it for granted that they had a beautiful indoor facility.

On the first day of winter workouts, we walked over to the indoor facility at 6:30 one morning, and as I walked inside, I looked around and thought, "You've got to be kidding me."

The turf must have been from about 1982. The ceiling was about 15 feet high, and there was a batting cage at the end of the field, which had a track around it. It wasn't exactly what I expected.

Then we started working out with coach [Jerry] Schmidt, who had just come from Florida with coach Stoops. He is as good a strength coach as anybody in the country. We ran for about an hour, and guys were throwing up in garbage cans. He blew the whistle and we thought, "Thank God, we are finally done."

No, that was the warm-up. We were in there for a long time. The fact is, we were a long way from where we needed to be. There were a lot of talented people in the building that day, but we weren't yet a football team.

I entered that spring as first-string on the depth chart, but the offense was not second nature to me yet. I called a play and thought, "Holy cow! This game is so fast here." It was the same feeling I had when I was a sophomore in high school. By the end of the spring, it slowed down for me a little. As I got more and more reps, I felt more comfortable.

I talked about all that tradition at Oklahoma, but there were a lot of down years when teams had not performed to that previous level. We may have felt that skepticism in the community. The big question was, "Would Oklahoma football ever get back to where it was?"

There was a lot to prove for all of us. A goal of mine had always been to win a conference championship and a national championship, but the pressure was on us. That summer was as long a summer as I ever experienced. I just never knew it could get that hot in Oklahoma. The workouts were long and hard, but it prepared us to be as good as we could be for the 1999 season.

There was an excitement to it all, but an underlying skepticism in the community, as I mentioned. You could just sense it. Everybody wondered what kind of team we would put on the field. I think back about that time now, and it feels so long ago.

I thought we had an opportunity to be a good football team, but I didn't know how good. You never know until you get out on the field and play a game.

I was extremely nervous before the season-opener against Indiana State, but I knew I was ready to play. We pulled up to the stadium and saw all of those people in crimson and cream out there tailgating. Then we came out and went through warm-ups about 50 minutes before kickoff, but there weren't many people in the stadium. It was not even half-full. I went back into the locker room and was thinking about everything I had gone through to get to this point and wondered if anybody would show up to see us.

I was always the last guy out of the locker room, so when I got down to the bottom of the ramp, I heard "Boomer Sooner" and looked up at that massive upper deck—it was packed with people.

I thought, "Yeah, this is a little different than Ephraim," where we had 1,200 fans at every game.

It was exciting. Your first touchdown pass and your first win are things you never forget.

We won those first three games [Indiana State, Baylor, and Louisville], and we were riding high. We went to Notre Dame and went ahead by 17 points in the third quarter. And then the wheels fell off. How did we let that slip away [a 34–30 loss]? I really don't know. We could have been 4–0 and cranking as we headed into the Red River Shootout.

I had always heard about the OU-Texas rivalry because it was the first thing some people mentioned to me during my recruiting trip.

We went down to Dallas and it was a smoking hot day, but I could tell it was the best atmosphere in college football. We got up by 17 again and the wheels came off again [in a 38–28 loss]. As good as we started, now we were 3–2 and fighting our tails off to have a winning record.

We lost the Independence Bowl [to Mississippi], but we were ahead in every game we had played that season. We came back home, and I was watching the national championship game [Florida State–Virginia Tech in the Sugar Bowl], when I mentioned to my roommate, "There is absolutely no reason we can't play in that game next year."

We had finished 7–5, and yet we could have won every one of the games we had lost.

I had heard the rumors about coach Leach leaving and then he called me. He told me he had a good opportunity [as head coach of Texas Tech], and I wished him the best. I thanked him for giving me the chance to play at Oklahoma. It was an easy change for us, really, because coach [Mark] Mangino had been there on the staff. We had great coaches at Oklahoma. Coach [Chuck] Long really helped my fundamentals and technique and helped me become a better football player in general.

In the first year of somebody's system, some kids question how you are doing things and why you are doing them. I know that happened with coach Stoops. In that off-season, some of the guys who weren't fully on board found other places to be. That really helped, too, because it took away any negative weight that we had during the 1999 season. Whenever that happens and those type of people leave, you get better as a team.

As we began workouts, we were able to handle more than the year before. We were in better shape and we were mentally tougher as a team. We had 100-percent attendance in our summer workouts, which we didn't have the year before. In those seven-on-seven sessions, everything went smoothly because we had been together for a year.

Before the 2000 season, we all talked about winning a national championship, but not many people outside of that locker room thought it was possible. We thought we had an opportunity to win every game because of how close we played every game the year before. If we took them one at a time, I knew we had a chance to win each game, but if we looked at it as a 13-game stretch—now that is a tough deal.

We started 4–0 [beating UTEP, Arkansas State, Rice, and Kansas] before we played Texas. I remember waking up that day in Dallas, and it was pouring down rain.

I looked out the window and thought, "This is not good. This is not what I want."

I was trying to grip the balls during the warm-ups, and I was probably throwing them end over end. We started the game with a quick drive, and I threw a fade to Andre [Woolfork] to put us up 7–0. Then it was 14–0, and 17–0. Now we remembered being up by 17 points a year earlier when we let it get away from us. On the sidelines, we just kept telling each other, "Let's keep rolling and not let up on them."

But we never figured it would get as out of control as it did [a 63–14 OU win].

It was a huge win for us, and the fans were really jacked about the outcome, but I don't want to say we were back just yet.

That next week, at Kansas State, was the most hostile environment I ever played in. You just felt that those fans hated you. There was a lot of history between those coaching staffs, because the Stoops brothers, coach Mangino, and coach [Brett] Venables had all coached there. Any time you go against people you are familiar with, there is some added spice to it. Coach Stoops never talked about it, but we sensed it a little. They were a great football team and were ranked No. 2. I remember it was Harley Davidson Day and about a hundred of those big hogs were on the field.

In the fourth quarter, they blocked a punt to get within seven points of us, and that was probably the loudest moment I had ever experienced of any game in which I played. We hung on to win [41–31], and I was totally exhausted after that game. I was sick. That is probably when a lot of fans jumped on our bandwagon. Not everybody did, but we gained a lot of them with that win.

Now we had to play the No. 1 team, Nebraska, but we had a week off to prepare for it. I think that any time you have a bye week, it is a good thing if you use it the right way. After playing Texas and K-State, we probably needed it.

It was an early kickoff and a beautiful fall day in Norman. I felt it was an opportunity to put Oklahoma back on top of the college football world. I knew if we won it, we would be ranked No. 1.

But we got down 14–0 right away, and I was struggling early in that game. I was not in rhythm at all. I remember sitting on the bench and hearing somebody in the crowd right behind our bench say, "I *knew* we weren't that good."

We never panicked, however. We never had that look of concern. We just picked it up and got started, but I never expected us to score

31 straight points to close out the game that way. I remember hearing horns honking until 2:00 a.m. after the game. I had about 50 friends and family members down for that game from South Dakota, where almost everybody roots for Nebraska. As a kid, I had an Oklahoma hat, not because I was an Oklahoma fan, but because I hated Nebraska.

So as you can imagine, it was a great night for me.

After we beat Baylor, Texas A&M set out to break the noise record for our next game. That place was swaying back and forth that day. I told the guys early in the game, "Let's just get some first downs and make some plays and we'll get this crowd out of the game."

We made a few first downs, but it didn't matter. That place just got louder, and it was like that nonstop for the remainder of the game. The huddle gets awfully tight in those games with people squeezing in like sardines trying to hear you call the plays.

We got down in that game, but we never panicked. We fought our way back, against a ranked team and against the loudest crowd. We put a drive together, and then Torrance Marshall picked off a pass. I was watching it on the Jumbotron and I grabbed my helmet, figuring we would get the ball in good field position. The next thing I knew he was coming all the way down the sideline for a touchdown.

Let me tell you that there is not a better feeling in sports than winning a tough, hard-fought game on the road in front of a hostile crowd. It is you versus everybody. There is a certain focus you must have to win games like that on the road. Winning that game [35–31] was one of those times. We were 9–0 and feeling pretty good.

We had a team with a lot of players who had chips on their shoulders. Take our offensive line, for example. That was a mix-and-match offensive line that became great. Frank Romero came in as a defensive lineman and probably weighed 210 when he got to Oklahoma. He became a great tackle. Howard Duncan was a junior college transfer from Kansas. Bubba Burcham was a walk-on. Mike Skinner was a sophomore. Scott Kempenich had been banged up and had knee surgery. Those were all guys who worked very hard to get where they were.

Our receivers, like Andre Woolfork and Curtis Fagan, had started their careers as defensive backs. Quentin [Griffin] wasn't highly recruited, either. We just had a lot of guys who had something to prove.

We had blown out Oklahoma State [44–7] the year before, so when we drove 99 yards on our first possession against them, we may have been thinking it was going to be another easy game. All of a sudden, they got into a three-man front and started dropping people into coverage. At times, they dropped 10 players into coverage, and I had never seen that before in my life. We struggled against it. And it was their coach's [Bob Simmons] last game, so they were fired up to play us.

Thankfully, our defense played great and we hung on [for a 12–7 win].

That win made it possible for us to play for the Big 12 championship in a rematch with K-State. It was a tight game and one of the coldest games I ever played in—and I came from South Dakota.

One of the key plays late in the game was when we were up seven points and ran an option play on fourth-and-1. That was a throwback to the glory days of Sooner football! I pitched it to "Q" and he ran about 22 yards. That set up a TD pass to Andre, and then Tim Duncan hit a 46-yard field goal to put us up by 10 points. They scored late to make it 27–24, but we recovered the onside kick and ran out the clock.

We were headed to the Orange Bowl to play in the national championship game—a game that I had mentioned watching a year earlier and thought we had a real shot of playing in.

There had been some preseason talk about me and the Heisman, but I didn't think about it at all. Until the night I was actually in New York, with all those Heisman winners around, I never gave it much thought. Then I walked into that old room with all the paintings of the past winners, and I met Andre Ware, whom I had a poster of on my wall, and it got me to thinking about winning it. People asked me if I was nervous. I never got nervous until he walked up to the microphone with that envelope—and called the wrong name! [Florida State's Chris Weinke finished with 1,628 points; Heupel was second with 1,562, making it the second-closest finish in Heisman Trophy history.]

It was a neat experience, but the next day I just wanted to get back with my team and prepare for the Orange Bowl.

It was Florida State's third national championship game in three years and the media was still very high on all of the Florida schools at the time. I think they probably questioned us because we had struggled against Oklahoma State and then beat K-State by three points in the Big 12 championship game.

I think people really underestimated the strength of the Big 12 that year. Nebraska finished fourth in the conference, and they beat Northwestern by about 60 points in the Alamo Bowl. Kansas State was as good as any team we faced, and they beat Tennessee in the Cotton Bowl by about 50 points. So I think people should have realized that this conference was pretty good as we headed into the Orange Bowl.

We were used to being underdogs. We weren't favorites that much all year long, especially going into the Texas game and the Nebraska game. Being an underdog fit our personality. None of us were that highly regarded coming out of high school. We didn't have this and we didn't have that, everybody told us.

On the other hand, Florida State thought strongly about their football team. I think they had 10 players drafted off that team, so they were very talented.

But yes, I feel that they definitely underestimated us. When they walked past our locker room that night before the game, we were ready to tear the doors down and go at it right there. I think we had an intensity that night that they did not have.

We tinkered with the game plan a little and didn't take many chances that night. We just knew that our defense was in control of what was happening as the game progressed. We put some drives together, but I threw a pick in the red zone once, and I think we had a big play and then fumbled at the end of it. We just didn't take advantage, and that's why we led only 3–0 at the half.

They were a man-to-man team, and I knew they would try to lock onto our receivers. We thought we could run some rub routes and get some guys open. One thing is true: they had a tremendous front four.

When we got it to 6–0, I felt pretty good because our defense was dominating. Once we got a turnover, we were in the red zone, and I knew any score would put them away. We called a trap, just trying to get "Q" loose. The little guy is tough to see, let alone tackle. He squeaked through that hole [a 10-yard touchdown run], and at that point, I knew it was over.

I still can't put into words how that [13–2 OU victory] feels, even today. It's as good a feeling as you can ever imagine. I can't imagine feeling any better than that. To be able to share that with 100 other individuals, from players to coaches to support staff . . . it is something special.

I have to thank coach Stoops, who gave me the opportunity. He believed in me enough while he was rebuilding the program. The way he treats everyone is the way I want to do it when I become a head coach one day. I will always be indebted to him.

To see where I came from just two years earlier, things like that don't happen very often. The thing I learned was that I enjoyed the process and the journey in getting there. That was the most fun. It was everything that led up to that night at the Orange Bowl. All of the hard work, the sweat, and the off-season conditioning . . . that's what makes it worth something.

I'll be honest with you, I could not tell you about one passing record or statistic I have from my time at Oklahoma. The things I remember about being a Sooner are the relationships I formed with people and what we accomplished as a team. I remember all the good times and bad times, on and off the field.

Few football programs in the country have the tradition of the University of Oklahoma, so to play at a university like this is a real honor for me.

The fans' enthusiasm and overwhelming support for the program is something that I will always remember and truly appreciate.

The great thing about the University of Oklahoma is all that tradition. Before I got there, there were six national championships and hundreds of All-Americans and thousands of other great players throughout history. Now there are seven national championships and even more players who have added to the tradition. There is something special about that place.

I have to say, I couldn't have planned my career any better than the way it actually happened.

In 2000 Josh Heupel led Oklahoma to a school-record 13 wins and a seventh national championship, and became Oklahoma's first consensus All-American quarterback. He also was a team captain in 1999 and 2000. He finished second in the Heisman Trophy balloting. He was named player of the year by the Associated Press, CBS, The Sporting News, and Walter Camp. He completed 654 of 1,025 passes for 7,456 yards and 53 touchdowns in his two-year career. Heupel was a graduate assistant coach at OU in 2003–2004 and became an assistant coach at the University of Arizona in 2005.

Roy Williams | Defensive Back | 1999–2001

I never watched football growing up in the Bay Area of California, although my dad was a big Dallas Cowboys fan. I would have much rather played the game than watch it. I tried T-ball, but that didn't work for me. I tried basketball, and that didn't work me. But football did.

I loved the game. I went to James Logan High School in Union City and started as a sophomore, playing cornerback and quarterback. We had a good program and played in the state championship game during my senior year, but lost. We ran the option and were basically a running offense, but we tried some of the run-and-shoot and West Coast offense when I was a senior. Let me put it this way: I wasn't an accurate quarterback, but I ran quite a bit.

I visited UCLA, Cal, Washington State, and Oklahoma. I was going to go to UCLA, and my buddy, Damian Mackey, was going to go to Stanford, but then he got hurt. Then we decided we would go to the same school, and I really wanted to get away from California.

Plus, John Blake at Oklahoma was a hell of a recruiter.

During my recruiting visit to Oklahoma, there were several guys—Curtis Fagan, Trent Smith, Damian and Frank Romero, and me—who got together and talked. We knew the program was down [coming off a 4–8 season in 1997], but we told each other, "Let's turn this around. Let's make it a top program again and let's do it together."

One by one, we finally said, "I am committing here, what about you?"

Everybody seemed to like everybody else and we all clicked. The campus was cool, but we were coming to play football. I really didn't know anything about OU history, and I am still learning it to this day.

Like I said, I didn't watch much football, but I was a Deion Sanders, Ronnie Lott, and Steve Atwater fan. Honestly, I don't get caught up in history. It doesn't mean anything, anyway, unless you do it yourself.

I understand Oklahoma won championships in the past, but that didn't help us win any championships. I know one thing: there was plenty of talent in Norman. John Blake could recruit, no matter what his record was. He was pretty laid back, but he could recruit.

I played a few games as a freshman, but I hurt my back in the TCU game [1998] and ended up redshirting.

I was in California when coach Blake got fired and I felt bad about it. People had told me before that it would happen, but I never knew what to expect. That proves it's a business, but life goes on.

We had a meeting after coach Blake got fired and told each other, "Whomever they bring in, we'll have to prove ourselves over again." Some people had taken advantage of the fact that Blake was laid back, not taking him seriously enough. I don't want to say we had no discipline, maybe just not enough.

We were over there chilling together when we should have been training, but when we met coach Stoops, that all changed. We embraced him from the beginning, but we didn't know a thing about him. He put his foot down right away. He gave the program a facelift and that is what was needed. It was for the best.

We knew this man was for real. He was all business. There was no more playing around anymore. We were going to do great things and we had to buy into what he was telling us.

I was saying, "Let's give this guy the benefit of the doubt and do what he asks of us."

The ones who were defiant, he ran them out right away. A few? No, I think he ran almost the whole defense off, about 11 of those guys were from the defense. Most of them just quit or transferred. I guess some of them just didn't like being told what to do.

Look what happened: we went to a bowl in our first season under coach Stoops.

The first big step we took in 1999 was learning we could win on the road, beating Louisville [42–21].

I really didn't know anything about the rivalry with Texas before I got to Oklahoma, but I had watched it as a freshman when I was hurt. Walking down that tunnel, you get such an adrenaline rush, and I really do hate Texas. If you don't when you get to Oklahoma, you learn to hate Texas.

We had a lead in my sophomore year, and I will never forget this—I bit on a post-corner route and the dude scored on me. I knew it was my fault. I thought right then, "I will get them back for that."

We headed up the tunnel at halftime and their quarterback, [Major] Applewhite, was talking trash to us. I couldn't believe it. I will never forget that. From that point on, I wanted to do something important every time we played Texas. We couldn't beat them by enough points to make me happy.

At the end of the Independence Bowl [a 27–25 loss to Mississippi], I knew we had the potential to be a great team the next year. Jay Hunt, Damian, and I were sitting in my apartment one day and we looked at our schedule for the next season. There wasn't a team on there that could beat us if we played well. We knew we could beat all of those teams. It was as if we had placed our order that we would win the whole thing. We had tasted a little bit of victory, won some games, got to a bowl, but it was an adjustment period. I knew then that we had the makings of a great team.

That off-season, [strength coach] Jerry Schmidt just worked us all the time. We were dedicated.

We were undefeated by the time we played Texas the next year, and so were they. It was a gloomy, rainy day, and Stoops gave one of those great motivational speeches. It ended with something like, "Let's go kick some Texas ass."

We did. It was like we had their plays down that day. We knew what they were going to run before they ran it. The defining play was when they had a fourth-and-1 early in the game and I filled the hole to stop the first down. Quentin [Griffin] then went wild and scored all of those touchdowns and it was a fun thing to watch.

Beating Texas is always special, but I really think that game [a 63–14 win] was a turning point for the whole program.

The Nebraska game was another big game. We shouldn't have let them score those 14 points [Nebraska led 14–0], but we were so excited that we were overrunning plays that day. We were very prepared for their offense, but we were just too excited.

Finally, Stoops said, "Calm down! We know what we are doing, just calm down and do it!"

Roy Williams, here laying a solid hit on an Oklahoma State player, became known as one of the hardest-hitting safeties in college football. He also made big plays, finishing his career with 34 tackles for loss. *Photo courtesy of Lisa Hall.*

We scored, created turnovers, and got back in the game. Our special teams, offense, and defense all clicked and we won it big [31–14].

Our goal that season was to win the national championship, but we were focused on one game at a time. We never looked ahead. Coach Stoops wouldn't have had it any other way. We got tested by Texas A&M and Oklahoma State, but we remained focused on what we wanted to do.

I still say that was the best defense in Oklahoma history. We had a phenomenal front four, great linebackers, and the secondary was pretty good, too. The great thing was, it wasn't just one guy. Everybody made plays. And I loved our scheme. It allowed me to make plays, attack and blitz and be around the football. Coach Stoops felt that where I could make plays was wherever the football was.

I knew heading into that Orange Bowl game that Florida State underestimated us. They thought we were a hillbilly school from the Big 12. We were walking down South Beach one day, and we always believed in good sportsmanship, but when we tried to speak to a few of their players, some of them were very cocky. They didn't even want to acknowledge us. We had heard about their tactics of running through our stretch drills, but we were so prepared for that game, nothing they did mattered to us.

We knew [Florida State quarterback Chris] Weinke wasn't mobile, so we would pressure him. All they had in running plays was a toss left and a toss right. Their game plan was so simple. We attacked them. We were relentless that night. I don't think they crossed the 50-yard line for a long time in that game. That was a great night [a 13–2 OU victory].

Finishing 13–0 and winning a national championship is the ultimate success. You know you've arrived when you do that. It is every kid's dream to win a national championship in college. Everybody wants to be a part of something great like that, but few get to do it. Even if I never win a Super Bowl ring, I know what it feels like because of that game and that season.

The next season, we didn't win them all, but we beat Texas [14–3] again. I had jumped up to try to rush the quarterback earlier in the year and got blocked where it hurt most. Mike Stoops had always yelled at me, "Don't jump!"

They had the ball deep in their territory and we were leading [7–3], when I knew they would try to cut [block] me again.

I thought, "If they do that, I am jumping over them."

They were on their own 2-yard line. I thought, "Well, if I get yelled at, I get yelled at, but I am making a play." I jumped up and hit [quarterback Chris Simms] and knocked the ball out. That's when it fell right into Teddy [Lehman]'s hands. That touchdown clinched the game. It was perfect.

Do we own Texas? Yes!

We should have won at Nebraska, but their quarterback trick play worked and ours didn't, and that was the story of the game [a 20–10 OU loss]. The toughest loss [16–13] was to Oklahoma State. They just wanted it more and they beat us. You can't make any excuses for it.

But we rebounded to beat Arkansas [10–3] in the Cotton Bowl. I had wanted to go out with a bang and do something special in my last game. I had about eight or nine tackles and two sacks, and we won.

Why would I come back for my senior season? I had won the Bronco Nagurski Award, the Jim Thorpe Award, had been the Big 12 Defensive Player of the Year, and had a national championship ring; so what was left for me to do?

Every year I had gotten better and the game was slowing down for me, so I needed a new challenge.

Coach Stoops tried to talk me into staying, saying that I would be number one on the Heisman list, but I didn't want to come back.

I put a lot of pain, blood, and sweat into my Oklahoma career. I love the University of Oklahoma. That's why I donate a lot of time and money to that school. It has done a lot for me. I want to thank Oklahoma for giving me the opportunity to play college football. My heart will always love Oklahoma. I think of those days every time I walk by my memorabilia room and I see all those Oklahoma items. I know I am a part of its history.

Roy Williams was an All-American strong safety in 2001, a season in which he won the Nagurski Award and the Thorpe Award. Despite leaving OU after his junior season, he finished his career with 287 tackles, including 34 for loss. He also broke up 44 passes and had 9 quarterback sacks in his career. He was named All–Big 12 in 2000 and 2001. He was taken in the first round of the 2002 NFL draft by the Dallas Cowboys.

Jason White | Quarterback | 1999–2004

I grew up in Tuttle, which is only about 20 miles west of Norman, and my earliest memories of sports were from playing baseball and from going to my sister's softball practices. Every time we would be leaving her practices, there was a guy standing there holding a pair of football pants, recruiting kids to play in Pop Warner.

Every time I walked by him, he would say, "It looks like these would fit you."

Every time it was the same thing.

"It looks like these would fit you."

Finally, one day, I said, "I will try it."

That first year, I played center and linebacker, and I didn't like it at all. My parents tell the story of how much I didn't want to go to practice. They would have to drag me to practice, but Dad wouldn't let me quit.

His philosophy always has been, "Once you start something, you finish it."

Dad was always a big sports fan. He loved watching football and he was always into softball and baseball. He coached my baseball team for a long time and helped me with my football career.

I guess his philosophy about not quitting something once you start it would stick with me once I got to college. It wasn't that I didn't like football that first year I tried it, but more than anything, I didn't like playing center and linebacker. That wasn't my thing. I played with the older guys, and I was always getting the crap beat out of me.

The very next year, I got to play running back. By the seventh grade, I started growing and maturing, and I became a quarterback and a running back. In the eighth grade, the high school coach in town told the junior high coaches, "Put him at quarterback and keep him there."

We went undefeated in the eighth and ninth grades. During my freshman season, I would play quarterback in the freshman games on

Thursday nights and then play free safety for the varsity on Friday nights because there was a junior quarterback starting at the time. The next year, when I was a sophomore, he and I started the season splitting time. I played receiver when I was not at quarterback.

Then we lost a game against Millwood, and I didn't play quarterback again that season. I think some of the seniors' parents put the blame on me for that loss and they got on the coach about it.

In my junior year, nobody thought we would be any good, but we went undefeated before losing in the second round of the playoffs. We tried to run a two-point conversion to win the game and didn't get it. In my senior year, we went undefeated again and made it into the semifinals.

One of the highlights of my career was making a 47-yard field goal to win a playoff game. And I did it with a concussion! I hadn't played the whole second half, and the coach came up to me and said, "You make it, we win. You miss it, we lose."

How's that for pressure?

The great thing in high school was that we ran a wide-open offense with a lot of variety that really helped me prepare for the college game.

Recruiting was pretty hectic for me. I was also playing basketball, and when I would come home after practice, the phone would be ringing off the hook. I had no time to relax. The phone just continued ringing all the time. I narrowed it down to a few schools really quickly just to get some other schools off my back.

I loved my visit to Miami and I had made up my mind to go there. Coach [John] Blake was still at Oklahoma, and I didn't think I fit into that OU offense at the time. I had pretty much ruled Oklahoma out when he was fired. Then coach Stoops came in, and I liked what the new offense looked like.

Growing up, I didn't watch many games on TV, so the only reason I knew anything about the Sooners was because my dad always talked about them. I never paid much attention to college football. I once went to a game during my junior year in high school to see them play California [a 13–12 OU loss], and it was awesome. The Sooners weren't doing well at the time, and still all these fans were there going crazy.

When I met coach Stoops, I could tell he had a fire lit under him from the get-go. Whatever he said, I believed it. He was so intense. I could tell then that he really wanted to get something done at Oklahoma. I met [offensive coordinator] Mike Leach and I also could tell he was a football genius.

I thought it was a great opportunity—to play in that offense and to stay close to home. So I forgot about Miami and committed to Oklahoma soon after my visit that January.

I went to Norman early that summer to the voluntary workouts to get a head start. I remember I was so worn out. I felt out of place and didn't know many people, so I spent most of my time in my room. I was always so tired. I had thought I was in pretty good shape, but I guess I wasn't. I was amazed at how hard it was. [Strength and conditioning] coach [Jerry] Schmidt about killed me that summer.

I got in those first two games in 1999 against Indiana State and Baylor when we got way ahead and Josh [Heupel] came out. After playing a little, I was so motivated to get back in there again it made me work even harder.

Then the week after the Louisville game, I got hurt in the weight room. As freshmen, we had to lift four days each week, and I hurt my back. I had some earlier back problems and I aggravated it. The school filed for a medical redshirt so that season wouldn't count against me even though I had played a little.

I jumped into Josh's back pocket that next summer. I always saw him working out by himself and asked him one day if he would mind if I worked out with him.

He said, "Sure, come along with me."

After we started, I was thinking, "This is a lot of work."

We did everything: throwing, agility drills, weights, [stomach] strengthening. That is one reason I stopped having back problems. I learned how to get my core stronger. Josh really helped me, and I could tell from the start that he was coaching material. When he told receivers how to run a certain route, he knew what he was talking about. He was awesome to me.

Jason White became the first Oklahoma quarterback and only the fourth Sooner to win the Heisman Trophy when he passed for nearly 4,000 yards and 40 touchdowns in 2003.
Photo courtesy of Lisa Hall.

As the 2000 season started, I was so down on the depth chart. Josh would come out of the game when we were beating somebody badly and Nate [Hybl] would go in. Then Patrick [Fletcher] would go in. Basically, I fell off the chart.

During practices, I was just standing around, so I decided to go to the quarterbacks coach with an idea.

"I am not getting any reps, so I would rather go run the scout-team offense," I told him.

He said, "OK, if that's what you want to do."

And that scout team wasn't bad. We took a lot of pride in playing well. If we ever scored a touchdown against that defense, we knew we had accomplished something. Our defense was awesome that year.

I felt good about contributing something. I wasn't just over there standing around. And at the same time, not many guys in college football ever get to experience a national championship team. We had a lot of fun that season just being part of the team, even if we didn't get to play.

After the Orange Bowl, I worked harder than I ever worked before. All the media had Nate Hybl slated as the starter when we went into the spring, but I had a pretty decent spring. Then the media was writing things like, "Now we don't know who it will be."

I worked hard that summer and I knew it was a close battle between him and me, but after one of those two-a-day practices, coach [Chuck] Long called me into his office and said, "We made a decision to start Nate."

I was devastated.

I went home that day with no desire to work hard anymore. I knew what I had put into it and I thought, "Maybe I am just not good enough to play the game at this level."

During those first four games, I was really down. I thought about transferring to a smaller school because I really wondered if I was good enough. Then coach Long told me, "You can play at this level. You are good enough. And I promise you that at some point, you will play here. It is very rare when one quarterback makes it through an entire season."

Sure enough, during the Texas game, the coaches yelled for me to warm up. They put me into the game when Texas had us pushed back to our own 10-yard line. I had trouble calling the plays because I was so nervous. I remember that on my first pass, I got hit hard in the back and that settled me down.

After [a 14–3 OU win], coach Long told me, "I told you so."

I was a different guy after that game. I looked forward to watching film and going to practice.

I played in the Kansas game [rushing for 117 yards and passing for 151 in a 38–10 win] and then made my first start against Baylor. I don't remember much about it other than it was hot and I think I passed for 300 yards [32 of 44 for 343 yards in a 33–17 win].

The next game was at Nebraska, and I remember how many interviews I had to do that week. I got caught up to speed on the importance of the rivalry real fast. On our first offensive series, I couldn't hear myself in the huddle because it was so loud. That place in Lincoln was rocking that day.

I didn't calm down until the second quarter when I started to make some plays. We had just started on a drive when I dropped back, felt the rush coming, and sprinted to the right. I saw Quentin [Griffin] wide open and threw him the ball, but I threw it awkwardly. I landed, coming down on my left leg, but all my weight was not in the right place. As soon as I landed, I heard my [left] knee pop. I couldn't move the bottom half of my leg.

When I got up, I started walking and thought, "This isn't too bad."

Then the doctors told me it was a torn ACL. They put a brace on it and I tried to play through it for a few weeks. Right before the Texas A&M game, I said, "This isn't working." I knew that I needed surgery.

I didn't want to fall behind the other quarterbacks, so I tried playing that next spring, but I couldn't do certain things. I think heading into that fall [2002], Nate and I were dead even again. Right before the season started, coach Long called me into the office. It was the same deal as the year before.

But this time, he told me I was the starter.

We had the jitters in that first game and led only 3–0 at the half against Tulsa. I know I didn't play too well, but we came back strong in the second half [in a 37–0 win]. In the first quarter of the next game, against Alabama, we were running the option, and I saw a gap, so I tried to cut it up and get a few yards. My [right] knee popped just like before, but this one hurt a lot more. I didn't get hit at all. It just popped real loud and I knew right away what that meant.

I already knew what it was, but I wanted to hear the doctor say it. He said, "Yes, you tore your ACL."

Again.

The first thing that came to my mind was, "Why? Why?"

"Am I supposed to be playing football?"

I wondered about that a lot. I thought maybe somebody was telling me I shouldn't be playing this game. I had surgery again and I leaned on my parents and my girlfriend and anybody I could. The coaches were at a loss for words, too. They were very supportive in whatever I wanted to do, but how could I not be discouraged?

The first time you go through that, it's very tough. The second time, it's not as hard physically because you've already gone through rehab and know what to do. You know you can come back because you came back from the first one. But in your mind, you wonder if you will have another injury.

The hardest thing about it is that your teammates are out there playing while you are inside rehabbing. They're doing things you love to do and you want to be out there with them. I came really close to quitting the whole thing.

That next spring, I tried to do everything the other two quarterbacks were doing, but my knee was killing me. It wasn't ready to go. I was so frustrated. Nothing was going right. One day I walked into coach Long's office, and he knew why I was coming to see him.

I was headed there to tell him I was done with football.

He told me, "Don't give up. Keep trying. Keep trying."

He convinced me to try again. After that meeting, I got it in my head to do what I needed to do to play again. I decided if I sat on the bench the rest of my career, at least I could look back and say I gave it my all. I wanted to finish my college career as a Sooner. I knew the way the fans and Sooner Nation treated its players was awesome, and I didn't want to give up on that. I wanted to finish as a letterman.

During that next summer, I started to get my confidence back. I felt like I was making strides. I was doing passing drills one day when coach Long told me, "Coach Stoops wants to name you the starter right now."

It was June 19, my birthday.

I was shocked. I was figuring on another two-a-days battle for the job. Once they told me, I worked extremely hard because I didn't want them to be wrong for giving me a shot. I think the coaches wanted it set in stone to let the other guys know who would be running the team.

Camp was really tough on me that year. I was struggling because I couldn't practice in two-a-days for two days in a row. I would practice one day and sit out the next because of my knee. I could only do so much. And if it hurt, I took a day off. I am sure it was a big concern for the coaches.

I thought, "I can't even make it through two-a-days, how the heck am I going to make it through the season?"

But coach Long had confidence in me and so did coach Stoops.

As the season started, I really didn't have any fear about getting hurt again. If it was going to happen, it was going to happen. I never even thought about it. I didn't want to play scared, so I just let it go. I had the mindset to give it all I had.

We went to Alabama in that second game and won [20-13], which was great, but it was a turning point mentally for me. I had been hurt in my second start of each season, so I figured if I could make it through the Alabama game, I could make it through the season.

After we beat Texas 65–13 [in which White completed 17 of 21 passes for 290 yards and 4 touchdowns], I knew we had a special team. I thought, "This team has what it takes."

I never read the newspapers, but after that game the guys were talking about me and the Heisman Trophy. I never gave it much thought. Every night of that season, as we won one game and then the next, and after every practice, I thought about how glad I was that I had stayed and not quit.

We got on a roll and didn't really have any close games. In that Texas A&M game [a 77–0 OU win], it wasn't just me, it was everybody. We got into a zone and scored every time we had the ball. It was amazing [completing 16 consecutive passes, an OU record]. I would drop back in the pocket and have all day to throw. It had rained that morning and everybody on the team had a muddy uniform but me.

After we beat Texas Tech to finish 12–0, the Heisman Trophy ceremony was coming up, but I never ever thought I was going to win it. I never wrote a speech. It is still all a blur to me. Even today, I guess I don't realize what I have done. More than anything, winning it changed my life. I went from being a small-town Oklahoma boy to being interviewed on all those national TV shows.

Then came the Big 12 championship game against Kansas State.

I still have no idea what happened that night. I have thought a lot about it. How did it happen? Still to this day, I do not know. We scored on that first drive and maybe everybody thought the game would end up like all the other games. We hadn't been challenged the whole year, so once we were, we didn't react the way we should have reacted. [OU lost 35–7.]

When we got the Sugar Bowl invitation, we knew we still deserved it. We had beaten some good teams by a lot of points and earned our way there. But we had to spend all that time answering questions about why we were in New Orleans. Everybody else said that we didn't deserve to be there.

That game was tough. I was pretty beat up and LSU had an awesome defense. When I dropped back to pass, it seemed like they had 12 guys on the field. But we never gave up, and that is what I am most proud of [in a 21–14 loss].

Those last two losses and winning the Heisman really wore on me. More than anything, the media said I didn't deserve to win the Heisman, and I got a lot of fan mail that disappointed me. A lot of people wrote me letters telling me that I didn't deserve it. And some of them got my e-mail address and did the same thing.

I would take my daughter and girlfriend out to dinner, and somebody would say something negative to me, and it would ruin my whole night. After a while, I stopped going out in public. I didn't even go to the grocery store.

I even thought about not playing my final season, but I figured I owed it to my teammates to stick around. All of those negative articles had motivated me. There was even talk around town that I wouldn't be the starting quarterback the next season. I knew after the Sugar Bowl that no matter what I did, I wouldn't have a chance to win the Heisman again. I could go out and put up better numbers than the year before, and they wouldn't vote for me.

Not winning the national championship definitely put a damper on that season. It would have made it all that much better. Don't get me wrong, the Heisman is a great honor, and all of the other Heisman winners tell me it will sink in as I get older, but I wanted to win a national championship.

My final year, my sixth year at Oklahoma, was the most fun of any season I had. The media got off my back and it was all about [freshman running back] Adrian [Peterson]. That was awesome for me. Reporters would ask me, "How do you feel about Adrian? Do you miss the spotlight?"

Are you kidding me? Miss the spotlight? I hated the media spotlight.

I told them, "I love it, because I don't have to deal with you guys anymore."

Our goal from the beginning was to get back to the Big 12 championship game and win it. That Kansas State game left such a bad taste in our mouths. So once we beat Texas [12-0], we knew we were in good position to win the Big 12 South and get there again.

That Texas game is so much fun to play in. That's why it is so exciting, because it is a big rivalry. Being part of it was a great experience for me. And we never lost to them, which makes it even more special.

Winning the Big 12 was the highlight of the season. The way we played [in a 42–3 win over Colorado] made it a great night to remember.

Going back to the Heisman ceremony, I knew I didn't have a chance to win it a second time.

Just winning it once and realizing how hard it would be to win it twice, it gives me a newfound respect for Archie Griffin. As far as winning two, I never even thought about it. I really didn't. I had been focused on helping us get back to the Big 12 championship game, winning it, and then winning the national championship game.

But once I got to New York and saw the trophy again, I wanted to win it. That is just me and how I am. If I am up for something, I want to win it. But at that point, there wasn't much I could do about it. I was disappointed, but I kind of knew going in that I wasn't going to win it. I was just honored to be back.

I was much more relaxed the second time around. I didn't know what to expect the year before. [USC's Matt Leinart] deserved what he got when he won it.

After that, I just wanted to get back with the team and prepare for the Orange Bowl.

We really wanted to establish the run against USC and throw the ball and do all the things we had done all year. But they played their best game of the season, and obviously, we did things we had never done before. Things took a turn for the worse early in the game and never got better.

We turned the ball over and that killed us. We had to play catch-up for the rest of the game. You have to give them credit. They played a great game and they were very well-coached. They were prepared to play. They had a great front-four and their team speed was extremely fast.

That [55–19] loss was very disappointing because I and all the other seniors worked so hard, and to not go out on top was tough on all of us. But you have to look back at all the positives. We won a lot of games as players at Oklahoma. We did a lot of things that people don't get the chance to do. I got to be on three teams that played in national championship games. Only two teams make it that far every year.

Coach Long once asked me, "How many quarterbacks would trade places with you even if they knew they would get to the national championship game and lose?"

And I know the answer—probably all but one of them.

I can sum up my feelings for Oklahoma in one word: family. I don't care if you played in 1940 or in 1980. You are part of the family. Those guys who played years before me treat me like family. They come back and watch practices and go to the games. It was always very humbling for me to walk down the hall and bump into one of them. They would tell you about the old days, and I could get a sense of their fond feelings for the school and the tradition we have at Oklahoma.

To be a part of that family . . . that's an awesome thing for me.

In 2003 Jason White became Oklahoma's fourth Heisman Trophy winner. He was also named the Player of the Year by the Associated Press, The Sporting News, and CNN. He also won the Davey O'Brien Award and the Jim Thorpe Courage Award. White completed 278 of 451 passes for 3,846 yards and 40 touchdowns in his award-winning season. He finished his career with 629 completions in 988 attempts for a .636 completion percentage. He finished his career 27–4 as a starting quarterback. White received six years of eligibility due to injuries and was a three-time team captain.